apartheid

the united nations & peaceful change in south africa

özdemir a. özgür

Transnational Publishers, Inc.
Dobbs Ferry, New York

The views expressed in this book are the author's personal views and do not necessarily reflect those of the United Nations.

Library of Congress Cataloging in Publication Data
Özgür, Özdemir A. (Özdemir Ahmet)
    Apartheid, the United Nations and peaceful change in South Africa.

    Bibliography: p.
    Includes index.
    1. United Nations—South Africa. 2. Race
discrimination—Law and legislation—South Africa.
3. Civil rights—South Africa. 4. South Africa—
Race relations. I. Title.
JX1977.2.S56095   341.23'68   81-23978
ISBN 0-941320-01-4   AACR2

Manufactured in the United States of America

In memory of my beloved ones
for their inspiring sense of justice and moral courage

CONTENTS

ILLUSTRATIONS

ACKNOWLEDGMENTS

I wish to thank Gisbert H. Flanz, Joel Larus, George Schwab, and Richard N. Swift for their helpful comments on the manuscript. I also wish to express my appreciation to all those who have helped in the production of this book.

Özdemir A. Özgür

New York
November 1981

INTRODUCTION

Few institutions in modern history have received the universal condemnation that the apartheid policy of the Republic of South Africa has received. Because of that policy, which is inherently discriminatory, South Africa has increasingly been isolated in the international community.[1] It has offended the international community's sense of justice as well as the dignity of all black people. Even those Western industrial democracies that have, for economic and strategic reasons, refused to withdraw military, economic, diplomatic and political support from the South African Government, in protest against that Government's policies of racial discrimination, have agreed with United Nations pronouncements describing apartheid as a violation of the Charter of the United Nations and the Universal Declaration of Human Rights (hereinafter to be referred to as the Charter, and the Universal Declaration, respectively).

Ironically, the practice of apartheid—which in Afrikaans means, literally, "apartness"—has set the minority Government of South Africa farther and farther apart from the world community. Through its policy of racial separation, South Africa, one of the founding members of the United Nations, has also separated itself from the moral, legal and political values of the United Nations. Indeed, instead of separating the races, the Government of South Africa has separated itself from all races and emerged as a foe of the one race to which all peoples belong: the human race.

In the past decade, because of the pressure of the international community, led very often by the United Nations, many embarrassed Western supporters of the South African Government have been spurred to use their influence to urge peaceful change on the leaders in Pretoria. Recently, however, a new administration in Washington has counselled "constructive engagement" as an alternative to isolation, and has de-emphasized human rights as an element of its foreign policy. This shift, while giving encouragement to the South African Government, has caused general disappointment the world over.

In view of this new attitude toward South Africa by one of its most influential trade partners and the increasing demands for more pressure and comprehensive sanctions against the apartheid regime, it seems timely to look at United Nations efforts to eliminate apartheid, the persistence of the

xiii

South African Government in maintaining apartheid and the positions of major Powers in the matter.

From the very first session of the General Assembly in 1946, the United Nations has had to deal with legalized racial discrimination, that is, racialized legal order, in South Africa as an official government policy. Declared as apartheid in 1948, South Africa's legalized racial discrimination has kept over 80 percent of its population outside the mainstream of political, economic, social and cultural life.

The Government of South Africa had legally practiced racial discrimination before the establishment of the United Nations in 1945. And although South Africa was a party to the Charter which specifically prohibited racial and other discriminations, the South African Government not only continued to practice legalized racial discrimination after joining the United Nations, but also began giving a doctrinaire and permanent character to its racial policies under the name of apartheid. In 1948, after the National Party ascended to political power on an apartheid platform, the policy of legalized and institutionalized racial segregation and discrimination became official government policy and has remained so ever since, with increasing vigor. Moreover, as internal opposition to apartheid has intensified, so have repressive and punitive measures by the authorities in South Africa.

The United Nations began in 1946 to "consider" the question of racial discrimination in South Africa upon the request of the Government of India, which complained that the South African Government was discriminating through legislative measures against people of Indian origin in South Africa.[2] Six years later, in 1952, the United Nations broadened its focus of attention and took up the question of apartheid as well. Since 1962, it has considered both questions under one item entitled "Policies of apartheid of the Government of the Republic of South Africa," covering discrimination against the population of Indian origin as well as discrimination against people of African and other origins.[3]

From the very beginning, the United Nations membership has unanimously regarded legalized racial discrimination as a violation of the Charter and of the Universal Declaration which was adopted in 1948 as a common standard for all peoples and nations and which today is generally accepted as an authoritative interpretation of the human rights provisions of the Charter.[4] Since the establishment of the United Nations, the states have taken numerous measures, individually and collectively, against racial discrimination, while the South African Government has been consolidating the system of apartheid as strongly as possible through such radical measures as bantustanization, that is, the policy of Bantu "homelands".[5]

The Government of South Africa has in the past thirty-five years resorted to legal technicalities, while also arguing on the merits of the case, to prevent the United Nations from considering the matter. It has maintained that apartheid is a matter essentially within its domestic jurisdiction and, therefore, the United Nations is not competent to consider the matter. Specifically, it has invoked Article 2 (7) of the Charter, which imposes a limitation on the Organization's jurisdiction with regard to such matters as human rights that are considered to be essentially within the domestic jurisdiction of a state, unless there is a threat to international peace and security. It proposed referring the issue of jurisdiction to the International Court of Justice, but was unable to convince enough Member States to go along. Pretoria has also claimed that since no definition existed of the human rights provisions of the Charter, it was not bound by any international obligations in that respect and that, in any case, it has not discriminated in terms of fundamental human rights.[6]

On substantive issues, the South African Government has argued that the structure of the South African society, with its different tribes and subcultures, requires apartheid. It has maintained that the several ethnic groups of people in South Africa are at different stages of development and that, therefore, separation of the groups will promote separate development. In 1947, a South African diplomat told the United Nations that in South Africa "certain distinctions and some segregations were the only way to minimize racial friction."[7]

The United Nations, in its efforts to have the racialized legal order changed in South Africa, has operated under both legal limitations, particularly the domestic jurisdiction clause of the Charter, and political ones. It has functioned within a system of imbalance between the authority of the General Assembly and that of the Security Council, where the former cannot normally take effective action beyond the stage of recommendation. Further, it has functioned in a decentralized system of enforcement action, where the veto of the permanent members of the Council has often blocked action.[8] Whereas in the Assembly a simple majority vote is needed to adopt a decision (except on "important issues" where a two-thirds vote is needed), in the Council the concurrence of all five permanent members is needed. The permanent members are China, France, the United Kingdom, the Soviet Union, and the United States. In contrast to the recommendatory powers of the Assembly, the Council's decisions under Chapter VII of the Charter are mandatory.

Despite South Africa's invoking the domestic jurisdiction clause, the United Nations has repeatedly appealed to Pretoria to revise its racial policies in order to bring them into line with the Charter and the Universal Declaration. It has called on that Government with the main purpose of achieving racial equality. In time, the Organization has also seen a threat posed by South Africa to international peace. On 4 November 1977, therefore, the Security Council adopted a mandatory arms embargo against South Africa [Security Council resolution 418 (1977)]. That action made South Africa the first and the only Member State against which the United Nations has so far adopted mandatory sanctions.[9]

Although the United Nations adopted an impressive number of resolutions from 1946 to 1980 concerning racial discrimination and apartheid in South Africa, it has not yet achieved its objective of racial equality in that country.[10] The South African Government has not implemented the United Nations resolutions, and at best has made only superficial changes in its racial policies. On the other hand, the news media shows a growing international awareness of the dangerous nature and implications of apartheid. As the United Nations has intensified its action against apartheid, world public opinion has become increasingly aware of the injustices inherent in apartheid, of the prospect of racial armed conflict in South Africa, and of the resultant implications for international peace. Thus, apartheid has become one of the major problems before the United Nations.

The grave, large-scale, legalized, and systematic violations of human rights in South Africa, based on a racialized legal order in flagrant violation of the Charter, certainly distinguishes the unique case of apartheid from other cases of racial discrimination. Apartheid is based on racial segregation, with inherent inequality.[11] The argument by the Government of South Africa that apartheid would lead to separate but equal development has never been convincing to the United Nations. In recent years, even Afrikaners have been questioning the premises of that policy.[12] In any case, violence has increased in South Africa in recent years, and so has the international outcry against apartheid.

Since the Second World War, racial discrimination has received much attention. As that war showed, racial discrimination is closely linked to the maintenance of international peace and security. It should not be forgotten that the United Nations was the product of that war and that it was established, as the Charter states, to "save the succeeding generations from the scourge of war," in an awareness of the role played by racist theories in the horrors of that epoch. In that sense, South Africa's racialized legal order stands in direct opposition to the *raison d'être* of the United Nations.

Certainly, there are other parts of the world where human rights are violated, although in most cases the reasons are political dissent, rather than race. However, in its large-scale and statutory discrimination on the grounds of race, South Africa is unique. In that country, one suffers the consequences of racial discrimination from birth and cannot avoid the violation of his human rights and fundamental freedoms by choosing to remain silent on political issues. Furthermore, such a policy as apartheid creates enormous political problems and forces people to become active against the political system. Some critics of the United Nations have objected to the Organization's activities against apartheid, accusing the United Nations of hypocricy in not attending to other violations of human rights in the world with the same force. Perhaps that criticism was best answered by a long-term and interested observer of the United Nations who noted: "It is sheer defeatism to dismiss the activities of the largest international forum in the world dealing with human rights because it is imperfect . . . The United Nations is not an association of demigods and sages . . . In this imperfect world it is trying to put up a few signposts toward a more just one."[13]

More to the point of the moral and political merits of the case, in comparison to other violations of human rights, a distinguished scholar of international politics has noted:

> To support the internal settlement [in Namibia], to yield to South Africa's manoeuvres in Namibia, to suggest to the South African regime that we would do no more than denounce apartheid verbally in exchange for its cooperation toward "moderate" solutions in Rhodesia and Namibia would be morally wrong and politically disastrous. To be sure, most black African regimes are not exemplary (violations of human rights being no less characteristic of "moderate" than of "radical" regimes). But their flaws or crimes in no way justify the continuing imposition of white-minority rule, open and repressive as in South Africa, or indirectly perpetuated in Rhodesia or Namibia.[14]

Because of its inhumanity and its danger to international peace, apartheid has become a matter of international concern. The world has seen enough of the consequences of racism. In the words of a contemporary intellectual historian: "With respect to the prospects of peace among nations and peaceful social change within nations, it is indisputable that nationalism and racism are prejudicial to their furtherance."[15]

The purpose of this book is to examine United Nations efforts from 1946 to 1980 to have the racialized legal order in South Africa changed to conform with the Organization's human rights standards, particularly with those on racial discrimination. It is the belief of this writer that, in the case of South Africa, the United Nations has striven to bring about internal peaceful change mainly on the strength of its human rights standards, despite the Charter's domestic jurisdiction clause.

For the purpose of this work, "internal peaceful change" is defined as the modification of the internal legal order of a state by primarily non-violent means. In that connection, it has been said that "the apartheid order is a legal order."[16] Also, although the traditional problems of peaceful change differ from those that arise in the case of South Africa, the definitions of "peaceful change" used by earlier authors are useful for the purpose of this book. The term "peaceful" has generally meant "primarily by non-violent means" or "primarily by means other than overt military warfare."[17] Moreover, a distinction has been made between "peaceful change," disputes *about* the legal order, and "peaceful settlement of disputes," disputes *within* the legal order.[18] With regard to peaceful change, the consensus seems to be that change has to do with the legal order, legal status quo, legal rights and interests of states, existing distribution of rights and possessions as established by the legal system.[19]

As will be seen, the means used by the United Nations to try to bring about change in South Africa have been primarily non-violent. The change sought by the United Nations has been *about* the internal racialized legal order; that is, the United Nations has tried to alter the internal legal order of a Member State and not to settle disputes *within* that order.

This work is not concerned with United Nations efforts for peaceful change by decolonization, but with United Nations efforts for internal peaceful change. Even though one can see in the case of South Africa the vestiges of colonialism and quasi-colonial internal rule, apartheid is not strictly-speaking a matter of colonialism. Legally speaking, South Africa cannot have a colonial status while it is a Member State of the United Nations.

Authors who have written on ''peaceful change'' have done so essentially from the perspective of decolonization. They have written on the transition of territories from one international political and legal status to another. In that respect, much has been written especially in the 1930s and the 1940s with regard to Article 19 of the Covenant of the League of Nations and Article 14 of the United Nations Charter. Some authors have briefly touched upon the question of internal peaceful change, but mostly insofar as it concerns the efforts of agents or forces within the society to bring about change, not an outside agent such as the United Nations. Even internal forces which support the status quo, such as the courts, are in fact supporting the existing internal legal order.[20] In other words, those authors have viewed internal peaceful change as the peaceful change of the internal legal order. Legal order is a common element between peaceful change at the international level and peaceful change at the national level. It has been aptly said that ''the UN treaties have gone much further than their predecessors, however, in that they have obligated signatory states to make changes—sometimes drastic changes—in their own domestic legal regimes to bring them into conformity with international law norms.''[21]

Nevertheless, peaceful change at both national and international levels is governed by Article 14 of the Charter. Indeed, in its first resolution regarding South Africa's racial situation in 1946, the Assembly implicitly referred to Article 14 by using the phraseology of that Article and saying that ''friendly relations between the two Member States [India and South Africa] have been impaired.'' Article 14 is concerned with the general welfare or friendly relations among nations and is known as having provided the legal avenue for peaceful change and as corresponding, with wider scope, to Article 19 of the League Covenant. In subsequent resolutions, the Assembly explicitly referred to Article 14. By these references, it indicated both that it pursued peaceful change and that it derived its competence mainly from that Article.

It would, therefore, be beyond the jurisdiction of the United Nations to concern itself with any kind of change in a Member State other than change related to the internal legal order and general welfare or friendly relations among nations. While in the case of South Africa it is obvious that its internal legal order is in violation of the Charter, any demand by the United Nations to change, for example, the form of government in any Member State would not find easy support in any provisions of the Charter.

Cases such as the Spanish case, which have been referred to as cases of internal peaceful change but have been included among the issues of peaceful change, do not fall within the definition of internal peaceful change in this book.[22] The Spanish case, which was brought before the United Nations in 1946, was concerned primarily with the form of government of Spain, not with the internal legal order. It was motivated by the military assistance that the Franco Government had received from the "ex-enemy" states and was aimed at changing the form of Government in Spain.[23] Spain was not then a Member State, and the case was based on Article 34 of the Charter, on provisions governing the pacific settlement of disputes, not on Article 14.[24]

It is this writer's belief that the legal order in South Africa violates the Charter most flagrantly, and that improvements in other aspects of life in that country will depend on altering the racialized legal order. The foundation of political, social, and economic orders in South Africa is apartheid, which is basically a legal order. As Zartman has noted, "the South African situation is not one of political change where a simple transfer of power is to be negotiated, whereupon the colonizer will go home; it is rather a situation of social change in which power is to shift within an expanded political system."[25]

The writer has limited his analysis to the efforts of the General Assembly and the Security Council, two principal organs of the United Nations. Of course, many resolutions have been adopted on racial discrimination and apartheid by other organs and bodies, such as the Economic and Social Council (ECOSOC) or the Commission on Human Rights. Moreover, the Assembly has adopted resolutions on items of broader human rights issues, of which racial discrimination and apartheid in South Africa are a part, at the recommendation of its Third (Social, Humanitarian, and Cultural) Committee and Fourth (Decolonization and Trusteeship) Committee. It is sufficient, however, to confine the inquiry to these two principal political organs of the United Nations, because it is the Assembly that has the primary responsibility for matters of peaceful change, and the Council that has a similar responsibility for the maintenance of international peace and security.

This book is in three parts. Part 1 examines the conflicting standards of the United Nations and South Africa on the subject of human rights and racial equality, and their relation to international peace and the domestic jurisdiction clause of the Charter. It also describes the population, the political system, and the racial legislation in South Africa.

Part 2 analyzes the United Nations resolutions, discussions, reports, statements, and similar documents on the racial situation in South Africa with regard to the Organization's objective and South Africa's response. It examines the 158 resolutions adopted by the Assembly and the twelve adopted by the Council during the period under review to ascertain the nature of change sought by the United Nations, the grounds on which such change was sought, and the limitations under which the Organization functioned. It traces discussions in the Assembly and the Council on the matter, covering both substantive and procedural arguments, and indicates how their positions have developed.

Part 3 deals with the impact of the United Nations efforts on South Africa, describing the United Nations pressures on South Africa and the changes made or proposed by the South African Government in its racial policies. It studies the internal opposition to apartheid and endeavors to make a prognosis about the fate of apartheid. Finally, it concludes with the effect that the United Nations has had in seeking peaceful change within a Member State, and on the Organization's potentialities in any similar situation in the future.

PART I

CONFLICTING STANDARDS

I. UNITED NATIONS STANDARDS

Human Rights in General

Background

Since the Middle Ages and the times of Grotius, there has been a growing recognition of the right to humanitarian intervention when a nation discriminates against its own people on the grounds of religion or language. Back in 1878, long before the League of Nations, the Congress of Berlin compelled the Ottoman Empire to undertake reforms with regard to all minorities in the Empire.

In the League of Nations period, treaties and declarations on the protection of minorities, under the guarantorship of the League, provided for the protection of the rights to life and liberty, political rights, equality before the law, freedom to choose religion and profession, and freedom to use their own languages and to administer their schools. Minorities were to enjoy the same civil and political rights as other inhabitants, and those obligations were binding. Such measures were of international concern and challenged the concept of absolute state sovereignty and its corollary—domestic jurisdiction.[26] Minority treaties were signed by Poland, Yugoslavia, Czechoslovakia, Rumania and Greece. Finland, Albania, Lithuania, Latvia, Estonia and Iraq made declarations concerning minorities when they were admitted to the League. Also, provisions for the protection of minorities were inserted in peace treaties involving Austria, Bulgaria, Hungary and Turkey.

Before the United Nations was established, a declaration signed in January 1942 by the original signatories of twenty-six nations expressed the conviction, in its preamble, that "complete victory over their enemies is essential to defend life, liberty, independence and religious freedom, and to preserve human rights and justice in their own lands as well as in other lands." At the San Francisco Conference, ensuring respect for the international rights and duties of man was stated as being one of the essential objectives of the Allies in World War II.[27]

Those same signatories also subscribed to the "common principles" of the Atlantic Charter (the joint Declaration by the United States and the United Kingdom) of August 1941. One of those common principles ex-

3

pressed respect for "the right of all peoples to choose the form of government under which they will live."

During the creation of the United Nations, the delegations of Brazil, the Dominican Republic, and Mexico submitted an amendment to the Dumbarton Oaks Proposals for inclusion in the Purposes. The amendment sought "to ensure respect for human rights and fundamental freedoms, without discrimination against race, sex, condition, or creed." As justification, they pointed out that their proposal was in accord with the progress and development of international law and policy, as had been affirmed by the Final Act of the Inter-American Congress on Problems of War and Peace, approved in Chapultepec, Mexico, on 7 March 1945.[28] Thus, they expressed their conviction that human rights had become a matter of international law and concern.

The Charter of the United Nations

With the establishment of the United Nations, the Charter and a number of international instruments provided explicitly for human rights and fundamental freedoms. Also, in peace treaties signed in February 1947 by former enemy states, Bulgaria, Finland, Hungary, Italy and Rumania undertook to observe human rights and fundamental freedoms for all the population of their territories, without discrimination on the grounds of race, sex, language, or religion.

The preamble of the Charter speaks of the peoples of the United Nations as determined, among other things, to reaffirm faith in fundamental human rights and in the dignity and worth of the human person. The dignity and worth of the human person is thus tied up with fundamental human rights.

One of the purposes of the United Nations, expressly stated in Article 1, paragraph 3, of the Charter, is "to achieve international cooperation in solving international problems of an economic, social, cultural, or humanitarian character, and in promoting and encouraging respect for human rights and for fundamental freedoms for all without distinction as to race, sex, language, or religion." In pursuit of the purposes of the United Nations, the Organization and its Members are required to act in accordance with certain principles enumerated in Article 2, which provides, among other things, that "all Members, in order to ensure to all of them the rights and benefits resulting from membership, shall fulfil in good faith the obligations assumed by them in accordance with the present Charter."

Article 13, paragraph 1 (b), of the Charter empowers the General Assembly to initiate studies and make recommendations for the purpose of, among other things, "promoting international co-operation in the economic, social, cultural, educational and health fields, and assisting in the realization of human rights and fundamental freedoms for all without distinction as to race, sex, language, or religion.'' The word ''realization'' in this Article implies a sense of active implementation.

Again, Article 55, paragraph c, provides that the United Nations shall promote, *inter alia*, ''universal respect for, and observance of, human rights and fundamental freedoms for all without distinction as to race, sex, language, or religion.'' This Article is linked to Article 56 which provides that ''all Members pledge themselves to take joint and separate action in co-operation with the Organization for the achievement of the purposes set forth in Article 55.'' It has been said that the word ''observance'' in Article 55 was added at the San Francisco Conference in order to imply active implementation by states.[29]

By still another article of the Charter, Article 62 (2), ECOSOC is empowered to ''make recommendations for the purpose of promoting respect for, and observance of, human rights and fundamental freedoms for all.'' Article 76, paragraph c, provides that one of the basic objectives of the trusteeship system of the United Nations is ''to encourage respect for human rights and for fundamental freedoms for all without distinction as to race, sex, language, or religion.''

Clearly, in the aforesaid Articles of the Charter racial non-discrimination is mentioned in conjunction with human rights and fundamental freedoms. The Charter provisions on human rights imply the right to equality before the law, of which the principle of non-discrimination is a corollary. The principle of non-discrimination emanates from the right to equality before the law. The principle of the equality of races is widely considered to be of supreme importance for the observance of human rights and fundamental freedoms. In fact, human equality is the basic foundation of human rights and fundamental freedoms. Without equality, the full enjoyment of these rights and freedoms is not possible. The repeated references to racial non-discrimination in the aforementioned provisions of the Charter constitute a clear indication to that effect. The meaning of these Charter provisions with regard to racial equality is beyond dispute, and no ''lack of definition'' can be argued in good faith to justify legalized racial discrimination. As noted by one expert in the field of human rights, the principles of self-determination, equality, and non-discrimination are fundamental for the protection of human rights.[30]

The principle of non-discrimination, including racial non-discrimination, is one of the keystones of the Charter and is fundamental to the enjoyment of human rights and fundamental freedoms. One of the main differences between the Charter and the Covenant of the League of Nations is that the Charter prohibits racial discrimination. The League Council was concerned with appeals made to it about violations of minority rights which were regulated by treaties or declarations. On the importance of Charter provisions on human rights, Goodrich has written that

> the Charter reflects a new approach to the protection of liberty and freedom born of the experience of World War II and the years immediately preceding it when flagrant violations of human rights and the denial of the basic dignity of man were the hallmarks of the régimes challenging and violating international peace and security. This approach is a denial of the proposition that the way in which a state treats its nationals is of no concern to the outside world and therefore beyond the proper competence of international agencies.[31]

The Universal Declaration of Human Rights

The principle of racial non-discrimination is contained also in the Universal Declaration, adopted in 1948 "as a common standard of achievement for all peoples and all nations." Its first preambular paragraph states that recognition of the inherent dignity and of the equal and inalienable rights of all members of the human family is the foundation of freedom, justice, and peace in the world. Article 1 of the Universal Declaration states that all human beings are born free and equal in dignity and rights. Article 2 states that "everyone is entitled to all the rights and freedoms set forth in this Declaration, without distinction of any kind such as race, colour, sex, language, religion, political or other opinion, national or social origin, property, birth or other status." Article 7 provides that all are equal before the law.

Although the Universal Declaration was adopted to elaborate on the general principles of human rights and fundamental freedoms of the Charter, the question whether the Universal Declaration is binding on Member States remains controversial. Nevertheless, it has received a high degree of recognition, both nationally and internationally. In 1962, the Legal Adviser of the United Nations said, upon the request of the Commission on Human Rights for clarification, that a declaration indicates a strong expectation that members of the international community will respect it and that, consequently, to the extent that the expectation is gradually justified by state practice, a declaration may by custom be regarded as laying down rules binding upon states.[32] Strict constructionists will, no doubt, regard this position as unacceptable.

A large number of resolutions of the United Nations contain references to the Universal Declaration. A number of national constitutions and regional organizations' charters have been inspired by, contain provisions of, or make references to the Universal Declaration. National courts and laws have cited the Universal Declaration, as have Judges of the International Court of Justice. In general, the Universal Declaration is accepted as an authoritative interpretation of the Charter provisions on human rights and fundamental freedoms, irrespective of the question of its binding or non-binding force.[33]

In his address to the United Nations on 2 October 1979, His Holiness Pope John Paul II referred to the Universal Declaration as the fundamental document of the United Nations and as a milestone on the long and difficult path of the human race. Linking the birth of the Universal Declaration to the tragedies of World War II, His Holiness elaborated:

> But my purpose in evoking this memory is above all to show what painful experiences and sufferings by millions of people gave rise to the Universal Declaration of Human Rights, which has been placed as the basic inspiration and cornerstone of the United Nations Organization. This Declaration was paid for by millions of our brothers and sisters, at the cost of their suffering and sacrifice brought about by the brutalization that darkened and made insensitive the human consciences of the oppressors and of those who carried out a real genocide. This price cannot have been paid in vain. If the truth and principles contained in this document were to be forgotten or ignored and were thus to lose the genuine self-evidence that so distinguished them at the time they were brought painfully to birth, then the noble purpose of the United Nations Organization would be faced with the threat of a new destruction.[34]

Notwithstanding the controversy over the binding force of the Universal Declaration, in 1972 the United Nations Security Council adopted resolution 310, which concerned labor relations in Namibia (South West Africa), calling on the South African Government to abolish any system of labor which may be in conflict with basic provisions of the Universal Declaration.[35] The preambular part of that resolution stated that the Council was "mindful of its responsibility to take necessary action to secure strict compliance with the obligations entered into by States Members of the United Nations under the relevant provisions of the Charter of the United Nations." The Council thus seems to have regarded the Universal Declaration as an instrument to be read in conjunction with the Charter and as binding on Member States. Since apartheid is being practiced by the Government of South Africa in both South Africa and Namibia, the Council's concern for the proper implementation of the Universal Declaration in Namibia is, a priori, applicable to South Africa, too. In fact, as will be seen later, the Council has adopted resolutions speaking of the inconsistency of apartheid policies with the Universal Declaration.

The International Covenant on Economic, Social and Cultural Rights, and the International Covenant on Civil and Political Rights

These Covenants, which were adopted in 1966 and entered into force in 1976, gave legal force to the Universal Declaration. With little difference, they provide for the same human rights and fundamental freedoms as does the Universal Declaration. As of 14 August 1981, seventy states had acceded to or ratified the former Covenant, and sixty-six states the latter. Article 2 of each Covenant prohibits discrimination on racial and other grounds.

The Covenants provide for implementation measures. States parties to the Covenant on Civil and Political Rights have elected a Human Rights Committee, composed of eighteen persons acting in an individual capacity, which considers reports submitted by the states parties. The Committee may address general comments to these states and to ECOSOC. Under the optional provisions of the Covenant, the Committee may consider communications from a state party claiming that another state party has not fulfilled its obligations under the Covenant. Under the Optional Protocol to this covenant, the Committee may consider communications from private individuals claiming to have suffered from a violation by a state party to the Protocol of any of the rights contained in the Covenant.

Under the Covenant on Economic, Social, and Cultural Rights, states parties submit periodic reports to ECOSOC on the measures adopted and progress made towards the realization of the rights set forth in that Covenant. ECOSOC may make general recommendations on those reports.

Some human rights experts regard the Universal Declaration and the two international Covenants, which have given form and content to the general human rights provisions of the Charter, as general instruments of positive international law of human rights.[36] One such expert has maintained that in the field of human rights no principle in the practice of the United Nations has been given so eminent a place as that of racial non-discrimination, and that, in light of the Charter, the members of the international community are bound by this principle even if they are not parties to international instruments providing against racial discrimination and apartheid.[37] One scholar has said that the Universal Declaration has become part of the customary law of nations and is thus binding on all states, whether they voted for it or not.[38]

Specific Instruments on Racial Discrimination

The International Convention on the Elimination of All Forms of Racial Discrimination

This Convention, which was adopted in 1965 and came into force in 1969, has defined racial discrimination as "any distinction, exclusion, restriction or preference based on race, colour, descent, or national or ethnic origin which has the purpose or effect of nullifying or impairing the recognition, enjoyment or exercise, on an equal footing, of human rights and fundamental freedoms in the political, economic, social, cultural or any field of public life" (Article 1). As of 2 September 1981, there were 109 states parties to this Convention, which exceeded two thirds of the United Nations membership. The Convention was preceded by the United Nations Declaration on the Elimination of All Forms of Racial Discrimination, adopted in 1963 by the General Assembly. The Declaration solemnly affirmed the necessity of speedily eliminating racial discrimination throughout the world in all its forms and manifestations, and of securing understanding of and respect for the dignity of the human person.

The Convention particularly condemns racial segregation and apartheid and prohibits racial discrimination both by states and by any persons, groups, or organizations. States parties undertake to review their legislation, repeal objectionable laws and regulations, and adopt legislative and other measures for the elimination of racial discrimination. They also undertake to adopt effective measures, particularly in the fields of teaching, education, culture, and information, in order to combat prejudices and to promote understanding, tolerance, and friendship among nations and national or ethnic groups.

For the implementation of the provisions of the Convention, a Committee on the Elimination of Racial Discrimination was established, consisting of eighteen experts serving in their personal capacity. The Committee considers reports submitted by states parties and makes proposals and general recommendations to the General Assembly. States parties undertake to submit reports on the legislative, judicial, administrative, or other measures which they have adopted and which give effect to the provisions of the Convention. The Committee may request further information from the states parties. In practice, the Committee has asked states parties to give information on measures taken under some provisions which the Committee has not regarded as self-executing.

Under article 14, a state party may at any time declare that it recognizes the competence of the Committee to receive and consider communications from individuals or groups of individuals within its jurisdiction claiming to be victims of a violation by that state party of any of the rights set forth in the Convention.

The International Convention on the Suppression and Punishment of the Crime of Apartheid

This Convention was adopted by the United Nations in 1973 and entered into force in 1976.[39] It establishes international criminal responsibility for individuals, members of organizations and institutions as well as representatives of states, who commit or are involved in the commission of the crime of apartheid. Article 1 declares that apartheid is a crime against humanity and that inhuman acts resulting from the policies and practices of racial segregation and discrimination are crimes violating the principles of international law, in particular the purposes and principles of the Charter, and constitute a serious threat to international peace and security. Article 2 defines the inhuman acts committed for the purpose of establishing and maintaining domination by one racial group of persons over any other racial group of persons and systematically oppressing them. States parties to the Convention undertake to submit periodic reports on measures that they have adopted to give effect to the provisions of the Convention. These reports are considered by a group of three persons appointed by the Chairman of the Commission on Human Rights. The Commission is also empowered to prepare a list of individuals, organizations, institutions, and representatives of states which are alleged to be responsible for the crimes under the Convention.

States parties undertake to adopt any legislative or other measure necessary to suppress and prevent any encouragement of the crime of apartheid and similar segregationist policies. They also undertake to adopt legislative, judicial, and administrative measures to prosecute, bring to trial, and punish persons responsible for the acts defined in the Convention. In other words, persons charged with the acts enumerated in article 2 may be tried by a competent tribunal of any state party to the Convention. This has been the most controversial provision of the Convention. As of 6 August 1981, sixty-three states had acceded to or ratified the Convention.

In its preamble, the Convention refers to the Convention on the Prevention and Punishment of the Crime of Genocide and to the Convention on the Non-Applicability of Statutory Limitations to War Crimes and Crimes Against Humanity. It observes that in the former Convention "certain acts which may also be qualified as acts of apartheid constitute a crime under international law" and that in the latter " 'inhuman acts resulting from the policy of apartheid' are qualified as crimes against humanity."

The Genocide Convention was adopted in 1948 by the United Nations General Assembly. Earlier at its first session, the Assembly had adopted resolution 95 (I) of 1946 affirming the principles of international law recognized by the Charter of the Nürnberg Tribunal and the Judgment of the Tribunal. This Convention defines genocide as meaning any of the certain acts which it enumerates, committed with intent to destroy, in whole or in part, a national, ethnic, racial, or religious group. In terms of the Convention, genocide has to do with denying the right of existence of human groups. The Convention on Apartheid, however, goes further in its definition of the acts that constitute the crime of apartheid. The acts constituting apartheid have a wider scope than merely denying the existence of a human group.

As noted, the Convention on War Crimes and Crimes Against Humanity qualifies inhuman acts resulting from apartheid as crimes against humanity. The Convention was not adopted specifically on racial discrimination, but on war crimes and crimes against humanity during the Second World War. As is widely known, the legality of the Nürnberg Trials, insofar as the Crimes against Humanity are concerned, has been contested by strict constructionists, who have said that the trials concerning those crimes were held on the strength of *ex post facto* legislation. It may also be noted that the Nürnberg principles were established by a number of states much less than the number of States Members of the United Nations, which have for so long a time recognized apartheid as a crime against humanity.

Judicial and Similar Standards

The International Court of Justice

The International Court of Justice (ICJ), principal judicial organ of the United Nations, has also made pronouncements on apartheid. In July 1970, it was asked by the Security Council for an advisory opinion concerning South Africa's presence in Namibia. In its advisory opinion on the *Legal Consequences for States of the Continued Presence of South Africa in Namibia*, the ICJ said in June 1971 that South Africa was under obligation to withdraw immediately and end its occupation of Namibia. The Court also stated that to establish and to enforce "distinctions, exclusions, restrictions, and limitations exclusively based on grounds of race, colour, descent or national or ethnic origin which constitute a denial of fundamental human rights is a flagrant violation of the purposes of the Charter."[40]

In a dissenting opinion delivered in 1966 in the case of South West Africa, World Court Justice Tanaka took the position that the norm of non-discrimination or non-separation on the basis of race had become a rule of customary international law. He cited the accumulation of authoritative pronouncements such as resolutions, declarations, decisions, and other instruments concerning the interpretation of the Charter by competent organs of the international community. He added that South Africa's obligations, therefore, were governed by this legal norm, in its capacity as a Member of the United Nations, either directly or at least by way of interpretation of Article 2, paragraph 2.[41] This Article, as has been seen, has to do with the performance of Member States' obligations in good faith. This opinion was given in connection with racial discrimination and apartheid in Namibia, but it is equally applicable to racial discrimination in South Africa itself, as racial discrimination in both cases emanates from the Government of South Africa and has the same legal basis and effect.

In 1971, when the Court took up the question of the continued presence of South Africa in Namibia, Justice Fouad Ammon said that the equality demanded by the Namibians and by other peoples of every color "is the foundation of other human rights which are no more than its corollaries" and that "it naturally rules out racial discrimination and apartheid."[42] In the same case, in his separate opinion, Justice Padilla Nervo said that "racial discrimination as official government policy is a violation of a norm or rule or standard of the international community."[43]

In its advisory opinion on the question of reservations regarding the Genocide Convention, the Court said in 1951 that the principles contained in that Convention were principles recognized by civilized nations, which are binding on states even in the absence of conventional obligations.[44] That position was confirmed and strengthened in 1970 in the *Barcelona Traction* case. In that case, the Court spoke of contemporary international law concerning not only acts of aggression and genocide but also the principles and rules of fundamental rights of human beings comprising the protection against the practice of slavery and racial discrimination.[45]

The ICJ, whose function is to decide in accordance with international law, is empowered under article 38 of its Statute to apply, among other things, international customary law as well as the general principles of law recognized by civilized nations. Apparently, the Court considers the principle of racial non-discrimination to have become one of the general principles of law recognized by civilized nations.

The International Law Commission

A further comment on apartheid has been made by the International Law Commission. The draft articles adopted by the Commission in 1976 relating to the responsibility of states for internationally wrongful acts constitute a recognition of the progressive development of international law. Draft article 19 on international crimes and international delicts, which includes apartheid, reads:

> 1. An act of a State which constitutes a breach of international obligation is an internationally wrongful act, regardless of the subject-matter of the obligation breached.
> 2. An internationally wrongful act which results from the breach by a State of an international obligation so essential for the protection of fundamental interests of the international community that its breach is recognized as a crime by that community as a whole, constitutes an international crime.
> 3. Subject to paragraph 2, and on the basis of the rules of international law in force, an international crime may result, *inter alia*, from:
>> (a) a serious breach of an international obligation of essential importance for the maintenance of international peace and security, such as that prohibiting aggression;
>> (b) a serious breach of an international obligation of essential importance for safeguarding the right of self-determination of peoples, such as that prohibiting the establishment or maintenance by force of colonial domination;
>> (c) a serious breach on a widespread scale of an international obligation of essential importance for safeguarding the human being, such as those prohibiting slavery, genocide and *apartheid*;
>> (d) a serious breach of an international obligation of essential importance

> for the safeguarding and preservation of the human environment, such
> as those prohibiting massive pollution of the atmosphere or of the seas.
> 4. Any internationally wrongful act which is not an international crime in
> accordance with paragraph 2 constitutes an international delict.[46]

In its commentary on that article, the Commission said that an objective examination of state practice in the United Nations enabled it "to conclude that the forcible maintenance of colonial domination and the application of a coercive policy of *apartheid* or absolute racial discrimination appeared to be considered within the legal system of the United Nations—and probably in general international law as well—as breaches of an established international obligation." The Commission added that such acts constituted internationally wrongful acts of a particularly serious character.[47]

The South African Government has neither voted for the Universal Declaration nor acceded to any of the human rights instruments adopted by the United Nations. Apparently, Pretoria wants to give the impression that so long as it does not accede to any of the international instruments on human rights it has no international obligation for its internal racialized legal order. Yet, racial non-discrimination is a keystone of the Charter of the United Nations, and by its membership in the Organization, South Africa has undertaken to fulfil its Charter obligations in good faith. Among those obligations is the prohibition of racial discrimination. The fact that South Africa has not voted for, or is not a party to, international human rights instruments cannot justify South Africa's violating the Charter.

As a Member State of the United Nations, South Africa is obliged to adjust itself to the progressive development of international law. In 1971, in the case of Namibia, the ICJ said that "an international instrument has to be interpreted and applied within the framework of the entire legal system prevailing at the time of interpretation."[48] In fact, Article 13, paragraph 1 (a), of the Charter empowers the General Assembly to initiate studies and make recommendations for the purpose of encouraging the progressive development of international law and its codification.

The conclusion is unavoidable that legalized racial discrimination as practiced in South Africa violates the relevant standards of the United Nations. But, to understand the competence of the United Nations with regard to the internal legal order of a Member State, it is necessary to consider such internal order in its relationship to both international peace and the domestic jurisdiction clause of the Charter.

Human Rights in Relation to International Peace and Domestic Jurisdiction

In its many instruments and decisions, the United Nations has clearly recognized the link between international peace and human rights violations.

Racial discrimination, of course, is a very serious form of human rights violation.

According to Article 1, paragraph 1, of the Charter, one of the purposes of the United Nations is to maintain international peace and security by, among other things, taking effective collective measures for the prevention and removal of threats to peace and by bringing about adjustment or settlement of international disputes or situations which might lead to a breach of peace. Paragraph 2 of the same Article provides that another purpose is "to develop friendly relations among nations based on respect for the principle of equal rights and self-determination of peoples, and to take other appropriate measures to strengthen universal peace." Universal peace is, therefore, linked to friendly relations among nations, and these relations are based on respect for the principle of equal rights and self-determination. The purposes of the Charter were understood at the San Francisco Conference to "form the *raison d'être* of the Organization."[49]

In Article 55 of the Charter, "the creation of conditions of stability and well-being which are necessary for peaceful and friendly relations among nations based on respect for the principle of equal rights and self-determination of peoples" is linked to "universal respect for, and observance of, human rights and fundamental freedoms for all without distinction as to race, sex, language, or religion." As stated earlier, under Article 56 all Member States pledge themselves to take joint and separate action in co-operation with the United Nations for the implementation of Article 55.

The Universal Declaration, too, has established a link between human rights and peace. Its first preambular paragraph states that the "recognition of the inherent dignity and of the equal and inalienable rights of all members of the human family is the foundation of freedom, justice and peace in the world." The second preambular paragraph adds that "disregard and contempt for human rights have resulted in barbarous acts which have outraged the conscience of mankind . . ." Even more explicit is the third preambular paragraph which says: "It is essential, if man is not to be compelled to have recourse, as a last resort, to rebellion against tyranny and oppression, that human rights should be protected by the rule of law."

The Covenants on human rights have established the same link. The first preambular paragraph of each Covenant is identical to the first preambular paragraph of the Universal Declaration. Furthermore, in its preamble, the International Convention on the Elimination of All Forms of Racial Discrimination reaffirms that discrimination between human beings on the grounds of race, color or ethnic origin is capable of disturbing peace and security among peoples. Moreover, the relationship between human rights and peace has been emphasized in many resolutions of the United Nations.

The link between human rights and international peace has been receiving increasing recognition, both inside and outside the United Nations. On 21 March 1979, at a meeting to observe the International Day for the

Elimination of Racial Discrimination, the Secretary-General of the United Nations said:

> More than ever today we understand that the international struggle against racial prejudice, inequality and injustice is very much related to the creation of conditions of stability and well-being which are necessary for peaceful and friendly relations among nations. In essence, these conditions must be based upon respect for the concept of equal rights and self-determination. In South Africa the policies of apartheid are diametrically opposed to this concept. There can be no peace while the overwhelming majority of its people are deliberately deprived of their human rights and excluded from the mainstream of their country's political, economic and social life.[50]

Similarly, in his address to the United Nations on 2 October 1979, His Holiness Pope John Paul II said:

> It is a question of the highest importance that in internal social life, as well as in international life, all human beings in every nation and country should be able to enjoy effectively their full rights under any political régime or system.
> Only the safeguarding of this real completeness of rights for every human being without discrimination can ensure peace at its very roots.[51]

The Final Act of the Conference on Security and Co-operation in Europe, adopted by thirty-five states in 1975, provides yet another example of the same relationship. In its Declaration on Principles Guiding Relations between Participating States, the Conference said that "the participating States recognize the universal significance of human rights and fundamental freedoms, respect for which is an essential factor for the peace, justice and well-being necessary to ensure the development of friendly relations and co-operation among themselves as among all States."

Reflecting the gravity of the racial situation in South Africa and its probable consequences for world peace, President Nyerere of Tanzania wrote that South Africa's

> organized denial of human rights to all but 17 per cent of its people, on the grounds of their race, makes South Africa's 'internal affairs' a matter of world concern. For nations have learned, and mankind has learned, that the hope for world peace and justice precludes indifference in the face of organized racialism.[52]

In the face of such racial discrimination as exists in South Africa then, and given the Organization's commitment to upholding human rights and preserving international peace and security, the question arises as to what competence does the Organization have in dealing with the menacing situation in South Africa.

The competence of the General Assembly and the Security Council is governed by the Charter provisions relating to their "functions and powers."

Both are limited, however, by Article 2 (7), the domestic jurisdiction clause, apart from political limitations on account of national or other interests. As for the Assembly, its functions and powers are governed by Articles 10 to 17, inclusive, but the article applicable to the racialized order in South Africa is evidently Article 14, which is designed for peaceful change. This article reads:

> Subject to the provisions of Article 12, the General Assembly may recommend measures for the peaceful adjustment of any situation, regardless of origin, which it deems likely to impair the general welfare or friendly relations among nations, including situations resulting from a violation of the provisions of the present Charter setting forth the Purposes and Principles of the United Nations.

The Report of the Rapporteur of Commission II to the plenary session at the San Francisco Conference stated that the Assembly would have ''wide powers of recommendation in economic, cultural, and humanitarian matters.''[53] The Assembly's decisions, however, are recommendatory, and its authority under Article 14 is restricted by Article 12, paragraph 1, which provides that ''while the Security Council is exercising in respect of any dispute or situation the functions assigned to it in the present Charter, the General Assembly shall not make any recommendation with regard to that dispute or situation unless the Security Council so requests.'' Subject to Article 12, the Assembly may discuss any questions relating to the maintenance of international peace and security and make recommendations to the states concerned or to the Security Council or to both. The Assembly may also call the attention of the Council to situations which are likely to endanger international peace and security (Article 11, paragraph 3).

Article 14 of the Charter is, to some extent, the counterpart of Article 19 of the League Covenant, which reads: ''The Assembly may from time to time advise the reconsideration by Members of the League of treaties which have become inapplicable and the consideration of international conditions whose continuance might endanger the peace of the world.'' Article 19 of the Covenant had aimed at the consideration of international conditions, mainly the revision of treaties and territorial changes, endangering international peace. Article 14 of the Charter is wider in scope; it aims at the revision of conditions, arising out of any source, impairing the general welfare or friendly relations among nations. In other words, while Article 19 of the Covenant applied in case of threat to international peace, Article 14 of the Charter operates even in situations before they threaten international peace. In case of such a threat, the Assembly has to refer the matter to the Council which is the principal organ vested with primary responsibility for the maintenance of international peace and security and which has to ''act in accordance with the Purposes and Principles of the United Nations,'' in terms of its functions and powers under Articles 24 to 26, inclusive.

Significantly, Article 14 does cover situations resulting from a violation of the provisions of the Charter. No doubt, the situation in South Africa is a result of the violation of the human rights provisions of the Charter and has, in the least, impaired friendly relations among nations. Indeed, in its first resolution on the matter in 1946, the Assembly asserted that friendly relations between South Africa and India had been impaired because of the racial policies of the Government of South Africa.

An interesting comment on this topic comes from three distinguished students of the international Organization, who state in their study of the Charter that

> more often the application of Article 14 has been discussed in connection with alleged violations of the Purposes and Principles of the Charter, especially those concerning human rights and self-determination. Article 14 has been invoked to justify action by the Assembly in these cases in the face of arguments that the questions being dealt with are matters of domestic jurisdiction.[54]

Meanwhile, as already noted, both the Assembly and the Council are restricted in competence by the domestic jurisdiction clause of the Charter, that is, Article 2, paragraph 7. This clause provides:

> Nothing contained in the present Charter shall authorize the United Nations to intervene in matters which are essentially within the domestic jurisdiction of any State or shall require the Members to submit such matters to settlement under the present Charter; but this principle shall not prejudice the application of enforcement measures under Chapter VII.

But, to determine whether a given matter is essentially within domestic jurisdiction, any organ has first to consider and study that matter. Many writers therefore believe that, irrespective of whether it is in the field of human rights, each organ of the United Nations can determine its own competence to consider, study, and make recommendations on any matter. Also, the power of recommendation, such as that given to the Assembly, necessarily entails the power of prior consideration and study.

With regard to the question of determining whether a given situation is within domestic jurisdiction, the Commission on the Racial Situation in the Union of South Africa concluded in its first report that "the authors of the Charter expressly manifested the intention that organs of the United Nations should themselves be called upon to interpret the scope of that Article [Article 2 (7)] in each case whether or not a given situation was within the domestic jurisdiction of a State."[55]

Nevertheless, domestic jurisdiction was limited by an understanding at the San Francisco Conference where the gravity of violations of human rights was not ignored. The Charter provisions should be interpreted not only in light of the progressive development of international law and teleologically but also historically on the grounds and meaning according to which they were adopted. Indeed, at the San Francisco Conference Sub-committee 1/1/A "held that assuring or protecting such fundamental rights [as contained in the Charter] is primarily the concern of each State. If, however, such rights and freedoms were grievously outraged so as to create conditions which threaten peace or to obstruct the application of provisions of the Charter, then they cease to be the sole concern of each State."[56]

Thus, the fathers of the Charter excluded human rights and fundamental freedoms from domestic jurisdiction in two cases: (a) where the violation of such rights becomes a threat to international peace and (b) where such violation obstructs the application of the provisions of the Charter. The existence of either one of these two conditions was deemed enough to consider such violation a matter of international concern and, therefore, beyond the scope of domestic jurisdiction.

It is generally accepted that with regard to human rights vis-à-vis the domestic jurisdiction clause, the Charter is not very clear. Yet, if the domestic jurisdiction clause were to be broadly interpreted, the human rights provisions of the Charter would become meaningless and the United Nations would have no say at all in such matters. If human rights were to have been regarded solely as a matter of domestic jurisdiction and entirely outside United Nations control, then there would have been no purpose for the founding fathers repeatedly to provide for human rights in general and for non-discrimination in particular within the Charter. The human rights provisions constitute one of the main purposes of the Charter and should be seen in balance, not in contradistinction, with domestic jurisdiction. In the words of the Rapporteur of the Committee 1/1 at San Francisco,

> the provisions of the Charter, being in this case indivisible as in any other legal instrument, are equally valid and operative. The rights, duties, privileges and obligations of the Organization and its Members match with one another and complement one another to make a whole. Each of them is construed to be understood and applied in function of the others.[57]

With respect to the domestic jurisdiction clause versus human rights, Lauterpacht concluded that Article 2, paragraph 7, does not exclude measures falling short of intervention as understood in international law. He added that inasmuch as the question of the observance of fundamental human rights and freedoms is a basic legal obligation of the Members of the United Nations it is outside the reservation of Article 2, paragraph 7.[58] He believed that the study, investigation, discussion, or recommendation by the Assembly or any other organ of the United Nations of any situation resulting from failure of states to observe their obligations with regard to human rights did not constitute intervention. Such action was not coercive, he continued, and did not constitute peremptory, dictatorial interference. Also, he maintained that extreme cases of human rights violations involving the peace of the world were outside domestic jurisdiction.[59]

One student of the issue has maintained that "competent international lawyers agree on the point that the matters of essentially domestic jurisdiction cannot be definitely determined in advance and that this point can only be decided after taking into consideration the particular facts at a particular time."[60] With regard to the competence of the Security Council, he concluded that the subtle distinction in the last part of Article 2, paragraph 7, designed to prevent the Council from intervening in every minor eventuality, did not serve the desired purpose and that in practice the Council has assumed competence even in cases involving domestic matters which constituted potential threats to international peace as against actual threats.[61]

In contrast to the narrow, technical interpretation given the term "intervention" in international law, as applied by Lauterpacht to Article 2 (7) of the Charter, others have given that term a broad interpretation. Reference has been made, for example, to Goodrich as one of those who have favored a broad interpretation and who believed that the creation of a commission of inquiry, the making of a recommendation, or the adoption of a binding decision constitutes intervention in terms of Article 2 (7).[62] Still others have held that a recommendation made by the United Nations to a specific, designated state, as opposed to a general recommendation, constitutes an intervention.[63]

One long-time observer of the United Nations has warned:

> The relative ease with which the majority of the States Members of the United Nations was able to sweep aside all constitutional scruples in the way of their massive attack on South Africa's internal policies was not so much a confirmation of the justice of their cause, as a warning of the inherent danger of an approach to international problems which is especially susceptible to political vagaries of the moment. The fact that practically the whole membership of the United Nations was moved to support the call for economic and diplomatic sanctions against the land of apartheid in no way resolved the constitutional ambiguities and uncertainties of their action.[64]

In the case of the Nationality Decrees in Tunisia and Morocco in 1921, which gave rise to a dispute between France and Great Britain, the Permanent Court of International Justice held in its advisory opinion that "the question whether a certain matter is or is not solely within the jurisdiction of a state is essentially a relative question: it depends upon the development of international relations."[65] The criterion of relativity with regard to domestic jurisdiction is still valid. Nothing has happened in the meantime to justify its abrogation.

As to whether a clear distinction can be established between the jurisdiction of the United Nations and the domestic jurisdiction (reserved domain) of states, one writer has noted that one cannot disregard the guiding principle of relativity as stated by the Permanent Court in the Nationality Decrees—particularly in relation to Article 2 (7) where no reference is made to international law—as a criterion for determining matters of domestic jurisdiction. The same writer has also noted that the Charter term "essentially," as compared to the term "solely" in the League Covenant, has brought an important change in the domestic jurisdiction clause by ensuring more flexibility for international political action.[66] He asserts that an ambiguity was created between Article 2 (7) and Article 56 of the Charter, and adds that Felix Ermacora had been mentioned as having maintained that a concurrent jurisdiction between Member States and the United Nations could be established in the subsequent practice of the United Nations as a result of that ambiguity.[67]

Ermacora has expressed the opinion that the answer to the question whether the implementation and safeguarding of human rights fall essentially within the domestic jurisdiction of a state should be sought in the handling of concrete human rights cases by the organs of the United Nations. From the precedents set by the organs of the United Nations, he has concluded that some human rights are no longer essentially within the domestic jurisdiction of states. These rights are, he believes, the promotion of the respect for human rights, the right to self-determination, and the protection of human rights in matters of discrimination as far as "gross violations" or "consistent patterns of violations" are concerned. He maintains that the aforesaid rights are, similar to the distribution of competence in federal states, "common matters of States and the international organization" and "are in their *concurrent jurisdiction*."[68] As apartheid has been considered by the United Nations a gross and persistent violation of human rights, it follows that he considers apartheid a matter within concurrent jurisdiction.

Brierly has stated that Article 2, paragraph 7, of the Charter

> . . . raises the query as to how far, if at all, the Organization is entitled to look into allegations of breaches of human rights by individual members as distinct from trying to encourage respect for human rights generally among members; and some even argue that the Charter clauses only contain a pious injunction to co-operate in promoting respect for human rights and do not impose any legal obligation on members with regard to their own nationals. The latter argument seems in any event to go too far, since a pledge to cooperate in promoting at least implies a negative obligation not so to act as to undermine human rights; for this reason South Africa's racial segregation policies appear to be out of harmony with her obligations under the Charter.[69]

In short, there has been a progressive development of international law on human rights and fundamental freedoms, and the United Nations has made them a matter of international concern. They are provided for in the Charter, which is an international treaty, as the constitution of an international and almost universal Organization. The Charter does not define human rights and fundamental freedoms, but it can be maintained that it does impose legal obligations on Member States in the field of human rights. Under Article 2, paragraph 2, of the Charter, those obligations have to be carried out in good faith.

The Charter provisions on racial non-discrimination are precise enough so as not to present any difficulty of interpretation. They should be interpreted according to the principle of good faith. In the meantime, those provisions have been strengthened by the adoption of a number of international human rights instruments, by the pronouncements of the International Court of Justice, by the work of the International Law Commission, and, as will be subsequently discussed, by the unanimous verdict of the international community against apartheid. There has also been strong recognition of the links between grave violation of human rights, such as legalized racial discrimination, and international peace. It seems reasonable to conclude, therefore, that racial non-discrimination has become a norm of customary international law.

Consequently, the fact that a Member State has not acceded to a human rights instrument prohibiting racial discrimination does not free that state from obligations under the Charter and international law. Otherwise, international concern with human rights could regress to pre-League days. It would be absurd to contend that the League could concern itself with minorities' rights but that the United Nations, whose Charter replaced the minority rights by its all-embracing provisions on human rights and fundamental freedoms all over the world, could not concern itself with such rights or, still worse, with legalized racial discrimination against majorities as in South Africa.

II. SOUTH AFRICA'S RACIALIZED LEGAL ORDER

Population

The population of South Africa is about 28,000,000.[70] The people in South Africa are classified on racial grounds by the Government as White (4,500,000), African (20,000,000), Asian (800,000), and Colored (2,600,000). It is generally accepted that race refers to a group of people socially defined according to physical characteristics. The white people (Europeans) are Afrikaans-speaking and English-speaking, with the former in the majority among the whites. By the term "African," the South African Government means the native (Bantu) people who are further classified by ethnic background as Xhosa, Zulu, Sotho, and Tswana. Whites constitute about 16.2 percent of the population and their proportion has been decreasing. Africans outnumber whites more than four to one. Blacks, as defined in this study, outnumber Europeans about six to one.[71] The Asians are mostly of Indian origin; some of the Asians come from the Chinese background. The Coloreds are people of mixed racial descent. Although whites are in the minority in South Africa, Afrikaans and English are the two official languages of the country. Bantu (African) languages are also official in the homelands which have achieved self-government. To understand the South African problem it is necessary to look briefly at the values and objectives of the whites and the blacks of South Africa.

White Population

The political values of the white population in South Africa relate to their political system which was established on a racialized legal order that guarantees what they call their vital interest. In practice, such an order guarantees the perpetuation of their domination. The white population would have others believe that their vital interests and their dominating status in the country are inextricably linked and that there exists no better alternative to apartheid. Of course, that simplistic view ignores the vital interests of the other people of the country.

In 1950, Prime Minister D. F. Malan said that total territorial segregation was impracticable in South Africa because the white people's "whole economic structure is, to a large extent, based on Native labor."[72] Clearly, that statement indicated the privileges of the white population rather than their "vital" interests. They have enjoyed those privileges so long that they virtually take them for granted. Consequently, any proposed change in the political and social system that would adversely affect those privileges would seem, to the white population, to affect their vital interests and values. To retain the racialized legal order that guarantees those privileges to whites, the cultural cleavages among ethnic groups have been extremely politicized by the Government.

Mahatma Gandhi, who lived and worked in South Africa for many years, tells of a chilling experience in the early 1880s when Indian leaders went to see President Kruger to make representation against a bill submitted to the Transvaal parliament which put restrictions on Indian trade and land ownership. President Kruger would not admit them into his house, and made them stand in the courtyard. He told them:

> You are the descendants of Ishmael and therefore from your very birth bound to slave for the descendants of Essau. As the descendants of Essau we cannot admit you to rights placing you on an equality with ourselves. You must rest content with what rights we grant to you.[73]

Gandhi did not fail in his writings to point out what the interests were of the Europeans in South Africa. Speaking of racial discrimination against the people of Indian origin in South Africa, he said:

> They [Europeans] were all out to amass the maximum of wealth in a minimum of time; how could they stand the Indians becoming co-sharers with them? Hypocrisy pressed political theory into service in order to make out a plausible case . . . The human intellect delights in inventing specious arguments in order to support injustice itself, and the South African Europeans were no exception to this general rule.[74]

South African politicians, for their part, have not disguised their purposes. In 1963, Prime Minister H. F. Verwoerd, speaking to the South African House of Assembly, said:

> Reduced to its simplest form the problem is nothing else than this: We want to keep South Africa White . . . Keeping it white can only mean one thing, namely, White domination, not leadership, not guidance, but control, supremacy. If we are agreed that it is the desire of the people that the White man should be able to protect himself by White domination . . . we say that it can be achieved by separate development.[75]

South African leaders have even gone so far as to cite divine mandates for their economic and political policies. In April 1979, the then Prime Minister B. J. Vorster said that he believed profoundly that Afrikaners had been appointed by Providence to play a role in South Africa.[76] Some students of South African affairs, however, believe that the concept of ethnic mobilization is the key for understanding South African politics. They maintain that, since 1948, the National Party's central concern has not been so much the apartheid ideology as the maintenance of Afrikaner identity as a means of preserving and promoting Afrikaner interests.[77] Others have cited social Darwinism, the dates of the arrival of racial groups in southern Africa, self-reliance, and the existence of four identifiable racial groups as the main values that led South Africa's whites to choose apartheid. These observers believe that Calvinism and economic factors have been given too much weight in the traditional analyses of apartheid.[78]

Afrikaners are for the most part members of the Dutch Reformed Church and are firm believers in its Calvinistic values. This church is a racially segregated one. There is a mother church for the whites and sister churches for other racial groups. Although not all the members of this church advocate apartheid or believe that apartheid exists on the authority of God, its teachings have had great influence. The secret Afrikaner society *Brotherhood* (Broederbond), which was established in 1918 and which played an important role in the build-up of the National Party, came up with the notion that Afrikaners are appointed by God to play a dominant role in South Africa, to form a separate nation identified with Western Christian civilization, and to take over the guardianship of other people who should develop separately. In an attempt to legitimize this notion through theology, some theologians from the Dutch Reformed Church in South Africa have asserted that in the Bible differences between races are as emphatically proclaimed as the unity of the human race. Critics have characterized such notions and assertions as serious forms of pseudo-theology, and regard apartheid as contrary to the Christian Gospel and the dignity of man.[79]

In view of the present progressive attitude of the Dutch people of the Netherlands, who profess the same Calvinistic religion, it is very doubtful that this theology is the main reason for the Afrikaners' concept of government. It is interesting, for example, to see what the representative of the Netherlands said in 1979, during the debate in the General Assembly on apartheid:

> This denial of freedom, justice and economic well-being is totally abhorrent to the Netherlands Government and people. There are those in South Africa who take pride in their European descent and frequently show their affinity with the Western world. We want them to know that their practice of arrests, bannings and intimidation is alien to our views on justice and fundamental aspects of society, which, unhappily, has become commonplace in the daily lives of the majority of South Africa, is in flagrant contradiction to our values. We want them to know too that we feel indignation about the way black people live in the so-called white areas, in total insecurity and in constant fear of being uprooted and separated from members of their family. The so-called pass laws, intended *inter alia* to stem black emigration to these white areas, lead to some

150,000 summonses a year. We therefore say once again that there is no common ground between this travesty of human justice and the heritage of moral and spiritual principles shared by the Western world.[80]

As far as South Africa's claim to being the preservers of Western civilization and democracy in South Africa, that position was challenged during a debate on the policies of apartheid in the General Assembly in November 1979. Speaking on behalf of the nine member states of the European Community, the representative of Ireland said:

This Assembly has repeatedly and unequivocally condemned *apartheid* in South Africa. The concept of separate development on a racial basis is contrary to the principles of equality and justice to which our countries firmly adhere and violates the most fundamental principles of the Charter of the United Nations. The *apartheid* system is based on racial segregation, discrimination, exploitation of human beings and repression. It has caused the majority of South Africans immeasurable suffering in the interests of ensuring the economic and political domination of white South Africans.

The Nine strongly deplore the grave injustice done by the Government of South Africa to the majority of its citizens by denying them their basic political rights and participation in the ordering of their own society. If this situation continues the Nine fear that opportunities for peaceful change in South Africa will be lost.

Freedom of political expression is, in our view, vital to the democratic process . . .

. . . These policies show how shallow is South Africa's claim to uphold democratic values, and demonstrate the risks it is prepared to take in its stubborn adherence to notions of separate development and racial superiority.[81]

There can be little doubt that apartheid is based on the doctrine of racial superiority.[82] For the Afrikaner that belief is part of a value system. Perhaps that belief is best summarized in the first report (3 October 1953) of the United Nations Commission on the Racial Situation in the Union of South Africa which concluded:

The doctrine [of apartheid] is based on the theory that the white race, as the heir to Western Christian civilization, is in duty bound to maintain inviolate and to perpetuate its position in Western Christian civilization, and must at any cost, although in a numerical minority, maintain its dominating position over the Coloured races. It refutes all dogmas of civil equality and therefore cannot grant the Natives or Bantus, or any other non-white groups such as the Coloured persons and Indians, the political rights which the white population enjoys and which confer on it the management of public affairs.[83]

As to the preponderous importance of economic interests over other causes for racial discrimination and apartheid, Michael Manley, former Prime Minister of Jamaica, spoke to that point in 1978 in the plenary meeting of the Assembly, when he stated:

But in fact it is impossible to understand *apartheid* and the entire structure of oppression in southern Africa without understanding the origins and continuing nature of imperialism. The three centuries which ended in 1945 witnessed an event unique in the history: the subjugation of three quarters of the globe by a technologically triumphant minority. Imperialism consisted of the military and political organization of the world for the purpose of economic exploitation. Half-empty territories were occupied, ancient and often glorious civilizations were destroyed in Africa, Asia and the Americas. The raw economic force of these events is without parallel in human history.

Racism was a terrible progeny of the process, but the human passions which it provokes must never be allowed to mask the true father of the process, which is the economic exploitation of nation by nation and, ultimately, of man by man. And it is precisely because racism is not the cause but the effect of injustice in southern Africa that we must look beyond the broken bodies of Soweto to find the true targets of our indignation and the real focus for our efforts.[84]

In short, apartheid policy seems more a product of Afrikaner interests than of values. The latter seem to have been shaped accordingly. The economic rewards accruing to the whites of South Africa as the result of extreme racial discrimination, legally institutionalized as apartheid, have been great. Black people in South Africa have been relegated to mere tools or units of labor. They are not partners with whites in any field. As has been aptly described by Deutsch, "in a country with racial discrimination, some of the economic relations among race groups take on the characteristics of international trade, just as some of the political relations among these groups assume several of the qualities of international relations, including its dangers."[85] In both types of relations, one can see a quasi-colonial status surrounding the black population in South Africa.

It is often said that the whites of South Africa cannot accept racial equality because their very survival will be threatened. Much depends on the meaning attributed to the term "survival." Is it their physical existence or their position of domination and exploitation that will be threatened? Survival does not necessitate domination and exploitation in a civilized society. On the contrary, history has shown that such practices inevitably engender violence, repression, and a threat to the very survival that the exploiters are trying to preserve.

In South Africa, the whites' survival has not been threatened by the African population. The black population has sought racial equality, not the riddance of the white population. If, in the future, the white population's survival should be threatened, it would be precisely because successive South African governments have never negotiated with the whole population in order to establish an agreed order or political system that would guarantee their rights and interests, whether in a unitary, federal, confederal, or partitionist system.

The whites have maintained their dominating and exploiting position by brute force within a racialized legal order, established without the participation or consent of the great majority of the people of South Africa. Even as late as November 1979, long after armed struggle was resorted to by the liberation movements of South Africa, the representative of the Pan Africanist Congress of Azania (PAC) said:

> To argue the anti-colonial nature of our struggle is not to deny the right of the white populace to a continued existence in our country, but it does deny them a position of power and privilege at the expense of the black majority. PAC maintains and will always maintain that there is only one race—the human race.[86]

With regard to the Afrikaners' concern for survival, two authors have observed that the formula of survival has emerged because ethnic chauvinism, cultural purity, or anti-communism have failed to provide the needed rationale for apartheid.[87] They have noted that the absence of an ideology beyond that of mere survival crucially weakens the cause of the white South Africans, that such a survivalist policy lacks moral principles worth defending, and that unquestioned right of survival is seen by the Western world as insufficient for supporting a racial minority. They have also argued that, as a mobilizing concept, the formula of survival represents no more than the minimum common denominator of an oligarchy bound together primarily on the basis of privilege maintenance.

It can, of course, be argued that the whites' fear concerns not so much their physical existence as the extinction of their culture, that is, their cultural survival. Yet, even in that regard, apartheid is not the only choice; nor is it a cogent justification for the continuation of the present system. To pretend otherwise, especially without negotiating, is nothing but an ostrich attitude. It has been aptly said that the Afrikaners "conceal the preservation of the whites' inordinate economic privileges under the cover of protecting 'white identity,' and more specifically 'Afrikaner identity.' "[88]

If the whites truly regarded integration as a threat to their survival, and wanted a peaceful alternative, they might have negotiated political, administrative, or territorial partition. For example, it has been suggested that to avert a massive and violent racial conflict a Cyprus-type solution should be contemplated.[89] Also, the idea of partition and the establishment of a "Whitestan" has increasingly been brought up in connection with South Africa.[90] As for Western pressure on South Africa to bring about internal peaceful change, it has been said that "despite the political rhetoric in South Africa, the West does not demand the destruction of the whites . . ."[91]

The idea of federation, too, has increasingly been brought up in connection with South Africa, both inside and outside that country. Beyers Naude of the Christian Institute of Southern Africa, who was among those "banned" by the South African Government in October 1977, is quoted as saying that it is his "clear conviction that, despite all efforts that the

Government [of South Africa] might currently or in the near future undertake to establish independent states, black majority rule for South Africa is inevitable either in a unified or in a federated State."[92]

Afrikaners have been in the majority among the whites, and they have formed the government since 1948. Obviously, their values and objectives have been dominant among the white population. There has been some opposition to the government's racial policies from among Afrikaners, but more has come from the English-speaking whites. The difference of opinion between those two factions of the white population and any reassessment by whites of their apartheid policy will be discussed later in connection with the impact of the United Nations on South Africa.

Black Population

As has been noted, the black population of South Africa consists of Africans, Asians, and the Coloreds. Africans are indigenous. The first Asians were people of Indian origin who came to Natal in 1860 as indentured laborers at the request made to the Indian Government by British settlers who wanted a stable labor force for their plantations. Racial discrimination was practiced legally long before apartheid was institutionalized in 1948. In 1926, the Governments of India and South Africa entered into discussions on the treatment of Indians. They achieved agreements in 1927 and 1931. Not only the Africans, but also the Indians and the Coloreds have been left outside the mainstream of the political, economic, and social life in South Africa. They have all long aspired to racial equality.

To understand the values and objectives of the black people of South Africa, one may look at the statements of some of their leaders. Chief Albert J. Luthuli, the President-General of the African National Congress of South Africa (ANC) and Nobel Peace Prize winner, at his Nobel lecture in Oslo on 11 December 1961, said:

> Our vision has always been that of a non-racial democratic South Africa which upholds the rights of all who live in our country to remain there as full citizens with equal rights and responsibilities with all others. For the consummation of this ideal we have laboured unflinchingly. We shall continue to labour unflinchingly.
>
> It is this vision which prompted the African National Congress to invite members of other racial groups who believe with us in the brotherhood of man and in the freedom of all people to join with us in establishing a non-racial democratic South Africa. Thus, the African National Congress in its day brought about the Congress Alliance and welcomed the emergence of the Liberal Party and the Progressive Party, who, to an encouraging measure, support these ideals. . . .
>
> We do not demand these things for people of African descent alone. We demand them for all South Africans, white and black. On these principles we

are uncompromising. To compromise would be an expediency that is most treacherous to democracy, for in the turn of events the sweets of economic, political and social privileges that are a monopoly of only one section of a community turn sour even in the mouths of those who eat them. Thus apartheid in practice is proving to be a monster created by Frankenstein. That is the tragedy of the South African scene.[93]

Robert Mangaliso Sobukwe, President of PAC who died on 26 February 1978 in Kimberley, where he lived under banning orders after his release in 1969 from the Robben Island prison, said at the inauguration of PAC in April 1959:

We aim, politically, at government of the Africans by the Africans, for the Africans, with everybody who owes his only loyalty to Africa and who is prepared to accept the democratic rule of an African majority being regarded as an African.[94]

Another black politician, Nelson Mandela, leader of ANC, who has been serving a life sentence on the Robben Island since 1964 and has been in jail since 1962, had this to say during his statement made at "Rivonia Trial" on 20 April 1964:

Above all, we want equal political rights, because without them our disabilities will be permanent. I know this sounds revolutionary to the Whites in this country, because the majority of voters will be Africans. This makes the White man fear democracy.

But this fear cannot be allowed to stand in the way of the only solution which will guarantee racial harmony and freedom for all. It is not true that the enfranchisement of all will result in racial domination. Political division, based on colour, is entirely artificial and, when it disappears, so will the domination of one colour group by another. The ANC has spent half a century fighting against racialism. When it triumphs it will not change that policy.[95]

Speaking in the Security Council on 31 October 1977, the representative of the United States quoted the late Steven Biko, who was tortured to death in detention, as saying:

We are looking forward to a non-racial, just and egalitarian society in which colour, creed and race shall form no point of reference. We have deliberately chosen to operate openly because we have believed for a very long time that through a process of organized bargaining we can penetrate even the deafest of white ears and get the message to register that no lie can live forever.

In doing this we rely not only on our strength but also on the belief that the rest of the world views the oppression and blatant exploitation of the black majority by a minority as an unforgivable sin that cannot be pardoned by civilized societies.[96]

The United States representative also quoted Percy Qoboza as saying that he still had faith that the point of no return had not yet been reached and that it was "never too late to build a South Africa where people of all races can live together in mutual respect and tolerance."[97]

The Freedom Charter of South Africa, adopted unanimously at the Congress of the People, held in Kliptown, near Johannesburg, on 26 June 1955, is in a similar vein. The Congress was convened by the African National Congress, together with the South African Indian Congress, the South African Colored People's Organization, and the Congress of Democrats (white organization). The Freedom Charter seeks equality for all people of South Africa: equality in rights, equality before the law, equality in political participation, and equality in the enjoyment of human rights. It should also be noted that, since ANC and PAC comprise not only Africans but also Asians and Coloreds, the statements by ANC and PAC leaders reflect the values and objectives of virtually all the black people of South Africa.

At its beginning, the Freedom Charter reads:

> We, the people of South Africa, declare for all our country and the world to know:
> —that South Africa belongs to all who live in it, black and white, and that no government can justly claim authority unless it is based on the will of all the people;
> —that our people have been robbed of their birthright to land, liberty and peace by a form of government founded on injustice and inequality;
> —that our country will never be prosperous or free until all our people live in brotherhood, enjoying equal rights and opportunities;
> —that only a democratic state, based on the will of all the people, can secure to all their birthright without distinction of colour, race, sex or belief;
> And, therefore, we the people of South Africa, black and white together—equals, countrymen and brothers—adopt this Freedom Charter. And we pledge ourselves to strive together sparing neither strength nor courage, until the democratic changes set out here have been won.[98]

Other black leaders who are known as moderates because they have been opposing apartheid from within the system, have also sought a fair sharing of power, land, and facilities, but never the destruction of the white population. These leaders are committed to change without violence. They include such personalities as Gatsha Buthelezi, Chief of KwaZulu; Manas Buthelezi, Bishop of the Evangelical Lutheran Church of Southern Africa and Chairman of the Black Parents' Association; Lucas M. Mangope, Chief of Bophuthatswana; Kaiser D. Matanzima, Paramount Chief of the Transkei; C. N. Phatudi, Chief of Lebowa; and Lennox L. Sebe, Chief of the Ciskei. Many black political, cultural, and educational organizations have pursued similar aims; never have they advocated the elimination, suppression, or the expulsion of white South Africans.[99] The black people of South Africa have consistently demanded that they be permitted to share in the government.

Until 1961, when the armed wing of the ANC, *Umkhonto we Sizwe*

(Spear of the Nation), was established, the African population of South Africa pursued its objective of racial equality through such peaceful means as meetings, conventions, statements, and recourse to the United Nations. Up to then, the power of the oppressed majority was no more than the power of persuasion. Through such instruments as the Freedom Charter of 1955, and speeches and statements by its leaders, the black people tried, by peaceful means, to persuade the international community that its rights and freedoms, its dignity and development were unjustly and adversely affected by the racial policies of the South African Government.

In 1960, both ANC and PAC, among other organizations, were banned by the South African Government. Since then both have gone underground and have increasingly resorted to armed struggle. They have been training young freedom-fighters in military and guerrilla combat, as revealed by court cases in South Africa. Indeed, the reason why the Terrorism Act of 1967 was made retroactive to 1962 was, according to the then Minister of Justice, because in 1962 the two banned organizations started training guerrilla fighters.[100] The armed wing of PAC, namely, *Poqo* (Purity), was established in 1962.

The Political System

After the Boer War (1899-1902), which led to the Peace of Vereeiniging, the four colonies in South Africa were united under one government. The South Africa Act of 1909 established the Union of South Africa. In 1931, South Africa became an independent state within the British Commonwealth of Nations. In 1948, the National Party came to power on the campaign platform of apartheid. That Party, which had emerged in the 1930s on militant Afrikaner nationalism, has been in power ever since.

As "parliamentary supremacy is basic to the constitutional structure of South Africa," in the words of one expert, and as the Afrikaners have constituted the dominant party in the House of Assembly, South Africa has, in effect, been governed by the Afrikaners since 1948.[101] On 31 May 1961, following a plebiscite, the Republic of South Africa Constitution Act No. 32 (25 April 1961) constituted the Republic of South Africa. That same year, the Republic was forced to withdraw from the Commonwealth due to increasing criticism and pressure by the new members from Africa and Asia, because of its apartheid policy.

South Africa is a republican, unitary, and parliamentary state. Until 1981, the Parliament consisted of two Houses: The House of Assembly and the Senate. Since then, the Senate has been replaced by the President's Council.[102] The legislative power of the Republic is vested in the Parliament. Political and executive power is vested in the Cabinet. The leader of the majority party in the House is appointed by the state president as prime minister, and the state president is elected by the parliament. Blacks are excluded from the Parliament and from national elections.[103] English and Afrikaans are official languages on an equal basis.[104] In addition to the Government of the Republic, the Cape, Natal, Transvaal, and Orange Free State have their provincial governments. Blacks are excluded from these governments, too.

In 1950, the National Party Government abolished the Colored Advisory Council which had been established in 1943. In 1956, the Colored people were removed from the common roll for elections to the House of Assembly. To represent them in the House, in 1958, they elected four whites. In 1968, this representation was ended and the Colored Persons' Representative Council was established.[105] This Council, which has recently been disbanded because of great opposition from the Colored comunity, could draft laws in some areas affecting the Coloreds, but any bill had to be approved by the Minister of Colored Affairs before it was introduced, and it had to be approved by the Cabinet (white) after it was passed, in order to be effective. After the establishment of the Council, a Department of Colored Relations was created to look after Colored matters outside the jurisdiction of the Council.

The Asiatic Land Tenure and Indian Representation Act of 1946 dealt with land and franchise rights of the people of Indian origin. With regard to franchise rights, the Act provided that Indian men in Natal and Transvaal, with stipulated educational and financial qualifications, could elect three white people to represent them at the House of Assembly. In the Senate, they would be represented by two white senators, one elected and one appointed. In 1948, this part of the Act was repealed by the new Government of South Africa. In 1961, a Minister of Indian Affairs was appointed in charge of the Department of Indian Affairs. The people of Indian origin have the South African Indian Council, established in 1968, with even more limited political capacity than was given to the Coloreds' Council. At the elections held on 4 November 1981 for this advisory body, 90 percent of the eligible voters boycotted the polls to show that they opposed apartheid and its separate institutions.

In 1976, an Inter-Cabinet Council was created. It consisted of some Cabinet Ministers (white) as representatives of the Indian and Colored Councils. Most factions of the Colored organizations declined to participate. The Africans were left outside this new endeavor.

The Representation of Natives [African] Act of 1936 gave the Africans advisory powers and deprived them of their franchise rights. It provided that African voters in the Cape should elect three whites to represent them at the House of Assembly and should thus be removed from the common roll. Also, all Africans in South Africa would elect four white senators. The Act established an advisory Natives' Representative Council. In 1951, three years after the National Party assumed power, the Bantu Authorities Act was adopted. The Act abolished the Natives' Representative Council of 1936 and provided for Bantu tribal and territorial authorities. The measure did not involve direct representation in the central administration.

Isolation of the Bantu people from having a voice in the government in Pretoria continued apace. In 1959, the Promotion of Bantu Self-Government Act, which resulted from the Bantu Authorities Act of 1951, abolished the parliamentary representation of Africans by whites and established the stepping-stone of the "homeland" policy. It aimed at gathering the Africans into the Reserves and turning those outside the Reserves into migrant laborers. In time, homelands were set aside under the Act. In Bantu homelands (termed Bantustans), there are homeland legislative assemblies where the Africans have limited self-government. Those homelands are the Ciskei, KwaZulu, Lebowa, Gazankulu, Qwaqwa, KaNgwane, Ndebele, Transkei, Bophuthatswana, and Venda.

In the Transkei, Bophuthatswana, and Venda, which were declared "independent" states by the South African Government in 1976, 1977, and 1979, respectively, the legislatures operate within the agreements signed with the Government of South Africa. Some towns and white farming areas of those territories have been excluded. The South African Government retains control of defence, external affairs, internal security, postal services, immigration, railways, currency, banking and customs, and excise. These territories have not been recognized as independent states by any Member State of the United Nations except by South Africa itself. The South African Government has announced its intention to grant independence to another homeland, namely, Ciskei, in December 1981.

Under the scheme of "bantustanization," the South African Government has allotted about 87 percent of the country's land to the white population and the remaining 13 percent to the rest which is the overwhelming majority of the people. The ten Bantu homelands consist of over one hundred small areas scattered all over the country. Most of them are non-contiguous. Under the Bantu Homelands Citizenship Act of 1970, Africans are required to adopt the citizenship of the Bantustans in which they live or to which they belong, even if they live and work in white areas; the Act thus deprives them of the South African citizenship.

One implication of this policy is that, since these people would not be South African citizens, the Government of South Africa would not feel obliged to entertain any complaint about their human or other rights. Another implication is that, by putting people into scattered, non-self-sustaining areas, the majority of the people would be forced into constant dependence on the whites for employment, thereby perpetuating the superior political and economic status of the whites. Eventually, every African is expected to become a citizen of a bantustan, whether or not he lives in one. As of now, most Africans do not live in bantustans. As foreigners in the white-designated areas, therefore, the Africans will provide the labor force so long as their work is needed. As with all other policies of the Government of

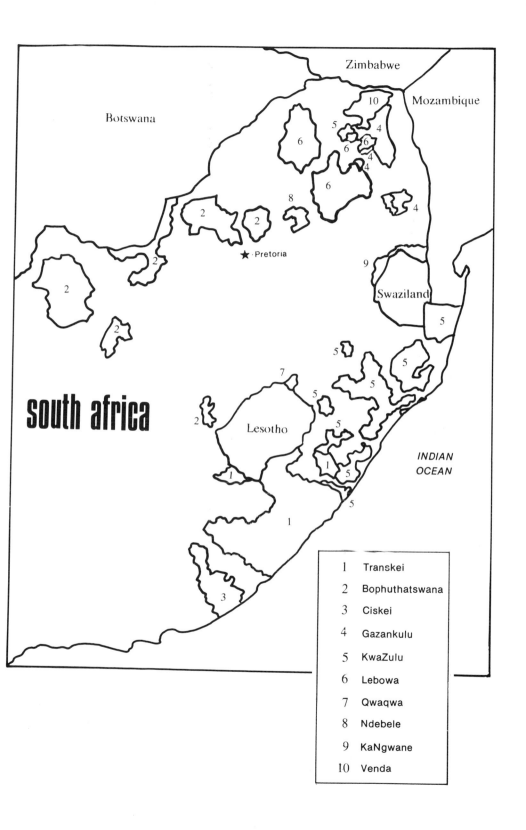

south africa

1	Transkei
2	Bophuthatswana
3	Ciskei
4	Gazankulu
5	KwaZulu
6	Lebowa
7	Qwaqwa
8	Ndebele
9	KaNgwane
10	Venda

South Africa, the scheme for bantustanization was not adopted in consultation with the majority of the people concerned.

The homelands policy is carried out on the basis of what the Pretoria government calls self-determination. As a member of the National Party explained during the House debate on the Status of Venda Bill on 14 June 1979, every nation in South Africa had an inalienable right to self-determination and what the Government was doing was merely granting independence to nations in South Africa in accordance with that right.[106]

Obviously, this is a bizarre way of applying the right to self-determination. The African people of South Africa as a whole have never been consulted about their own future. They have been forced into homelands. The homelands policy has nothing to do with the concept of self-determination. The people concerned have not determined their political status or the size of the territory freely. It is hypocritical, to say the least, that the white minority government should determine the future of the Africans and call it *self* determination.

The white minority Government has been trying to find collaborators for its homelands policy on the basis of ethnic grouping. Strangely enough, to point out the disparity in South Africa's approach, while the Africans are divided into ten homelands on the basis of separate ethnic groups, the Afrikaners and the English-speaking people in South Africa are considered one nation. In addition to these manipulations, it should be noted that these small, scattered and barren areas of homelands cannot survive without South Africa's financial aid. Nevertheless, the homelands policy is the main pillar of the apartheid system.

Other Racial Legislation and Practices

Racial discrimination, both as an attitude and as a policy, existed in South Africa before that state became one of the founding Members of the United Nations. The Masters and Servants Acts, passed between 1856 and 1904, regarded breach of contract as a criminal offence and applied to unskilled work generally involving the black people. These Acts were also in force after the Union was established. The title itself is self-indicting.

The Colour Bar Act (Mines and Works Act) of 1911 and a similar Act of 1926 gave the Government power to decide who could do skilled work in mining and engineering. The Native Labour Regulation Act of 1911 set out the conditions for the recruitment of African labor and made breach of contract by African workers a criminal offence. The Natives Land Act of 1913 prohibited Africans from acquiring any land outside the native "reserves," into which they were forced. The Natives Trust and Land Act of 1936 provided more land to the Reserves and extended the application of the 1913 Act to the Cape as well.

The Natives (Urban Areas) Act of 1923, as amended in 1930, segregated areas for African residence and provided for the control of the influx of Africans as well as for the removal of surplus persons. The Industrial Conciliation Act of 1924, as amended in 1937, excluded African male workers from the definition of "employee," thus excluding them from registered trade unions. African unions were not officially recognized, and strikes by Africans were illegal. Under the "civilized labour" policy of 1924 concerning the Public Service, white workers were paid "civilized" rates without regard to the skilled or unskilled nature of their work. The Factories, Machinery, and Building Works Act of 1941 gave the governor-general power to provide different accommodation and facilities to workers of different colors or races. The Immorality Act of 1927 prohibited extra-marital intercourse between whites and Africans, as had been done under similar laws of 1902 and 1903. The Native Administration Act of 1927 authorized the governor-general to move people forcibly from one place to another. Under the Natives Laws Amendment Act of 1937, the acquisition of land in urban areas by Africans from non-Africans was forbidden.

After the establishment of the United Nations, the Asiatic Land Tenure and Indian Representation Act of 1946, as already mentioned, prevented Indians from living or owning property in white residential areas. It also provided for qualified Indian men to elect white male representatives to represent Indians. This form of representation was unacceptable to the whole black population, who demanded full franchise rights. These, however, were then generally regarded as ad hoc measures.

Under the Population Registration Act of 1950, apartheid segregates and classifies people according to their race and color. This Act superseded earlier laws on definitions of racial groups and provided for the compilation of a register of the population and for identity cards. Such classification adversely affects the basic human rights of blacks. Under the apartheid laws, "the individual's political, social and economic status in society is dependent on the racial group, and sometimes sub-group, to which he belongs."[107] Race classification determines, among other things, where a person may live or work and with whom a person may enter into marital or sexual relationship.

Not only do the black people in South Africa have no right to stand for national elections, but they also have no equality of opportunity with the whites in any sphere.[108] Under the Prohibition of Mixed Marriages Act of 1949, whites cannot marry members of other racial groups. The Act was amended in 1968 to nullify mixed marriages of South African citizens abroad. Incredibly, partners in such marriages can be prosecuted upon their return to South Africa, a practice reminiscent of Nazi laws prohibiting the marriage of Jews to non-Jews in Germany. Sexual intercourse between whites and blacks is forbidden by the Immorality Act of 1957 which consolidated the Immorality Amendment Act of 1950 and the Immorality Act of 1927. According to the Minister of Police, from 1 July 1977 to 30 June 1978, that is, in one year, there were 363 investigated cases of contravention of this Act, and 295 of the people involved were charged.[109] Racially-mixed sports teams have been prohibited under the impact of a variety of laws, as have been racially-mixed political parties under the Prohibition of Political Interference Act of 1968 (more will be seen on sports policies in part 3).

Under the notorious "pass laws," such as the Natives (Urban Areas) Consolidation Act of 1945, Masters and Servants Laws, and Vagrancy Laws, Africans are obliged to show their passes upon demand by the authorities anytime and anywhere. In 1952, the passes were replaced by more comprehensive "reference books." Mass demonstrations and campaigns by African women against "pass laws" in 1956 culminated in the 1960 Sharpeville incidents. Hundreds of thousands of African people are arrested and tried under these laws each year. In 1978 alone, 224,910 male Africans and 47,977 female Africans were arrested for offences relating to reference books.[110] This discriminatory measure, the so-called "influx control," is used as a means of controlling the movement and residence of Africans. In terms of the "pass laws," even married couples who come from different areas cannot live together unless they have obtained special permission. Generally, Africans cannot visit urban or proclaimed (white designated) areas for longer than 72 hours without a permit, and they are required to obtain curfew passes if their job requires them to move around after curfew hours. On 18 April 1978, curfew regulations applied to 377 towns and villages in South Africa.[111]

Africans can, in any case, be compulsorily removed under the Group Areas Act and the Bantu Trust and Land Act. The former controls all interracial property transactions and changes of occupation by subjecting them to permit. Whole townships have thus been abolished and moved. Under that Act, 74,909 Colored families, 35,013 Indian families, and 2,234 white families had been moved as of 17 March 1980 and many would still be moved.[112] Similarly, during the 1960s alone, nearly one million Africans were expelled from white areas.

Legal strikes by African workers were not possible until 1973, when they were legalized under strict conditions by the Bantu Labour Act. Until 1953, strikes were not possible because of the Masters and Servants Acts. The Bantu Labour (Department of Disputes) Act, adopted in 1953, retained that prohibition. Its definition of the term "employee" excluded all Africans, so that Africans could not become members of registered unions.

Under the Industrial Conciliation Act of 1956, which discriminated openly against Africans, certain jobs were classified as "skilled jobs" and were reserved for whites. That Act defined an "employee" as any worker other than African. The Act, as amended in 1959 and 1961, also provided that no further mixed trade unions of both white and Colored (including Indians) would be registered, and that if more than half of the members of the one racial group wished to break away they could apply for separate registration. In brief, African trade unions could not, until recently, be registered, and mixed trade unions were prohibited by law. Although African trade unions had not been illegal, they had not been recognized. African workers had not, therefore, had the right to collective bargaining.[113]

It has been said that the denial of trade union rights and freedom of movement prevented the African worker from selling his labor to the highest bidder and from securing a better deal for himself. Moreover, intrepid African workers who challenged the system risked banishment to homelands, as idle or undesirable Bantus, where they joined the vast pool of unemployed Africans ready to become migrant workers.[114] Those workers are usually forced, because of their need to work, to live apart from their families. Indeed, the apartheid régime regards all Africans in white areas as migratory without entitlement to political and social rights.

In public facilities, segregation has led to discriminatory inferior services for the blacks. Segregation has been implemented in trains, buses, taxis, schools, hospitals, clubs, post offices, benches in public parks, public rest rooms, elevators, and other public services and institutions. Some moves to eliminate the social segregation, known as "petty apartheid," to appease blacks and to create a better image abroad have not succeeded. The Reservation of Separate Amenities Act of 1953, meanwhile, has led to unequal public facilities.

Another critical area affected by apartheid is education. African education in South Africa is governed by the Bantu Education Act of 1953. That Act is based on the premise that Africans should not receive such education as to be encouraged to expect that education would do away with discrimination in South Africa. In 1953, Hendrik F. Verwoerd, the Prime Minister who was assassinated in 1966, said that Africans had to be trained and taught in accordance with their opportunities in life and that there was no place for Africans among the whites above the level of certain forms of labor.[115] Such a policy has created a vicious circle. On the one hand, the Government of South Africa maintains that Africans are not developed enough; on the other hand, Africans are not given the opportunity for proper education and training. The purpose is clear. But because of the "Bantu Education" Act, the world witnessed the tragic events in Soweto and other African townships in 1976. Under the University Education Act of 1959, Bantu education was extended to university education. In the opinion of Africans, the concept of Bantu education is "a system designed to perpetuate black inferiority," entailing an immense gulf in quality between white and African schooling.[116] With regard to education, the Coloreds and Indians are in a situation similar to that of the Africans.[117]

The residential quarters of racial groups have been legally separated in urban areas since the Group Areas Act of 1950, as amended in 1957 and 1966. Those measures followed the Asiatic Land Tenure Act of 1946 designed to bar the Asians from living or owning property in the residential areas of the Europeans. In the Orange Free State and the Transvaal, there were laws enacted as early as the nineteenth century forbidding Indians from buying land.

Under a number of laws, applicable to all people but in effect designed to suppress black opposition, people are liable to detention and restriction indefinitely and without charge. The detainees have no right to consult lawyers or see family members. Under section 17 of the General Law Amendment Act of 1963, a senior police officer can arrest without warrant and detain for up to 90 days for interrogation. If the detainee has not replied "satisfactorily" to all questions, he can be repeatedly arrested. Under the same Act, by what is known as the "Sobukwe Clause," the minister of justice can authorize the continuation of the imprisonment of a political prisoner after the expiration of his sentence. That provision was deemed convenient in 1963 because Robert M. Sobukwe, President of PAC, would have shortly completed his three-year prison sentence but the Government was not willing to set him free.

The Internal Security Amendment Act of 1976, which replaced the Suppression of Communism Act of 1950, empowered the minister of justice to order arrest for preventive detention. The same Act empowered the attorney-general to order arrest and detention for 180 days, extending even to potential witnesses. Section 6 of the Terrorism Act of 1967, made retroactive to 1962, enables indefinite detention without trial. Under both the Terrorism Act and the Internal Security Act, the onus of proof is on the accused. Trials under the Terrorism Act are held summarily, without preliminary hearing before a magistrate. The General Law Amendment Act of 1962 introduced the offence of sabotage, also with the onus of proof on the accused.

As of 9 February 1979, there were fifty-two persons detained under section 6 of the Terrorism Act; six persons under section 10 and seventeen persons under section 12B of the Internal Security Act; four persons under section 185 of the Criminal Procedure Act; and seventeen persons under section 22 of the General Law Amendment Act.[118] Because of the Soweto incidents of 1976 and 1977, the number of detainees under various security laws was much higher at the end of 1977.

People in South Africa have been "banned" or banished to other areas under the Internal Security Act, the Riotous Assemblies Act, and the Bantu Administration Act for having opposed the policies of apartheid. Banned persons cannot be quoted by the press and they cannot associate with other people. Works of distinguished writers have been banned under the Publications Act of 1974. Banning orders are imposed without trial and are designed to restrict the freedom of movement and political activity of the opponents of apartheid. Under the Internal Security Act, as of 9 February 1979, there were 145 banned persons, of whom 23 had left the Republic.[119]

The array of legislation designed to suppress dissent is formidable and relentless. Under the Unlawful Organizations Act of 1960, organizations may be declared unlawful, as were ANC and PAC in 1960, the Congress of Democrats in 1962, and the International Defense and Aid Fund for Southern Africa in 1966. Under the Bantu (Prohibition of Interdicts) Act of 1956, Africans cannot get an interdict from court against a banishment order. Under section 25 of the Criminal Procedure Act of 1977, police may enter and search any place and question anyone there without a warrant if the police officer has reason to believe that the delay to be caused by the issue of a warrant would defeat the purpose of the search. Under the Bantu (Urban Areas) Consolidation Act and Police Amendment Act (1965), a policeman can enter any premise any time, without a warrant, if he alone suspects that an African is illegally residing or employed therein. Moreover, there is no allowance for redress against an abuse by police. According to the Indemnity Act of 1961, no civil or criminal proceedings may be brought against the Government in respect of detentions.

The press can be heavily penalized and shut down under the Internal Security Act and the Riotous Assemblies Act. The publication or dissemination of any speech or writing by any listed or banned person, without the permission of the minister of justice, is prohibited. Also the state president can prohibit the printing, publication, or dissemination of any publication on grounds of state security or public order.

The Publications Act of 1974 increased censorship on "political and moral" grounds—of course, the moral values and political beliefs of the Afrikaner elite. The Affected Organizations Act of 1974 empowered the Government to disallow the receipt of funds from abroad by organizations, if such organizations are believed to have engaged in politics with aid abroad. In 1977, the South African Government made a huge crackdown on a number of persons and organizations, banning and/or detaining about sixty persons and eighteen organizations. The large-scale bannings and detentions, coupled with the death of Steve Biko—leader of the Black Consciousness Movement in South Africa and under torture while he was in police detention—made an impact on world public opinion. South African authorities defended their actions by saying that they were necessary for curbing the incitement of racial hatred, and maintaining law and order.[120]

The Abolition of Juries Act of 1969 abolished the jury system in South Africa. Capital punishment may be given for murder, treason, sabotage, terrorism, rape, and kidnapping. In 1978, 132 people were hanged in South Africa. All were black, except one. There are growing reports about torture of political detainees.[121] Most deaths in detention are said by police to be suicides. From 1963 to 1976, about 23 detainees died mysteriously in police custody in South Africa. From 24 March 1976 to mid-July 1978, 24 people died while in detention.[122]

Amnesty International has reported that from May 1978 to April 1979 waves of people were detained under section 6 of the Terrorism Act, many of whom were later transferred to preventive detention under section 10 of the Internal Security Act. Some of them who were ultimately released were restricted or banished under banning orders. Until the end of 1978, convicted political prisoners were usually banned, under the authority of the minister of justice, upon completion of their sentences. Since then, as a new trend, many people have been banned after long periods in detention without any charge whatsoever. Also, until 1978, the police were empowered to detain potential state witnesses in political trials and hold them *incommunicado* for up to 180 days. In that year, the Criminal Procedures Act was amended to eliminate that limit. Many detainees had been held *incommunicado* for over a year before they were charged.[123]

In 1980, to suppress news coverage of rising black militancy, the South African Government further restricted the freedom of the press by enacting several new laws. Of these, the Second Police Amendment Act (1980) makes it an offence to disclose the names or any other information about people arrested under the Terrorism Act, without the permission of the Minister or the Commissioner of Police. Consequently, the relatives or lawyers of persons detained under the Terrorism Act are left unaware of the detainees' whereabouts. The National Key Points Act (1980) prohibits, without proper authorization, the disclosure of information about security measures, terrorist activities, sabotage, espionage or subversion at strategic places. The Armaments Development and Production Amendment Act (1980) prohibits the disclosure of information concerning the acquisition, supply, marketing, importation, export, development, manufacture, maintenance or repair of, or research in connection with, armaments. Freedom of the press in South Africa, in so far as it exists, is restricted by about one hundred laws.

The Rule of Law has been greatly eroded in South Africa. The International Commission of Jurists, whose principal preoccupation is with the Rule of Law, has reported that "recent developments demonstrate that the erosion of the Rule of Law in South Africa continues unabated."[124]

South African authorities have a peculiar interpretation of the Rule of Law. They argue that the Rule of Law is being observed in South Africa in the sense that the Executive organ acts on the authority of laws enacted by Parliament. This argument, however, emphasizes only the procedural aspect of the Rule of Law rather than its substance. It ignores the injustice inherent in the apartheid laws and the fact that the overwhelming majority of the population cannot participate or be represented in the making of the laws. More fundamentally, it ignores the generally-accepted meaning of the Rule of Law that the individual should be protected against the arbitrary power of the Government, that there should be equality before the law for all, and that the rights and freedoms of the individual should be subject to effective judicial remedies. For their own purpose, South African authorities

Segregated rest rooms in Capetown

Children behind a fence that separates them from the white Community near Johannesburg

A beach reserved for the whites of Durban

A train stop for the whites at Durban

Segregated bus services in Johannesburg

Poor Living conditions in the black township of Soweto

A residential area for the whites, near Capetown

50

View of a village in a Bantustan in Zululand

prefer to stress legal positivism. They confuse the Rule *of* Law with the rule *by* law, irrespective of the source and validity of the law.[125]

In fact, South Africa's racialized legal order perpetrates legal violence against the majority of the country's population. The South African Government cannot distinguish legality from legitimacy. Laws made by minority rule in South Africa are devoid of legitimacy, and, used as a means for minority domination, they are also immoral. Force used for the implementation of these laws and immoral ends has become state violence against the majority of the country's people.

One of the characteristics of any state is its monopoly of the legitimate use of physical violence, that is, force. But, to be legitimate, its use of force has to devolve from the consent of the majority. As one writer has noted, "for violence to qualify as legal punishment, it must be imposed by duly constituted public authority for an act within its jurisdiction that is publicly judged to violate a legal rule promulgated before the act took place."[126] As the majority of South Africa's population has no say at all in the making of the laws, the laws punishing the black population are devoid of legitimacy.

Naturally, the illegitimate use of force by the South African Government gives rise to resistance by the black population who lack basic democratic rights. Deprived of constitutional avenues for peaceful change, blacks have been compelled to increase their resistance, and doubtlessly will further intensify their struggle to obtain elementary human rights. One writer makes a case for the belief that whenever in a state a substantial section of the population feels that it is underprivileged, or deprived of elementary political rights, its protest is likely to take the form of direct action.[127]

In sum, almost every article of the Universal Declaration has been violated by South African laws that do not regard all the people of South Africa as equal before the law.[128] The existing legal order humiliates and degrades the black people of South Africa, as well as all black people anywhere; it keeps South African blacks outside the political system as well as outside the mainstream of economic and social life, and is contrary to the specific provisions of the Charter and other human rights standards.[129]

PART II

ACTION-REACTION

III. INTERNAL PEACEFUL CHANGE

General Assembly

Treatment of People of Indian Origin in the Union of
South Africa; The Question of Race Conflict in
South Africa Resulting from the Policies
of Apartheid of the Government of the
Union of South Africa (1946-61)

The General Assembly first dealt with the matter of racial discrimination against people of Indian origin in South Africa in 1946.[130] On 8 December of that year, the Assembly adopted its first resolution on the item of the Treatment of Indians in the Union of South Africa.[131] It expressed the opinion that the treatment of Indians in the Union of South Africa should be in conformity with the international obligations under agreements concluded between the two Governments [India and South Africa] and the relevant provisions of the Charter. The Assembly added that friendly relations between the two Member States, that is, India and South Africa, had been impaired because of that kind of treatment and that, unless a satisfactory settlement was reached, their relations were likely to be further impaired. The language about "friendly relations" was an implicit reference to Article 14 of the Charter, which empowers the Assembly to recommend measures for peaceful change in situations which impair the general welfare or friendly relations among nations. The Assembly requested the two Governments to report to the Assembly at its next session on measures adopted in that regard.

In 1949, the Assembly adopted its second resolution on the same issue, inviting the Governments of India, Pakistan, and the Union of South Africa to enter into discussion at a round-table conference and to take into consideration the purposes and principles of the Charter and the Universal Declaration.[132] As the Universal Declaration had been adopted in the preceding year, the Assembly referred to it because it was considered to have been adopted in order to define and strengthen the Charter provisions on human rights.

In 1950, the Assembly adopted its next resolution on the item of the treatment of people of Indian origin.[133] It considered that "a policy of racial

55

segregation (apartheid) was necessarily based on doctrines of racial discrimination" and recommended that the three Governments concerned proceed to hold a round-table conference to negotiate, bearing in mind the Charter and the Universal Declaration, and that, in the event that they failed to do so within a certain time-limit, those Governments and the Secretary-General should establish a commission of three members to assist in carrying through negotiations. The resolution called on the Governments concerned to refrain from taking action which would prejudice the success of negotiations and urged the South African Government not to implement the Group Areas Act, pending the conclusions of negotiations.

Negotiations could not take place because the South African Government did not accept Assembly resolution 395(V) as a basis for a round-table conference. Nonetheless, the Assembly continued to take up the item and to recommend courses of action. In 1952, in resolution 511(VI), the Assembly repeated its earlier recommendation for the establishment of a commission of three members to assist the parties in carrying through appropriate negotiations. This commission was never established. The Assembly once again called upon the South African Government to suspend the implementation of the Group Areas Act. Both resolution 395(V) and resolution 511(VI), in their preambles, recalled Assembly resolution 103(I), concerning racial persecution, and resolution 217(III), relating to the Universal Declaration. Resolution 511(VI) repeated the statement of resolution 395(V) that a policy of racial segregation is necessarily based on doctrines of racial discrimination, and asked the Secretary-General to assist negotiations.

In 1952, in another resolution the Assembly went one step further in its attempt to initiate negotiations. It established a United Nations Good Offices Commission consisting of three members nominated by the President of the General Assembly, with a view to arranging and assisting in negotiations between the Governments concerned "in order that a satisfactory solution of the question in accordance with the Purposes and Principles of the Charter and the Universal Declaration" might be achieved.[134] It again called on the South African Government not to implement the Group Areas Act. It also noted that the South African Government had expressed its inability to accept resolution 511(VI) for negotiations.

The Assembly adopted all these resolutions under the item of the Treatment of People of Indian Origin in the Union of South Africa. Accordingly, it recommended negotiations among the Governments of South Africa, India, and Pakistan with the aid of the Good Offices Commission. In 1953, however, the Commission expressed its regret that, in view of the response of the South African Government, it had "been unable to carry out its task to arrange and assist in negotiations between the Governments concerned."[135] The following year, the Commission expressed regret that it had been "unable to submit any proposal likely to lead to a peaceful settlement of the problem, on account of the unco-operative attitude of the Government of the Union of South Africa, which had even prevented the Permanent Representative of South Africa from meeting with the Commission."[136]

Meanwhile, the Assembly was adding a new dimension to its consideration of South Africa's legalized racial discrimination. On 5 December 1952, it adopted its first resolution on the question of race conflict in South Africa resulting from the policies of apartheid of the Government of the Union of South Africa.[137] In Part A of the resolution, the Assembly established a three-member commission

> to study the racial situation in the Union of South Africa in the light of the Purposes and Principles of the Charter, with due regard to the provisions of Article 2, paragraph 7, as well as the provisions of Article 1, paragraphs 2 and 3; Article 13, paragraph 1 B; Article 55c, and Article 56 of the Charter, and the resolutions of the United Nations on racial persecution and discrimination, and to report its conclusions to the General Assembly at its eighth session.[138]

In Part B of the resolution, the Assembly declared that

> in a multi-racial society harmony and respect for human rights and freedom and the peaceful development of a unified community are best assured when patterns of legislation and practice are directed towards ensuring equality before the law of all persons regardless of race, creed or colour, and when economic, social, cultural and political participation of all racial groups is on a basis of equality.[139]

In the latter part, the Assembly also affirmed that governmental policies of Member States which are not directed towards these goals, but which are designed to perpetuate or increase discrimination, are inconsistent with the pledges of the Members under Article 56 of the Charter, and called on all Member States to bring their internal policies into conformity with the Charter to promote the observance of human rights and fundamental freedoms. This kind of recommendation is known to be a general recommendation, in contrast to a specific recommendation made to a designated state. Some authors believe that a general recommendation is not barred by the domestic jurisdiction clause.[140]

Over the next three years, the Commission on Racial Situation submitted a report each year. Its first report was submitted on 3 October 1953. That report stated that the racial policy of the Government of South Africa was contrary to the Charter and the Universal Declaration and that the continuance of that policy was likely to impair friendly relations. It considered that the doctrine of racial differentiation and superiority on which the policy of apartheid was based was scientifically false, extremely dangerous to internal peace and international relations as had been proved by the tragic experience of the world in the preceding twenty years, and contrary to the dignity and worth of the human person.[141]

The Commission also expressed the opinion that the United Nations might suggest ways and means such as

> a round-table conference of members of different ethnic groups of the Union,
> which would, in an effort towards conciliation, make proposals to the Govern-
> ment to facilitate the peaceful development of the racial situation in the Union
> of South Africa. The United Nations might offer its help to that conference by
> sending a number of United Nations representatives, so that all parties might
> be sure that the principles of the Charter would guide the debates.[142]

In its second report (1954), the Commission reiterated its earlier conclusions and stated that the measures taken in pursuance of the policy of
apartheid were incompatible with the Charter and the Universal Declaration.
It reaffirmed its "profound conviction" that apartheid constituted a gross
threat to the internal situation and foreign relations of South Africa as well
as to the future of peaceful relations between ethnic groups. Under its new
terms of reference, by which it was requested "to suggest measures which
would help to alleviate the situation and promote a peaceful settlement,"
the Commission repeated the suggestion for a round-table conference in
South Africa to facilitate the peaceful development of the racial situation
in that country.[143]

Although the South African Government continued to ignore the Commission's recommendations, the Commission persisted in expressing concern about the potential damage that apartheid might do to friendly relations
among nations. In its third report (1955), the Commission stated:

> The policy of apartheid is a seriously disturbing factor in international relations,
> and the least that can be said of it is that it is likely to impair the general welfare
> or friendly relations among nations. This, then, is one of those situations which,
> under Article 14 of the Charter, may form the subject of recommendations by
> the General Assembly.[144]

That statement had found a similar expression in the Commission's
first report. Nevertheless, the third report was merely a progress report and
did not offer any fresh conclusions. It gave an account of the developments
in South Africa during the period of one year from August 1954 to August
1955. It referred to South Africa's isolationist policy and expressed the wish
that South Africa might reconsider its policy towards the United Nations
and enter into close and extensive co-operation with the Organization.[145]

In 1953, in connection with the item on the Indian people, the Assembly
took note of the report of the Good Offices Commission and in particular
its conclusion that "in view of the response of the Government of the Union
of South Africa, it has been unable to carry out its task to arrange and assist
in negotiations between the Governments concerned." The Assembly regretted that the South African Government refused to use the Commission's
good offices, that it continued to implement the provisions of the Group
Areas Act, and that it proceeded with further legislation contrary to the

Charter and the Universal Declaration. The Assembly also considered that these actions were not in keeping with South Africa's obligations and responsibilities under the Charter.[146]

In the same year, on the question of race conflict resulting from apartheid, the Assembly noted with concern the conclusion of the study of the Commission on Racial Situation that the policies of apartheid and their consequences were contrary to the Charter and the Universal Declaration. It stated that continuing the apartheid policy would "endanger friendly relations among nations" and would "make peaceful solutions increasingly difficult." It also requested the Commission to continue studying the development of the racial situation in South Africa in relation to, among other things, Charter provisions, in particular Article 14, and to suggest measures that would promote a peaceful settlement.[147] This resolution marked the Assembly's first explicit reference to Article 14 in its consideration of the South African racial situation. The Assembly also stated that lasting peace depended "especially upon respect for and observance of human rights and fundamental freedoms for all."

In resolutions adopted in 1954, 1955, and 1957 on the treatment of Indian people, the Assembly again urged the parties to negotiate a solution.[148] In 1954, it also requested the Secretary-General to designate, if need be, a person to facilitate contacts between the parties. Accordingly, the Secretary-General designated Ambassador Luiz de Faro, Jr., of Brazil to assist negotiations. The Governments of India and Pakistan informed the Secretary-General that they would co-operate with Ambassador de Faro. The Government of South Africa, however, declined to co-operate lest it should prejudice its juridical stand on the domestic jurisdiction clause.[149] It persistently maintained that the matter was within the domestic jurisdiction of South Africa alone. In 1955, in considering the Secretary-General's report on the item, the Assembly "noted" that negotiations, as envisaged, had not taken place.

In 1954, in its resolution on race conflict, the Assembly noted the suggestions of the Commission on Racial Situation for facilitating a "peaceful" settlement of the problem.[150] Noting further the profound conviction of the Commission that the policy of apartheid constituted a grave threat to the "peaceful" relations between ethnic groups in the world, the Assembly invited the South African Government to consider the Commission's suggestions for a peaceful settlement of the racial problem. By taking note of the Commission's reports, the Assembly, in effect, approved of the reports and, in referring explicitly to Article 14, the Assembly was, in fact, encouraging peaceful change in South Africa.

In 1955, South Africa recalled its delegation from the tenth session of the Assembly, and in 1956 it announced that it would maintain only token representation at the United Nations. In 1958, it returned to participate fully, but continued to refuse to discuss its racial policies and stated that it would ignore any resolutions of the Assembly in respect of its racial policies.[151]

In its resolution on race conflict in 1955, the Assembly reminded the Government of South Africa of the faith that South Africa had re-affirmed, in signing the Charter, in the fundamental human rights and in the dignity and worth of the human person. It asked that Government to observe the oglibation contained in Article 56 of the Charter, that is, the pledge to take joint and separate action in co-operation with the Organization for the promotion of universal respect for, and observance of, human rights and fundamental freedoms for all without distinction as to race, sex, language, or religion.[152] It recalled its resolution 377 A (V) of 1950 in which it had expressed its conviction that a genuine and lasting peace depended also upon the observance of all the principles and purposes established in the Charter and especially upon respect for, and observance of, human rights and fundamental freedoms for all. It also reiterated its resolutions 103 (I) of 1946 and 616 B (VII) of 1952 in which it had declared that it is in the higher interests of humanity to put an immediate end to religious and racial persecution and discrimination.

In 1957, the Assembly adopted two resolutions on race conflict appealing to the Government of the Union of South Africa to revise its policies of racial discrimination. In one, the Assembly requested the Secretary-General to communicate with the Government of South Africa in order to carry forward the purposes of that resolution, that is, to revise its racial policies. It also ''deplored'' South Africa's not having observed its Charter obligations.[153] Accordingly, the Secretary-General transmitted the text of that resolution to the Government of South Africa.[154] In the other resolution, the Assembly again ''deplored'' the South African Government for not revising its policies and for not co-operating.[155]

Subsequently, in its resolutions on the people of Indian origin in 1957 and 1958, the Assembly again appealed to the South African Government to participate in negotiations.[156] It invited Member States to use their good offices to bring about negotiations, and noted that the Governments of both India and Pakistan had reiterated their readiness to enter into negotiations with the Government of South Africa. Most significantly, it expressly declared that such negotiations would not in any way prejudice the position of any of the parties with regard to their respective juridical stands on the question of domestic jurisdiction in the dispute.

In 1958, in connection with the item on race conflict, the Assembly affirmed that perpetuating discrimination was inconsistent with Article 56 of the Charter, and called upon all Member States to bring their policies in line with the Charter. It also regretted that the South African Government had not yet responded to the Assembly's appeals.[157]

The following year, on the same item, the Assembly expressed the view that racial discrimination was prejudicial to international harmony and contradicted the observance of human rights and fundamental freedoms. It called upon ''all States'' to bring their policies into conformity with their obligation under the Charter to promote the observance of human rights and fundamental freedoms.[158] Again it regretted that the South African Government had not responded to Assembly appeals to reconsider its policies which impair the right of all racial groups to enjoy the same fundamental rights and freedoms. It appealed to all Member States to use their best endeavors to achieve the purposes of that resolution.

Continuing in its efforts towards peaceful change through negotiation, the Assembly, in its next resolution on the people of Indian origin, appealed to the Union Government to enter into negotiations with the Governments of India and Pakistan, which had long indicated their readiness for negotiations, and invited Member States to use their good offices to facilitate that goal.[159]

In 1960, the Assembly did not adopt any resolution on either race conflict or the people of Indian origin. The following year, it adopted its final resolutions on both items. With regard to the Indian people, it again urged the South African Government to negotiate with the Governments of India and Pakistan, and invited Member States to use their good offices to bring about negotiations.[160] In one of the resolutions on race conflict, the Assembly, introducing a new element, requested ''all States to consider taking such separate and collective action as is open to them, in conformity with the Charter of the United Nations, to bring about the abandonment of these policies.'' It also reminded the Government of South Africa of the requirement in Article 2, paragraph 2, of the Charter that all Members should fulfil in good faith the obligations assumed by them under the Charter.[161] The Assembly had never before requested all states to consider taking action against South Africa. Another new element in this resolution was the Assembly's observation that policies based on racial discrimination had led to international friction and that their continuance endangered international peace and security.

In the other resolution on race conflict in 1961, the Assembly again urged all states to take separate and collective action and again reminded the South African Government of the ''good faith'' Article of the Charter.[162] It also called the attention of the Security Council to Article 11, paragraph 3, of the Charter, whereby it is provided that the Assembly may call the Council's attention to situations likely to endanger international peace and security. As will be seen in due course, the Assembly pursued these new elements in increasingly stronger terms after 1961 in connection with the combined item.

Despite all these appeals by the United Nations, the Government of South Africa continued adopting measures which furthered its segregationist policies. During the General Debate in the Assembly on 28 September 1959, about fourteen years after the United Nations began to deal with the matter, the South African Minister of External Affaires ''outlined measures being taken to develop South Africa's traditional policy of separation between the two races to provide for the peaceful co-existence, on the one hand, of separate Bantu communities which could eventually attain full self-government and, on the other hand, of a separate community or State controlled by South Africans of European descent."[163]

Between 1946 and 1961, the Assembly adopted a total of twenty-four resolutions on the items of the treatment of people of Indian origin and the question of race conflict resulting from the policy of apartheid of the South African Government. The first resolution on the people of Indian origin, 44(I) of 1946, was adopted by 32 votes in favor, 15 against, and 7 abstentions. On the same item, the last resolution, 1662(XVI) of 1961, was adopted unanimously, South Africa not participating. On the item of race conflict, the first resolution, 616(VII) of 1952, was adopted in two parts. Part A was passed by 35 votes to 1, with 23 abstentions; Part B by 24 votes to 1, with 34 abstentions. The last resolution adopted on this item, 1663(XVI) of 1961, was passed by 92 to 2, with 1 abstention. If progress in South Africa was non-existent, there was growing opposition in the United Nations to South Africa's racial policies.

The item on the treatment of the people of Indian origin was first referred by the Assembly for consideration to the Joint Committee of the First (Political and Security) Committee and the Sixth (Legal) Committee. The item on race conflict resulting from apartheid was first referred for consideration to the Ad Hoc Political Committee. Later, both items were referred to the Ad Hoc Political Committee, subsequently (in 1956) named Special Political Committee, which shared the work of the First Committee. Believing that the problem had political overtones, the Assembly considered the racial situation of South Africa more in political organs and bodies rather than in juridical ones, and continued to exert political and moral pressure rather than using legal means.

From 1946 to 1961, then, as means for peaceful change in South Africa, insofar as the people of Indian origin were concerned, the Assembly made repeated recommendations for holding negotiations between India and Pakistan, on the one hand, and South Africa, on the other.[164] It asked the Secretary-General to assist the negotiations and to consult with the Government of South Africa. It asked Member States to use their good offices to facilitate negotiations. It established a Good Offices Commission and had a distinguished person designated to assist negotiations. While the Assembly was the policy-making body, the Good Offices Commission, the Secretary-General, and Ambassador de Faro were the executive bodies. With regard to the race conflict resulting from the policy of apartheid, the Commission on Racial Situation and the Secretary-General were the executive bodies while the Assembly was again the policy-making body.

In retrospect, it appears that it was unnecessary for the Assembly to consider the matter in two concurrent items. Both items concerned the racialized legal order of South Africa and could have been dealt with as one item as from 1952 when the item on race conflict resulting from apartheid was introduced. Although some people of Indian origin had British passports, most were South African nationals. The fact that the people of Indian origin were covered by international agreements should not have made any difference for the United Nations, since both items related to statutory racial discrimination.

From the very beginning the Assembly considered the racial situation in South Africa as having impaired "friendly relations between nations." This language echoed Article 14 of the Charter having to do with peaceful change, but later the Assembly explicitly referred to Article 14, recommending negotiations and appealing to the parties concerned to negotiate. It also appealed repeatedly to the South African Government to suspend certain discriminatory legislation and revise its racial policies to bring them into line with the Charter and the Universal Declaration. It reminded that Government of its obligations under the Charter, particularly Articles 56 and 2(2), that is, the pledges of Member States under human rights provisions and their obligations under the "good faith" provision.

The South African Government, meanwhile, did not co-operate, did not negotiate, and did not heed the Assembly's appeals. Instead, it went ahead with enforcing and strengthening its policies of racial segregation.

Although Assembly resolutions are not, strictly speaking, binding on Member States, they do have moral and political weight, particularly when they are adopted by unanimity or by a large majority. The frequency and the consensus or unanimity with which the substances of certain resolutions have consistently been adopted are generally regarded as indications of the quasi-legislative functions of the Assembly, and not all of the Assembly's resolutions are merely recommendatory or non-binding.[165] Moreover, the Assembly's consistent and unanimous calls for racial equality during its first fifteen years certainly reflected the values and conscience of mankind. Nevertheless, up to 1962, the Assembly did not achieve its objective of racial equality through peaceful change in South Africa. The Assembly's subsequent efforts to promote peaceful change in South Africa are to be seen presently.

The Policies of Apartheid of the Government of the Republic of South Africa (1962-1980)

In 1962, the General Assembly began considering both the treatment of the people of Indian origin and the race conflict as one combined item, namely, "the Policies of Apartheid of the Government of the Republic of South Africa."[166] In its first resolution on the combined item, the Assembly established a Special Committee that began its work in 1963, and has since kept apartheid policies under review in reports to the Assembly and the Security Council.[167] The Committee has heard petitions, studied communications and documents, followed developments in South Africa, sent visiting missions, held special sessions and seminars in various countries, made recommendations for dealing with the problem, and constantly encouraged the growth of an international campaign against apartheid.

The Assembly has taken note yearly of the reports, recommendations and work of the Special Committee. In 1966, it amended the Special Committee's terms of reference, authorizing it, among other things, to hold sessions away from Headquarters or to send a sub-committee on a mission to consult specialized agencies, regional organizations, states, and non-governmental organizations on ways and means to promote international campaigns against apartheid and to investigate various aspects of apartheid.[168]

The Assembly's resolution which established the Special Committee in 1962 also introduced two new elements into the Assembly's handling of the South African situation. The Assembly requested Member States to take specific measures, separately or collectively, in conformity with the Charter, to compel South Africa to abandon the policies of apartheid. It recommended breaking off diplomatic relations with the Government of the Republic of South Africa, closing ports to all vessels flying the South African flag, boycotting South African imports and exports (including all arms and ammunition), and refusing landing and passage facilities to South African aircraft. In that resolution, the Assembly also requested the Security Council to take appropriate measures, including sanctions, to secure South Africa's compliance with Assembly and Council resolutions and, if necessary, to consider action under Article 6 of the Charter, relating to the expulsion of Members from the United Nations.

In 1962, then, the Assembly for the first time suggested to Member States specific measures against South Africa. Later, the Assembly would repeat such calls on Member States and address requests to the Security Council in even stronger terms, including requests that the Council adopt an arms embargo. As from 1963, the Assembly would also appeal to Member States to comply with the Council's resolutions calling upon all states to cease the sale and shipment of arms, ammunition of all types and military vehicles to South Africa.[169] In 1965, the Assembly asked, for the first time, that the Council impose mandatory sanctions on South Africa, under Chapter VII of the Charter, on the ground that the South African situation constituted a threat to international peace. The Assembly has repeated that request to the Council in numerous resolutions.[170]

Since 1963, beginning with resolution 1881 (XVIII) of that year, the Assembly has annually adopted resolutions on political prisoners and trials in South Africa, asking the South African Government to release unconditionally all political prisoners and detainees.[171] In the first of such resolutions, the Assembly noted that the harsh repressive measures instituted by the Government of South Africa frustrated the possibilities for ''peaceful settlement.'' The Assembly also requested the Secretary-General to report to the Assembly and the Council on the implementation of that resolution. The Secretary-General reported later that the Permanent Representative of South Africa had informed him that ''no reply can be expected to a resolution which the United Nations was clearly not entitled to adopt since it constitutes flagrant interference in South Africa's judiciary.''[172]

In 1963, the Assembly urged Member States and organizations to provide humanitarian assistance to the families of persons persecuted in South Africa for their opposition to apartheid. Because of the United Nations' financial crisis in 1964, no resolution on South Africa's racial situation was adopted in that year when, indeed, few decisions were taken. In 1965, it established a Trust Fund for grants for legal assistance and relief to the victims of apartheid, to be financed by voluntary contributions. Since then it has repeatedly called for such voluntary assistance.[173]

The Assembly at the same time began expressing support for the opponents of apartheid and recognizing the legitimacy of their struggle. In resolution 2054A (XX) of 1965, it ''firmly'' supported all those opposing the policies of apartheid and particularly those combating such policies in South Africa. In 1967, it adopted resolution 2307 (XXII) which, among other things, affirmed its recognition of the legitimacy of the struggle of the people of South Africa for human rights and fundamental freedoms for all the people of South Africa, irrespective of race, color or creed. The Assembly also appealed to all states and organizations to provide appropriate moral, political, and material assistance to the people of South Africa in their legitimate struggle for the rights recognized in the Charter. Since then, the Assembly has affirmed its recognition of that legitimacy in a large number of resolutions.[174] But, while in 1967 and 1968 the Assembly extended its recognition on the grounds of human rights and fundamental freedoms, in 1969 (resolution 2506B) it began justifying its recognition on the grounds of self-determination and majority rule.

Beginning in 1970, relevant Assembly resolutions recognized the legitimacy of the struggle of the people of South Africa ''by all means at their disposal'' or ''by all means available.'' The Assembly began getting increasingly annoyed at the defiant position of the South African Government. During the discussions on apartheid in the Special Political Committee in 1970,

> a number of Members including Algeria, the Central African Republic, Ethiopia, Iraq, Morocco, Nigeria and Poland pledged continued moral, material and military assistance for the oppressed peoples of southern Africa. Others, among them Cuba and Sudan, argued that an armed struggle was the only solution to the evils and endless exploitation and humiliation of *apartheid*. The

representative of Ethiopia said that if the alternatives were either to use force
or to abandon the cause of freedom and justice, force must be resorted to as
the lesser of the two evils.

On the other hand, some Members, including Denmark, Norway, and
Japan contended that the United Nations could not be a party to violence and
the use of armed force. They said that non-violent means might in the long run
be more effective and that the primary task of the United Nations was peace-
keeping.[175]

During the discussion of the text of the relevant draft resolution in the
same committee in that year, the representatives of Colombia, Uruguay,
Sweden, Denmark, Finland, Iceland, Norway, and others expressed concern
or objections to a provision that they believed was an endorsement of the
use of force.[176] The use of force, they said, was implied in the expressions
"by all means at their disposal," and "by all means available." The spon-
sors of a draft resolution, however, do not always justify or clarify each
and every provision of the text.

Then, in 1977, for the first time, the Assembly explicitly endorsed
"armed struggle" in South Africa. It declared

> that, in view of the intransigence of the racist regime, its defiance of resolutions
> of the United Nations and its continued imposition of the criminal policy of
> *apartheid*, the national liberation movement has an inalienable right to continue
> its struggle for the seizure of power by all available and appropriate means of
> its choice, including armed struggle.[177]

Objections were raised to the draft resolution but it was adopted with
112 votes in favor, 9 against, and 17 abstentions. The negative votes were
cast by Belgium, France, the Federal Republic of Germany, Japan, Lux-
embourg, the Netherlands, the United Kingdom, the United States, and
Uruguay. In explanation of vote before the draft resolution was put to vote,
the representative of Belgium spoke on behalf of the nine countries of the
European Community and said:

> As an example of a questionable formulation, I will point to the statement
> that the South African Government is illegitimate. South Africa is, in fact, an
> independent Member of the United Nations. Any suggestion to the contrary
> would be in contradiction with the principle of the universality of our Orga-
> nization.
>
> This is why the Nine, without minimizing the role played by political
> organizations formed from the ranks of the oppressed, consider that their efforts
> are primarily aimed at the establishing of equal rights for all the inhabitants,
> regardless of race or colour. For the Nine, the call for "the seizure of power
> by all available . . . means . . . including armed struggle" as envisaged in
> draft resolution A/32/L.29 is not acceptable, because of the well-known views
> of our countries on the subject.
>
> Moreover, as we pointed out in our joint statement, we feel that it is our
> responsibility not to close all channels of communication, and to continue to

make our views known to South Africa. We hope that this critical dialogue will
finally contribute to the abolition of *apartheid*, without resort to violence.[178]

The representative of New Zealand, one of the abstainees, speaking
before the vote, said that his delegation would not support the resolution
because "New Zealand does not agree that there is no alternative to armed
struggle as a means of achieving the legitimate rights of the disenfranchised
majority of South Africans."[179] After the vote, the representative of Sweden,
speaking on behalf of the five Nordic countries, said that it had "consistently
been the stand of the Nordic countries not to condone paragraphs containing
expressions of explicit support for the use of armed force."[180]

In 1979, the Assembly adopted a Declaration on South Africa declaring
that "all States shall recognize the legitimacy of the struggle of the people
of South Africa for the elimination of apartheid and the establishment of
a non-racial society guaranteeing the enjoyment of equal rights by all the
people of South Africa, irrespective of race, colour or creed." It also declared that "all States shall recognize the right of the oppressed people of
South Africa to choose their means of struggle."[181]

The following year the Assembly reaffirmed "the legitimacy of the
struggle of the oppressed people of South Africa and their national liberation
movement by all available means, including armed struggle, for the seizure
of power by the people, the elimination of the *apartheid* regime and the
exercise of the right of self-determination by the people of South Africa as
a whole."[182]

In recognizing the legitimacy of the struggle against apartheid, the
Assembly also appealed to Governments, specialized agencies, national and
international organizations, and individuals to provide every assistance to
the national liberation movement of South Africa.[183] In 1976, it declared
that the South African régime had no right to represent the people of South
Africa and that the liberation movements recognized by the Organization
of African Unity were the authentic representatives of the overwhelming
majority of the South African people.[184] Later, it recognized the importance
of providing all necessary assistance to the national liberation movement
of South Africa in its struggle for the eradication of apartheid and the
establishment of a non-racial society.[185]

While the Assembly has spoken increasingly in stronger terms about
the legitimacy of the struggle of the opponents of apartheid, it has also
continued to speak of the necessity for peaceful solution. In 1965, it drew
the attention of the Security Council to the fact that action under Chapter
VII of the Charter was essential and that universally applied economic
sanctions were the only means of achieving a "peaceful solution."[186] In
1967, the Assembly expressed the same conviction.[187] Later, it revised its
position by saying that mandatory and universally applied economic and
other sanctions constituted "one of the essential means of achieving a peace-

ful solution'' of the grave situation in South Africa.[188] In 1973, the Assembly expressed its strong conviction that the release of leaders of the oppressed people of South Africa from imprisonment and other restrictions was essential for a ''peaceful solution of the grave situation in South Africa.''[189] The following year, it said that the United Nations should intensify efforts to secure a ''peaceful change'' in South Africa.[190]

In examining the various Assembly resolutions, it becomes clear that the Assembly has from early on felt that the United Nations was duty-bound to resolve the South African problem. In 1969, in resolution 2506B (XXIV), the Assembly ''recognized the obligations of the United Nations to take urgent and effective measures to resolve the situation [in South Africa] in accordance with the purposes and principles of the Charter.'' That recognition grew stronger by 1975 when, in resolution 3411C (XXX), the Assembly proclaimed that the United Nations and the international community ''have a special responsibility towards the oppressed people of South Africa and their liberation movements, and towards those imprisoned, restricted or exiled for their struggle against *apartheid*.'' The Assembly reaffirmed that ''special responsibility'' in other resolutions.[191]

Since 1965, the Assembly has attached much importance to world public opinion. It has requested the Secretary-General to intensify the dissemination of information on the evils of apartheid with a view to promoting national and international action for the elimination of apartheid.[192] It has requested all states, specialized agencies and other organizations to intensify the dissemination of information on apartheid and to co-operate in these activities.[193] It has requested UNESCO to prepare an educational kit on racial discrimination and apartheid in Southern Africa.[194] It has advised assisting the various anti-apartheid movements in disseminating information on apartheid,[195] and recommended action by inter-governmental and non-governmental organizations in this respect.[196]

The Assembly has also addressed itself to the Secretariat in its efforts to mobilize public opinion against apartheid. It has requested the Secretary-General to reinforce the Unit on Apartheid for the purpose of intensifying United Nations action against apartheid.[197] It has recommended that the Unit on Apartheid and the Office of Public Information expand dissemination of information against apartheid.[198] It has requested the Special Committee against Apartheid and the Unit on Apartheid to re-double their efforts to publicize the cause of all those persecuted for their opposition to apartheid in South Africa,[199] and requested the Secretary-General to rename and strengthen the Unit on Apartheid.[200] The Unit subsequently became the Centre against Apartheid.

To counteract South Africa's propaganda efforts, the Assembly has established a Trust Fund for Publicity against Apartheid,[201] and requested the Special Committee and the Centre against Apartheid to utilize the Fund particularly for the production of audio-visual material and for assistance to appropriate organizations so that they might disseminate information on apartheid. It has appealed to all governments to contribute to the Fund. It has also requested the Secretary-General to undertake a regular programme of radio broadcasts directed at South Africa, and has commended UNESCO, ILO, WHO, FAO and the UN High Commissioner for Refugees for having intensified their activities in disseminating information against apartheid.[202]

The Assembly then began to adopt stronger terms to refer to the Government of South Africa and its apartheid policies. In 1966, the Assembly condemned apartheid as "a crime against humanity."[203] Later, it referred to the South African Government as the "racist minority Government of South Africa."[204] In 1972, the Assembly referred to that Government as the "South African regime."[205] In the following year, it referred to the same Government as the "*apartheid* regime."[206] Also in 1973, the Assembly adopted the International Convention on the Suppression and Punishment of the Crime of Apartheid.[207] In resolution 3324D (XXIX) of 1974 and other subsequent resolutions, the Assembly has also referred to the South African Government as the "racist regime."

Over the years, the Assembly has intensified its efforts against apartheid. In 1966, it endorsed the proposals of the Special Committee for an international campaign against apartheid under United Nations auspices.[208] The following year, it invited all states to encourage the establishment of national organizations for further enlightening public opinion on the evils of apartheid.[209] It has adopted programmes of action against apartheid to be implemented by governments, intergovernmental organizations, trade unions, churches, anti-apartheid and solidarity movements, and other non-governmental organizations.[210] To step up the international campaign against apartheid, and as recently as 1977, the Assembly proclaimed the year beginning on 21 March 1978 International Anti-Apartheid Year and requested all governments, organizations, and institutions to co-operate in the effective observance of that Year.[211] It authorized the Special Committee to organize a World Conference for Action against Apartheid in 1977, and that year it endorsed the Declaration adopted by the Conference.[212] After the expiration of the International Anti-Apartheid Year, the Assembly called upon all governments and intergovernmental and non-governmental organizations to join in the international mobilization against apartheid.[213]

In 1968, the Assembly, for the first time, referred to the question of apartheid in sports and requested all states and organizations to suspend cultural, educational, sporting, and other exchanges with South Africa. In 1970, the Assembly repeated its request.[214] In 1971, however, the Assembly adopted its first resolution exclusively related to apartheid in sport.[215] That year, the Assembly declared its unqualified support for the Olympic principle of non-discrimination, and called upon all national sports organizations to uphold that principle and deny support to sporting events organized in violation of that principle. The Assembly also appealed to all individual sportsmen to refuse to participate in segregated sports events, urged all states to promote adherence to the Olympic principle, and specifically condemned the actions of the Government of South Africa.

Sporting links with other countries is a matter that has given some worry to the South African Government.[216] Beginning with its resolution of 1971, the Assembly has intensified its action against apartheid in sports. In resolution 3411E (XXX) of 1975, also adopted exclusively on apartheid in sports, the Assembly reaffirmed its resolution of 1971 and requested the Secretary-General for the widest distribution of information against apartheid in sports. Significantly, although the Assembly's resolution in 1971 was adopted with the abstentions of the United Kingdom, France, and Australia, which are among South Africa's regular partners in sports, its resolution on the topic in 1975 was adopted unanimously.

Subsequently, the Assembly established an Ad Hoc Committee on the Drafting of an International Convention against Apartheid in Sports and requested that Committee to prepare a draft declaration on the subject as an interim measure.[217] On 14 December 1977, the Assembly adopted and proclaimed the International Declaration against Apartheid in Sports.[218] The Declaration provides, *inter alia*, that states shall take all appropriate action to bring about the total cessation of sporting contacts with any country practicing apartheid. It also provides that states shall publicly declare and express full and active support for the total boycott of all teams and sportsmen from the racist apartheid sports bodies, take appropriate actions against their sporting teams and organizations participating in sports activities in any country practicing apartheid, and deny visas to sports bodies or sportsmen from any country practicing apartheid.

At the time of the writing of this book, the Ad Hoc Committee was still working on a draft convention. The main difficulty confronting the Ad Hoc Committee was the so-called "third-party" principle. That principle would require, on the one hand, that states take all necessary action to ensure that their nationals refrain from participating in sports events which include individuals or teams from a country practicing apartheid; on the other hand, that same principle would require that states prevent their nationals from participating in sports events which include individuals or teams that engage in sports activities with teams and individuals from a country practicing apartheid.[219] In other words, United States athletes, for example, could not compete in a sporting event involving South Africa directly. Moreover, if New Zealand, for instance, was known to have played South Africa in any sport, then United States individuals and teams would not be allowed to play against New Zealand either.

In the meantime, Assembly resolutions had become bolder and introduced new concepts. In 1968, the Assembly stated for the first time that it "recognized that the policies and actions of the Government of South Africa constitute a serious obstacle to the exercise of the right of self-determination of the oppressed people of southern Africa."[220] This recognition, incidentally, came after the adoption of the two Covenants on human rights in 1966, both of which contain, in their first articles, the provision that "all peoples have the right of self-determination." While the preamble of the 1968 resolution spoke of the right of self-determination of the people of "southern Africa," the operative part reaffirmed "the urgent necessity of eliminating the policies of apartheid so that the people of 'South Africa' as a whole can exercise their right to self-determination and obtain majority rule based on universal suffrage."

In 1969, the Assembly, for the first time, specifically endorsed "the struggle of the oppressed people of South Africa for the exercise of their inalienable right of self-determination, and thus to attain majority rule based on universal suffrage."[221] Thus, the Assembly now supported both the struggle for attaining human rights and fundamental freedoms, and the objective of self-determination and majority rule. In subsequent years, the Assembly many times explicitly recognized the right of the South African people to self-determination and/or majority rule.[222]

Self-determination and majority rule for South Africans had now become new United Nations objectives. It will be recalled that the Assembly had so far pursued the objective of racial equality in South Africa. The right of peoples to self-determination is not contained in the Universal Declaration, apparently because that Declaration was intended to proclaim individual rights and freedoms rather than collective rights such as self-determination. As a right, distinct from a principle, self-determination was first contained in Assembly resolution 421D (V) of 1950 and later in a declaration known as the Declaration on decolonization (Declaration on the Granting of Independence to Colonial Countries and Peoples) contained in Assembly resolution 1514 (XV) of 1960. In the former resolution, it was described as a fundamental right. As a human right, self-determination is contained also in the International Covenants on human rights. But, for blacks in South Africa self-determination and racial equality are virtually the same. With the establishment of full racial equality in South Africa the need for self-determination would automatically disappear, as the majority would then rule.

The claim to self-determination as a human right is controversial. Questions have been raised as to whether it is a political right, a legal right, a human right, or a principle. Some writers contend that inserting self-determination in the International Covenants on human rights is problematic because self-determination is not a human right but a collective right.[223] It has been asked who the people entitled to self-determination are. One writer asserts that "the difficulty results from the attempt to transform a political principle into an enforceable right."[224]

The right of self-determination as contained in Assembly resolution 421D (V) of 1950 and in the Declaration on decolonization of 1960 seems to have been meant for colonial peoples and territories. The situation in South Africa is not a matter of colonialism *strictu sensu*, but a matter of legalized racial inequality. South Africa is an independent state and a Member of the United Nations. A Member State of the United Nations cannot be a colony. True, there are vestiges of colonialism and remnants of settler-colonialism in South Africa where the situation can be described as internal colonialism. If, however, the Assembly had thought the matter was essentially one of colonialism, it could have referred the matter to the Committee on decolonization, otherwise known as the Committee of 24, instead of establishing the Special Committee against Apartheid.

Some have contended that self-determination should be exercised by different ethnic communities separately. On the other hand, the Declaration on decolonization stipulates that "any attempt at the partial or total disruption of the national unity and the territorial integrity of a country is incompatible with the purposes and principles of the Charter of the United Nations." However, the people of South Africa as a whole have never been given the opportunity to exercise their right to self-determination. Nevertheless, it has been observed that the United Nations had theoretically had all colonial peoples in mind for self-determination but has not proved consistent in practice.[225]

Most likely, the Assembly regarded the right of self-determination not only as a human right but also as a prerequisite for the enjoyment of human rights and fundamental freedoms. But the Assembly does not appear to have been consistent with regard to the application of the right of self-determination or majority rule in all the cases brought before it, such as the cases of Cyprus, Gibraltar, Western Sahara, and South Africa. In some cases, it has only recommended negotiations between the parties concerned. By making substantive recommendations in the case of South Africa, the United Nations has attempted to play more or less a conciliatory role, while in some other cases it has merely recommended negotiations and has thus played the lesser role of mediation.

On the subject of South Africa's homelands policy, however, the Assembly has been thoroughly consistent. Since 1970, the Assembly has condemned the establishment of African homelands, formerly called native reserves and Bantustans, and the forcible removal of the African people to those areas as a violation of their inalienable rights. It has expressed the conviction that the establishment of homelands in South Africa was designed to deprive the majority of the people of their inalienable rights and to destroy the unity of the South African people.[226]

In 1971, in a resolution specifically adopted on Bantustans, the Assembly again condemned the establishment of Bantustans.[227] Later, it reaffirmed "that the establishment of bantustans is a measure essentially designed to destroy the territorial integrity of the country in violation of the principles enshrined in the Charter of the United Nations."[228] In 1976, it rejected the declaration of "independence" of the Transkei (one of the ten homelands) and declared that action invalid. At the same time, it called upon governments to deny any form of recognition to the Transkei and to take effective measures to prohibit all dealings with it.[229] Subsequently, it denounced the declarations of "independence" of Bophuthatswana and Venda, proclaimed in 1977 and 1978, respectively, as well as any other bantustans which might be created by the South African regime.[230]

In 1971, the Assembly declared that the then tactics of the South African Government in pursuance of its so-called "outward policy" were designed to obtain acquiescence in its racial policies, to confuse world public opinion, to counter international isolation, to hinder assistance to the liberation movements, and to consolidate white minority rule in southern Africa. It requested all states to take more effective action for the elimination of apartheid and to dissuade their nationals from emigrating to South Africa. At the same time, it proposed that the United Nations and Member States should intensify their efforts to solve the situation in South Africa in accordance with the principles of the Charter and the Declaration on decolonization.[231]

In 1974, the Assembly suspended the South African Government from participation in the work of the Assembly, because of its continued enforcement of apartheid and its disregard of relevant resolutions of the United Nations. Earlier, in 1970 and 1971, the Assembly had refused to approve the credentials of the South African delegations.[232]

Also in 1974, an attempt was made to expel South Africa from the United Nations. A draft resolution with that intent was submitted to the Security Council on 30 October, but was rejected because of a veto by three permanent members of the Council—France, the United Kingdom, and the United States. The Assembly cannot expel a Member State from the Organization without the recommendation of the Council.

Since 1974, the Government of South Africa has not been able to participate in the Assembly, although it has tried. On 23 May 1979, South Africa reoccupied its seat in the Assembly session in connection with the Namibia question. On the following day, however, the Assembly voted to reject South Africa's credentials and to prevent it from participating in the debate on Namibia, as a result of which the South African delegation immediately walked out.[233] South Africa was confronted with the same fate in March and September 1981, when it attempted again to take its seat in the Assembly, in connection with the issue of Namibia.

In recent years, at the Assembly's invitation, the South African liberation movements (ANC and PAC), both of which are recognized by the OAU, have participated in the debate on apartheid in the Special Political Committee and other bodies. In October 1976, these liberation movements were for the first time invited by the Assembly to participate in the debate on apartheid in plenary meetings of the Assembly.

In 1975, after its repeated requests to the Council to impose a mandatory arms embargo against South Africa had proved fruitless, the Assembly formally expressed its regret that France, the United Kingdom, and the United States had prevented adoption of the embargo by what the Assembly termed an "abuse" of their veto power.[234] Earlier, the Assembly had condemned the strengthening of political, economic, military, and other relations between South Africa and some countries.[235] In 1976, it called upon the Governments of France, the United Kingdom, and the United States to facilitate the adoption of a mandatory arms embargo against South Africa.[236]

The Assembly has also advised strongly against military, nuclear, and economic collaboration with South Africa, and against investments in South Africa, and advocated national and international trade union action against apartheid.[237] It has deplored collaboration with South Africa and called for the end of such collaboration.

At its thirty-third session, which began in September 1978 and extended into 1979, the Assembly adopted fifteen resolutions on the South African situation. In essence, the Assembly expressed its conviction that the United Nations had an important and vital role to play in the promotion of international action for the elimination of apartheid, and appealed to anti-apartheid movements, solidarity committees, trade unions, churches, youth organizations, non-governmental organizations as well as governments and intergovernmental organizations to join in a mobilization for that end.[238]

Apparently, the Assembly and the Council were influencing each other. After the Council adopted the mandatory arms embargo against South Africa, upon the Assembly's persistent requests over quite a number of years, the Assembly must have felt further emboldened. In 1979, the Assembly adopted eighteen resolutions on the item of "The Policies of Apartheid of the Government of South Africa." Most of them covered aspects of apartheid that had been dealt with in previous resolutions, and repeated previous recommendations or calls. In one resolution, the Assembly proposed an international conference to promote the Assembly's conviction that economic and other sanctions should be adopted against South Africa.[239] In other resolutions, the Assembly requested the Security Council to consider mandatory economic sanctions against South Africa, to declare that military or nuclear collaboration with South Africa was a threat to international peace and to take mandatory measures against such collaboration, to consider urgently a mandatory oil embargo on South Africa, and to consider the taking of effective steps for ending foreign investments in, and financial loans to, South Africa.[240]

In 1980, the Assembly again adopted eighteen resolutions on apartheid. It mainly repeated its earlier calls. On the nature of change in South Africa, it noted that the racist minority régime, through its system of institutionalized racial discrimination, exploitation and oppression, continued to deprive the majority of the South African people of avenues of peaceful change and legal courses of action to secure their inalienable rights to self-determination.[241]

Since 1962, in dealing with the combined agenda item on the South African situation, the Assembly has increased its efforts and demands and widened the scope of its consideration to include more aspects of apartheid. It has increasingly demanded more action not only from governments and the United Nations Secretariat but also from the international community. It has used stronger language and has brought in new concepts and elements. The Assembly has thus intensified its pressure against apartheid in a variety of directions.

These pressures were also manifest in the procedure that the Assembly followed. It first considered the combined item in the Special Political Committee and later in the plenary meetings of the Assembly without reference to a Main Committee. The ascendance of the combined item to the plenary meetings indicated that the Assembly attributed more importance as well as higher political attention to the item. Also, the Assembly has adopted an increasing number of resolutions from year to year. In 1962, when the combined item was first considered, the Assembly adopted one resolution on it; at its thirty-fifth session in 1980, it adopted eighteen. In all, during the period of nineteen years (1962-80), the Assembly has adopted 133 resolutions on this item, averaging seven a year.

The first resolution on the combined item, resolution 1761 (XVII) of 1962, was adopted by 67 votes in favor, 16 against, and 23 abstentions. The last resolution on the item, resolution 35/206R of 16 December 1980, concerning the United Nations Trust Fund for South Africa, was adopted without a vote, an indication of the growing international opposition to apartheid. It should also be noted that from 1962 to 1980 United Nations membership greatly increased, and that new members were mostly Afro-Asian countries. As newly independent countries, those members strongly supported United Nations efforts for decolonization, self-determination, and liberation.[242] The Afro-Asian members were easily able to muster the necessary votes to pass any resolution in the Assembly on the South African situation.

Despite the economic and other measures that the Assembly urged Member States to adopt against South Africa and despite its requests to the Security Council to adopt mandatory sanctions against South Africa, the Assembly can be said to have pursued internal change in the case of South Africa primarily by peaceful means. Progressively, it has sought racial equality, self-determination, and majority rule in South Africa. The economic measures and mandatory sanctions suggested by the Assembly do not involve violent means. So long as no military measures are adopted, or suggested, under Article 42 of the Charter, the sanctions already adopted against South Africa, or those requested by the Assembly, fall within the definition of the term "peaceful" in the Charter, in international law and in this book.

The Assembly's recognition of the legitimacy of armed struggle, however, remains controversial. United Nations speakers on apartheid are often confronted with the question whether it is appropriate for the United Nations, created to maintain international peace and security, to extend legitimacy to armed struggle. It is asked whether the United Nations is not encouraging violence, despite Article 1, paragraph 4, of the Charter, which provides that the United Nations should be a center for harmonizing the actions of nations in the attainment of the common ends, and Article 2 (3) providing that all members shall settle their international disputes by peaceful means. In case violent measures have to be used, it is asked, should they not be used collectively as provided by the Charter.

There are no legally satisfactory answers to these questions. Rebellion cannot easily, if at all, be defended on legal grounds. The right of rebellion is a moral issue. The Assembly is a political organ and takes political decisions, without any obligation to give or seek legal justification for its actions. Elementary justice and common sense, however, cannot accept the legal positivist argument against the use of force when there is no remedy to grave injustice, such as the case in South Africa. One writer, indeed, maintains that a citizen has the moral right to rebel in certain circumstances, such as when the state offers no remedy to evident injustices, when the state is unnecessarily repressive, when there is no normal outlet for dissent, and when a system is clearly not acceptable to the overwhelming majority of the population.[243] These circumstances fit precisely the South African situation, over which the international community has long given its moral verdict.

At the same time, the Assembly has never called for violence. It has merely taken note of a *de facto* situation where many blacks have been arrested, detained, tried, and convicted in the growing opposition to apartheid. Armed struggle in South Africa did not start at the instigation of the Assembly. On the contrary, the Assembly merely recognized the legitimacy of that struggle long after it started. One may also argue that the Articles of the Charter, referred to above, govern relations between nations, not relations between groups within a nation. Thus, the use of force in anti-colonial and anti-racist struggles was not considered inconsistent with the United Nations purposes and was not directed, under Article 2 (4), against the territorial integrity or political independence of any state. By the time the Assembly recognized the legitimacy of armed struggle in South Africa, such struggles for liberation had already been internationalized and legitimized in a gradual process, characterized by a broader interpretation of the United Nations Charter.[244]

Understandably, as the Assembly's requests to the Security Council for collective and non-violent measures were repeatedly frustrated, the Assembly ultimately recognized the legitimacy of armed struggle to put further pressure on South Africa. Moreover, since the Universal Declaration and the Declaration of Independence of the United States have recognized the right of rebellion, the Assembly would not seem to be setting a precedent in recognizing that people struggling to obtain rights enshrined in the Universal Declaration and in the Charter might lawfully rebel. As stated in the Declaration of Independence, "Whenever any Form of Government becomes destructive of these ends [unalienable rights including Life, Liberty and the Pursuit of Happiness], it is the right of the People to alter or to abolish it, and to institute a new Government . . ." That description applies very well to the situation in South Africa where the form of government has been destructive of blacks' inalienable rights.

The Assembly, however, did draw the line at proposing that states take violent measures such as military action against South Africa.[245] Furthermore, it was a full thirty-one years after the Assembly first took up the South African situation that it recognized the legitimacy of the armed struggle and only three years before the end of the period covered by this book. The Assembly was far from being impetuous. Primarily, the Assembly sought change in South Africa by peaceful means. But, apparently because the Assembly has legitimized the struggle in South Africa, something regarded as aggressive by Western countries, repeated efforts since mid-1960s to get Western states to serve on the Special Committee against Apartheid have failed. At the time of this writing, no Western state was serving on that Committee.

In retrospect, between 1962 and 1980, the Assembly repeatedly expressed its belief that the legislative racial measures in South Africa hindered peaceful change in South Africa. It stated that the release of leaders of the oppressed people of South Africa was an essential factor for a peaceful solution of the problem. It also expressed its conviction that the United Nations should intensify its efforts to secure a peaceful solution. At first, it considered that mandatory sanctions were the only means for achieving a peaceful solution to the crisis in South Africa, but later it considered that mandatory sanctions were only one of the essential means for achieving a peaceful solution.

Proclaiming that the United Nations and the international community had a special responsibility towards the struggling people of South Africa, the Assembly asked for assistance to be given to the people concerned. It also rejected the independence of certain homelands, announced by the Government of South Africa. It adopted the International Declaration against Apartheid in Sports, and recommended making world public opinion aware of the true nature of apartheid. It promoted an international campaign against apartheid, mainly in order to isolate the Government of South Africa.

In other actions, the Assembly asked governments and intergovernmental and non-governmental organizations to co-operate in international action against South Africa and not to collaborate with the Government of that country. It requested the Security Council to adopt mandatory sanctions against South Africa. It requested Member States to take specific diplomatic and economic measures to help bring about an end to apartheid, and suspended South Africa from participation in its work. It further requested the Council to consider the expulsion of South Africa from United Nations membership. It branded the South African Government as racist and adopted the Convention on apartheid.

In brief, from 1962 to 1980, that is, for nineteen years, the Assembly again pursued internal change primarily by peaceful means. In fact, in some resolutions, the Assembly expressed at the same time both its wish for a peaceful change in South Africa and its recognition of the legitimacy of the struggle of the oppressed people of South Africa to attain their human rights and fundamental freedoms.[246]

The South African Government, meanwhile, ignored the Assembly's appeals and recommendations although, obviously, there was a growing opposition to apartheid and stronger demand for action against South Africa. The South African Government went ahead with its policies of segregation and bantustanization. However, it made some changes, apparently to stem the growing black unrest in the country and to present a better face to the outside world.[247] But, the Assembly's objective of peaceful change in South Africa was not achieved. During the period under review, moreover, the Assembly repeatedly urged the Security Council to take action for peaceful change in South Africa.

Security Council

The Security Council considered the racial situation in South Africa for the first time in 1960. Its seizure of the issue is significant because Council consideration of a matter normally implies a linkage to a threat to international peace, imminent or potential. It will be recalled that it was soon after the consideration by the Council in 1960 that the Assembly for the first time requested Member States to take specific measures against the Government of South Africa, and that Assembly action against apartheid was intensified after 1960.

The Council began to consider South Africa's racial situation fourteen years after the Assembly. During the twenty-one years of Council consideration covered by this book, the Council adopted twelve resolutions employing increasingly stronger terms. It sought the same objectives as did the Assembly, and usually followed the Assembly in its demands, condemnations, and descriptions of apartheid. It recommended measures against South Africa, usually at the Assembly's repeated requests, but it has not yet taken all the measures requested by the Assembly. At the end of 1980, the Assembly was still exerting pressure on the Council to impose comprehensive mandatory sanctions on South Africa.

In its first resolution on South Africa's racial situation (1960), the Council deplored the policies and actions of the Government of the Union of South Africa.[248] It linked the consequences of such policies to the continued disregard by that Government of the resolutions of the Assembly, which called upon it to revise its policies in conformity with its obligations and responsibilities under the Charter. It called upon that Government "to initiate measures aimed at bringing about racial harmony based on equality" and to abandon its policies of apartheid and racial discrimination. It also asked the Secretary-General to consult with that Government and make such arrangements as would adequately help in upholding the purposes and principles of the Charter.

In 1960, the Secretary-General reported that it was agreed between him and the South African Government that consultations would be undertaken on the basis of his authority under the Charter, and that this would not require the prior recognition from that Government of the United Nations' authority. However, in January 1961, he reported that he had visited South Africa in that month but that "no mutually acceptable arrangement" had been found.[249]

The Council adopted its second resolution on the matter in August 1963.[250] The Council repeated its call to the South African Government to abandon the policies of apartheid and racial discrimination. It strongly deprecated the racial policies of South Africa as being inconsistent with the principles of the Charter and contrary to its obligations as a Member of the United Nations, and called upon that Government to liberate all persons imprisoned for having opposed apartheid. For the first time it called upon all states "to cease forthwith the sale and shipment of arms, ammunition of all types and military vehicles to South Africa." As the call was not made under Chapter VII of the Charter, it was not a mandatory measure. And, because it does not involve measures provided for under Article 42, such action does not alter the peaceful character of the measures by the United Nations to attain change in South Africa. The reason for adopting such voluntary measures, the Council indicated, was its concern that South Africa's arms build-up was being used in the furtherance of that Government's racial policies. The Council also regretted the failure of the Government of South Africa to accept its invitation to delegate a representative to appear before it. The Council further requested the Secretary-General to keep the situation under observation and to report by 30 October 1963.

The Secretary-General reported on 11 October 1963 that he had communicated with the Minister for Foreign Affairs of South Africa, who had informed him that the South African Government did not then wish to comment on the matter except to say that its views had often been stated in the past and were well known. In another letter, dated 11 October 1963, from the Minister for Foreign Affairs of South Africa, the Secretary-General was informed that the South African Government had never recognized the right of the United Nations to discuss or consider a matter which fell solely within the jurisdiction of a Member State. Referring to the arms embargo provisions of the resolution, the Foreign Minister maintained that those provisions were in essence a denial of the spirit of Article 51 of the Charter concerning the right of self-defence. He further held that the Council did not have the judicial power in those circumstances to take the action envisaged by the resolution and that it could not, therefore, have any binding effect on South Africa or any other Member State.[251]

In its next resolution (1963), the Council again pointed out the inconsistency of the racial policies of South Africa with the Charter principles and membership obligations.[252] It expressed the firm conviction that a positive alternative should "be found through peaceful means" to the policies of apartheid and racial discrimination as those policies were abhorrent to the conscience of mankind. It urgently requested the South African Government to cease its "discriminatory and repressive measures which are contrary to the principles and purposes of the Charter and which are in violation of its obligations as a Member of the United Nations and of the provisions of the Universal Declaration of Human Rights." It requested the Secretary-General to establish a small group of recognized experts to examine methods of resolving the situation in South Africa, through full, peaceful, and orderly application of human rights and fundamental freedoms to all inhabitants of the territory as a whole, regardless of race, color, or creed, and to consider what part the United Nations might play in the achievement of that end.[253]

By that same resolution, the Council invited the Government of South Africa "to avail itself of the assistance of this group in order to bring about such peaceful and orderly transformation," and solemnly called upon all states to cease forthwith the sale and shipment of equipment and materials for the manufacture and maintenance of arms and ammunition in South Africa. It also deplored South Africa's refusal, as confirmed in the reply of the Minister of Foreign Affairs, to comply with the Council's previous resolution and to accept the repeated recommendations of other United Nations organs.

The Group of Experts submitted its report on 20 April 1964. As a primary principle, the Group concluded that all the people of South Africa should be brought into consultation and should thus be enabled to decide the future of their country at the national level. Regarding the constitutional framework, the Group expressed its belief that, keeping in mind the overriding purpose of ensuring the rights of all, some kind of a federal system of government in South African conditions might be advisable, provided that representation should not be on any racial basis, but on a national or regional basis through a fully democratic franchise on a common voters roll.

With regard to the question of sanctions, the Group noted that the African leaders had vigorously rejected the argument that sanctions should not be imposed on South Africa because they would harm the black population. It concluded that for sanctions to be rapidly effective they should be imposed by a unanimous decision of the Security Council, and recommended that the Council examine the logistics of sanctions. It also recommended that, if no satisfactory reply was received from the South African Government by a date to be stipulated, the Council should apply economic sanctions. It concluded that "a political, economic and social system built on the domination of one race by another by force cannot survive."[254] The Group further noted that on 5 February 1964 the South African Government had informed the Secretary-General of its refusal to grant facilities to the Group or to co-operate with it in any form.[255]

In June 1964, the Council adopted two resolutions on South Africa's racial situation. In the first one, it noted with regret that the Government of South Africa had rejected the appeal of the Secretary-General of 27 March 1964, and urged that Government to renounce the execution of those sentenced to death, to end the Rivonia trial, and to grant amnesty to all political prisoners.[256] It also invited all states to exert all their influence on South Africa to induce it to comply. In the second resolution, the Council took note of the report of the Group of Experts and endorsed and subscribed in particular to the main conclusion of the Group that "all the people of South Africa should be brought into consultation and should thus be enabled to decide the future of their country at the national level."[257] The Council requested the Secretary-General to consider what assistance the United Nations might offer to facilitate such consultations among representatives of all elements of the population in South Africa. It invited the Government of South Africa to accept the main conclusion of the Group of Experts, to co-operate with the Secretary-General, and to submit its views to him with respect to such consultations by 30 November 1964.

At the same time, the Council established a Committee of Experts, composed of representatives of all Council members, to undertake a technical and practical study as to the feasibility, effectiveness and implications of measures which could, as appropriate, be taken by the Council under the Charter. This was a step taken in accordance with the recommendation of the Group of Experts, as seen above. The Council also appealed to the Government of South Africa to abolish the practice of imprisonment without charges, and invited the Secretary-General to establish an educational and training programme for South Africans.

The Permanent Representative of South Africa replied to the Secretary-General's letter of 9 June 1964, which transmitted the Council resolution of that day to the South African authorities. He reiterated that South Africa regarded intervention by the United Nations in the judicial processes of a

Member State as illegal and *ultra vires* the United Nations Charter.[258]

On 19 June 1964, the Secretary-General sent a letter to the Minister of Foreign Affairs of South Africa transmitting the Council's resolution of that date. In his reply, the Minister of Foreign Affairs said that it was "difficult for the South African Government to conceive of a more far-reaching example of attempted intervention in matters falling within the domestic jurisdiction of a sovereign Member of the United Nations than is represented by the terms of the resolution in question."[259]

In March 1965, the Committee of Experts reported on the importance of total embargoes on such items as trade, petroleum, and arms, but noted difficulties in world-wide implementation. It pointed out that South Africa was not immune to damages from economic sanctions, although it would not be readily susceptible to such measures. It expressed its belief that the degree of effectiveness of such measures would depend on the universality of their application, especially by South Africa's traditional trade partners, and on the manner and the duration of their enforcement.[260]

From 19 June 1964 to 22 July 1970, or for about six years, the Council did not adopt any resolution in the matter. This inactivity was quite strange for a responsible organ which had initiated action by establishing an expert committee, by asking the Government of South Africa to co-operate and submit its views, and by calling upon all states to cease the sale of arms and ammunition to South Africa. The Council was so reluctant to consider the matter during that span of time that the Assembly had to urge it repeatedly to do so. In 1967, the Assembly requested the Council to resume consideration of the question of apartheid.[261] In 1968, the Assembly noted that the Council had not considered the problem of apartheid since 1964 and requested it to resume urgently the consideration of the matter.[262]

Under Article 11, paragraph 3, of the Charter, the Assembly may call the attention of the Council to situations which are likely to endanger international peace and security. The Council, however, does not have to consider a matter submitted to it in the form of a general recommendation. A formal request to the Council entails a dispute or a situation which might lead to international friction or give rise to a dispute, brought to its attention by any Member State or States, under Article 35, or by the Secretary-General, under Article 99. Thus, when on 19 December 1967 the Secretary-General transmitted the text of Assembly resolution 2307 (XXII) to the Council, the latter did not discuss the matter.[263]

Similarly, the Council did not discuss Assembly resolution 2396 (XXIII) transmitted to it by the Secretary-General on 12 December 1968.[264] Perhaps the Unilateral Declaration of Independence by Southern Rhodesia in 1965 diverted the Council's attention from South Africa. Also, the strong cause provided by the 1964 political trials for the Council's meetings did not exist in the ensuing few years.

In 1970, when the Council adopted its next resolution on South Africa's racial situation, it condemned the violations of the 1963 arms embargo and called upon all states to strengthen the arms embargo by certain ways it suggested.[265] It also recognized, for the first time, the legitimacy of the struggle of the oppressed people of South Africa in pursuance of their human and political rights as set forth in the Charter and the Universal Declaration.[266] Similar phraseology would appear in some of its subsequent resolutions.[267]

The Council, for its part, has never qualified the struggle in South Africa by such terms as "by all means" or "armed," as was the case with the Assembly. It has used more moderate terms. Nor has it specifically mentioned the liberation movements. It has spoken only of the "oppressed people of South Africa." The liberation movements, however, are composed of the most militant of the oppressed people of South Africa. Nevertheless, the explanation given earlier with regard to the effect of the recognition of the legitimacy on the peaceful character of the means used by the Assembly is equally applicable here, the more so because the Council did not extend recognition specifically to armed struggle.

In its resolution of 1972, on the racial situation in South Africa, the Council deplored the persistent refusal of the South African Government to implement the resolutions adopted by the Council in order to promote a "peaceful solution" in accordance with the Charter of the United Nations.[268] At the same time, it again recognized the legitimacy of the struggle of the oppressed people of South Africa. It called on all states to observe strictly the arms embargo, and expressed the conviction that it (the Council) ought to take urgent measures to secure the implementation of its resolutions. As a matter of urgency, it decided to examine methods for resolving the situation arising out of apartheid policies. It called upon the South African Government to release all political prisoners, and called for generous contributions to United Nations Funds for humanitarian and training purposes of South Africans.

Yet, despite its decision urgently to take measures and examine methods, the Council did not discuss the matter for four more years (between 5 February 1972 and 18 June 1976). During that period, the Assembly continued to adopt resolutions requesting the Council urgently to consider the situation with a view to taking effective measures under Chapter VII.[269] But the Council did not discuss the matter until 19 June 1976, just after large-scale killings and wounding of Africans in Soweto and other black townships had taken place, when 176 were shot dead and over a thousand injured. Then in resolution 392 of 19 June 1976, adopted by consensus, the Council strongly condemned the South African Government for massive violence against African people, reaffirmed that the policy of apartheid is a crime against the conscience and dignity of mankind, and recognized the legitimacy of the struggle of the South African people for the elimination of apartheid and racial discrimination.

Significantly, in October 1977, the Council affirmed, for the first time, the exercise of the right to self-determination by all the people of South Africa as a whole, irrespective of race, color or creed.[270] It demanded, among other things, that "the racist régime of South Africa abolish the policy of bantustanization, abandon the policy of *apartheid* and ensure majority rule based on justice and equality." It thus branded the South African régime as racist. It also requested all governments and organizations to take all appropriate measures to implement these and other demands, and to contribute assistance to the victims of violence and repression, including student refugees from South Africa. It further requested the Secretary-General to follow the situation and report to the Council not later than 17 February 1978. As the Assembly had done nearly a decade ago, the Council now added self-determination and majority rule to its objective of racial equality in South Africa.

The Secretary-General submitted his report on 28 April 1978. He informed the Council that he had transmitted the text of the resolution to the Ministers for Foreign Affairs of all states and that he had asked for information on measures taken by their governments under that resolution. He supplied the list of those states which had replied. South Africa was not among them.[271]

In the meantime, in November 1977, the Council took the historic decision on voting a mandatory arms embargo against South Africa. Acting under Chapter VII of the Charter, the Council determined that "the acquisition by South Africa of arms and related matériel constitutes a threat to the maintenance of international peace and security." It decided "that all States shall cease forthwith any provision to South Africa of arms and related matériel of all types . . ." It further decided "that all States shall refrain from any co-operation with South Africa in the manufacture and development of nuclear weapons."[272]

At the time of the adoption of the mandatory arms embargo, the Council had other draft resolutions to consider, ones which would impose economic and other sanctions on South Africa. It did not go along with the request of African countries to adopt such sanctions under Chapter VII, because of the opposition of certain Western permanent members of the Council. The Council's action marked a significant change. Fifteen years earlier the Council would not even adopt a simple condemnatory resolution against South Africa, but in 1977 it adopted mandatory sanctions against a Member State, one of the founding members of the Organization.

The Council's decision to adopt a mandatory arms embargo against South Africa was also significant because it was the first time in United Nations history that the Council had adopted mandatory sanctions against a Member State. In addition, the Council had always maintained that it could not adopt measures under Chapter VII unless it could determine the existence of a threat to the peace, breach of the peace, or act of aggression.

In its earlier resolutions, therefore, the Council had avoided saying that the situation in South Africa constituted a threat to international peace. But, in resolution 418 (1977) it devised a new phraseology. It linked the acquisition by South Africa of arms to a threat to peace. It did not say that the racial situation itself in South Africa constituted a threat to peace. Finally, with the imposition of this partial embargo, it became clear that other steps such as mandatory economic sanctions might follow more easily. Significantly, immediately after the adoption of the arms embargo the representative of the Soviet Union in the Council said, among other things, that he regarded that "step by the Council not only as an important advance but as a basis for further effective measures to be taken by the Council in its fight against *apartheid* in South Africa."[273] Since 1977, the Assembly has been putting increasing pressure on the Council to adopt mandatory economic sanctions against South Africa.

The mandatory sanctions adopted by the Council are of peaceful character as they do not involve the use of violence and they are not measures adopted under Article 42. Notably even during the discussions surrounding the adoption of resolution 418 (1977), Council members were asserting that their aim was to achieve peaceful change in South Africa. For instance, immediately after the Council adopted the mandatory arms embargo, the representative of the United States stated, *inter alia*:

> At the same time, however, we must stress the other side of the picture and make clear to the Government of South Africa our desire for reconciliation, provided South Africa is willing to begin progress towards the end of *apartheid* and the full participation of all South Africans in the political and economic life of their country. . . .
> As far as the United States is concerned, it looks forward to the day when progress in South Africa will make it possible for this Council to remove the stigma which this resolution places on South Africa.[274]

At the same meeting, the representative of the United Kingdom said:

> At the same time, and perhaps more importantly, we view the action which the Council has taken as both a warning and an appeal to South Africa—a warning that the international community is in earnest about the need for change, and the desire to see . . . a peaceful and democratic transformation, rather than a disintegration into violence. . . .
> Today's decision is therefore of profound significance, in the view of my Government—both as a reflection of the way in which we can, if we wish, make the United Nations a reality, and also in the signal that it sends to the South African Government. That signal is clear, unremittable and precise: namely, that the world expects changes to be made and, what is more, will do what it can to ensure that they are.[275]

Again at the same meeting, the representative of the Federal Republic of Germany expressed the hope that the Council's serious warning would "encourage those forces which continue to work with all the energy at their command, but without bloodshed, towards a speedy transition of Namibia and Rhodesia into independence and towards the necessary changes in South Africa."[276]

In December 1977, the Council established, in accordance with rule 28 of its provisional rules of procedure, a Committee of the Security Council, consisting of all the members of the Council, to examine the progress of the implementation of the measures adopted in the previous resolution imposing the arms embargo. The Committee was also authorized to study ways and means to make the embargo more effective.[277]

On 13 June 1980, the Council adopted its last resolution on the item, within the period under review.[278] It strongly condemned "the racist regime of South Africa for further aggravating the situation and its massive repression against all opponents of apartheid . . ." It also expressed "its hope that the inevitable change in South Africa's racial policies can be attained through peaceful means . . ."

The Council resolution on the mandatory arms embargo was adopted unanimously, including the votes of the traditional political friends and economic partners of South Africa. Obviously, there was a growing consensus within the Council on the need to take some action with regard to the racial situation in South Africa. In all, between 1960 and 1980, the Council adopted twelve resolutions on the matter. The first resolution was adopted with two abstentions, while the last one was adopted unanimously.

The Council began to consider the South African situation much later than the Assembly. At first, it demanded racial harmony based on equality in South Africa. Later, long after the Assembly had done so, it demanded self-determination and majority rule for the whole people of South Africa. It deplored the racial situation in South Africa and called upon the Government of South Africa to revise its racial policies in conformity with the Charter and the Universal Declaration.

Over the years, the Council has asked the Secretary-General to consult with South Africa so that the principles and purposes of the Charter might be upheld. It has also requested the Secretary-General to keep the situation under observation and report. It has established a Group of Experts to examine methods of a peaceful solution, a Committee of Experts to study the feasibility and effectiveness of sanctions against South Africa, and a committee of its own to see about the implementation of the mandatory arms embargo.

The Council has consistently called for a solution to be found through peaceful means. It has deplored the persistent refusal of the South African Government to comply with its resolutions in order to promote a peaceful solution. It has adopted the mandatory arms embargo against South Africa in order to prevent the racial situation in South Africa from worsening and to avoid the eruption of violent racial conflict in that country. Even during the adoption of the mandatory embargo, statements made by the members of the Council clearly indicated that the Council's objective was the peaceful change of the racial situation in South Africa.

The Council, too, recognized the legitimacy of the struggle of oppressed people of South Africa, although it did not extend the legitimacy to armed struggle. It affirmed apartheid as a crime against the conscience and dignity of mankind, but fell short of affirming it as a crime against humanity. Also, as the Assembly had done, the Council branded the South African Government as racist. The Council expressed the conviction that it ought to take urgent measures to ensure the implementation of its resolutions.

The executive bodies were the Secretary-General, the Group of Experts, the Committee of Experts, and the Committee of the Security Council, while the policy-making body was the Council. As means, the Council resorted to appeals, consultations, demands, deplorations, condemnations, political and moral pressure, and voluntary as well as mandatory arms embargoes.

Despite the Council's many resolutions, however, the South African Government has not co-operated or heeded any recommendations. It has never recognized the authority of the United Nations in the matter. The Council began to consider the matter quite late and usually followed the Assembly in its actions. It adopted the mandatory embargo fourteen years after it adopted the voluntary embargo and declined to adopt mandatory economic sanctions. Moreover, for long periods of time it did not consider the matter. Nevertheless, despite recognizing the legitimacy of the struggle of the oppressed people of South Africa and adopting the mandatory arms embargo against South Africa, the Council persistently pressed, albeit in vain, for peaceful change of the racial situation in South Africa.

IV. MATTER OF HUMAN RIGHTS AND OF THREAT TO INTERNATIONAL PEACE

General Assembly

Treatment of People of Indian Origin in the Union
of South Africa; The Question of Race Conflict
Resulting from the Policies of Apartheid of
the Government of the Union of South Africa (1946-61)

We have seen that the United Nations has sought to change South Africa's racialized legal order primarily by peaceful means, although ultimately it recognized the legitimacy of the struggle within South Africa. Has it sought peaceful change in South Africa because of human rights or because of a threat posed by South Africa's racial situation to international peace and security, or both? The present chapter deals with these questions.

As stated earlier, from 1946 to 1961 the Assembly repeatedly invoked the Charter provisions on human rights as well as the Universal Declaration, called attention to its resolutions on racial discrimination, and declared racial segregation to be inherently discriminatory. It called upon the South African Government to suspend the implementation of certain discriminatory legislation, declared that it would be in the higher interests of humanity to end racial discrimination, and linked peace with respect for, and observance of, human rights and fundamental freedoms. It deplored South Africa's racial policies, and found those policies to have impaired friendly relations between nations, to be harmful to ethnic relations in the world, and to be prejudicial to international harmony. In 1961, the Assembly called the Security Council's attention to those policies on the grounds that they were likely to endanger international peace.

Also during its first fifteen years, when considering the treatment of the people of Indian origin in South Africa, the Assembly repeatedly invited the parties, namely, India, Pakistan and South Africa, to enter into negotiations, keeping in mind the purposes and principles of the Charter and the Universal Declaration.[279] It frequently expressed its regret at South Africa's refusal to co-operate,[280] that South Africa had continued to implement the Group Areas Act,[281] and that it proceeded with further legislation contrary

89

to the Charter and the Universal Declaration. It also stated that South Africa's actions were not in keeping with its obligations and responsibilities under the Charter.[282] After 1957, the Assembly began appealing specifically to the Government of South Africa to co-operate and enter into negotiations,[283] drawing that Government's attention to its repeated appeals, and inviting Member States to use their good offices to bring about negotiations.[284]

To encourage the South African Government to negotiate with regard to the treatment of people of Indian origin, the Assembly, as early as 1958, repeatedly noted that the Governments of India and Pakistan were prepared to negotiate with South Africa, and that they had declared that such negotiations would not in any way prejudice the juridical stand in the dispute of any of the negotiating Governments.[285] As will be seen in relation to the question of domestic jurisdiction, from the beginning, the main objection to taking strong measures against South Africa was the argument that human rights were matters of domestic jurisdiction and that, therefore, the United Nations was not competent to take such action.

In its first resolution on the question of race conflict in South Africa, the Assembly said that one of the purposes of the United Nations was to achieve international co-operation in promoting and encouraging respect for human rights and fundamental freedoms for all, without distinction as to race, sex, language or religion. It called upon all governments to conform to the letter and spirit of the Charter, and requested the Secretary-General to provide the Commission on Racial Situation with the necessary staff and facilities and invited the Government of South Africa to extend its full co-operation to that Commission.[286]

Subsequently, the Assembly repeated some of its earlier points and affirmed that governmental policies designed to perpetuate or increase discrimination were inconsistent with the pledges of the Members under Article 56 of the Charter. It solemnly called upon all Member States to bring their policies into line with their obligations under the Charter to promote the observance of human rights and fundamental freedoms.[287] As yet, there was no mention of a threat to international peace.

In 1953, the Assembly stated that

> enduring peace will not be secured solely by collective security arrangements against breaches of international peace and acts of aggression, but that a genuine and lasting peace depends also upon the observance of all the Principles and Purposes established in the Charter of the United Nations, upon the implementation of the resolutions of the Security Council, the General Assembly and other principal organs of the United Nations intended to achieve the maintenance of international peace and security, and especially upon respect for and observance of human rights and fundamental freedoms for all . . .[288]

The Assembly thus linked human rights with international peace, but did not find in South Africa's racial situation any threat to international peace. The Assembly also agreed with the report of the Commission on Racial Situation that it was highly unlikely that the policy of apartheid would ever be accepted by the masses subjected to discrimination.

In 1954, the Assembly pointed out the pledges of Member States under the Charter to respect human rights and noted with apprehension the adoption of new laws by the South African Government, which were also incompatible with the obligations of that Government under the Charter. It invited that Government to reconsider its position in the light of the Charter, and to take into account the valuable experience of other multi-racial societies as set forth in chapter 7 of the report of the Commission. It further invited the South African Government to take into consideration the Commission's suggestions. It also requested the Commission to keep under review the problem of race conflict in South Africa.[289]

The following year, the Assembly recalled its earlier conviction about the maintenance of a genuine and lasting peace, reminded the Government of South Africa of the faith it had reaffirmed in fundamental human rights and in the dignity and worth of the human person, and called on that Government to observe the obligations contained in Article 56 of the Charter. It commended the Commission for its constructive work and recommended that the Government of South Africa take note of the Commission's report.[290] There was still no mention of any threat to international peace.

In two resolutions in 1957, the Assembly did not mention international peace or threat thereto.[291] It repeated earlier statements on racial doctrines and obligations under the Charter. In one resolution, it affirmed its conviction that perseverance in discriminatory policies was inconsistent not only with the Charter but also with the forces of progress and international co-operation in implementing the ideals of equality, freedom, and justice. It also expressed its conviction that

> in a multi-racial society, harmony and respect for human rights and freedoms and the peaceful development of a unified community are best assured when patterns of legislation and practice are directed towards ensuring a legal order that will ensure equality before the law and the elimination of discrimination between all persons regardless of race, creed or colour.

Clearly, the Assembly was conscious of the fact that the foundation of the racial inequality in South Africa was the legal order. In the other resolution in 1957, the Assembly appealed to the Government of South Africa to revise its racial policy in the light of the purposes and principles of the Charter and of world opinion, emphasizing the Organization's human rights standards.

In 1958 and 1959, the Assembly repeated its earlier statements and expressed its regret that the South African Government had not yet responded to its appeals to reconsider governmental policies which impaired the right of all racial groups to enjoy the same fundamental rights and freedoms. It stated that "government policies which accentuate or seek to preserve racial discrimination are prejudicial to international harmony." That was not, yet a judgment that a threat existed to international peace. At the same time, the Assembly expressed its conviction that the practice of racial discrimination and segregation was opposed to the observance of human rights and fundamental freedoms. It also expressed its opposition to the continuance or preservation of racial discrimination in any part of the world.[292]

In 1961, the Assembly adopted its last two resolutions on race conflict.[293] It deprecated and condemned policies based on racial discrimination and superiority as reprehensible and repugnant to human dignity. It also reminded the South African Government of the requirement in Article 2, paragraph 2, of the Charter that all Members should fulfil in good faith the obligations assumed by them under the Charter. It noted with grave concern that the policies of apartheid had led to international friction, and that their continuance endangered international peace and security. It requested all states to consider taking such separate and collective action as is open to them, in conformity with the Charter, to bring about the abandonment of apartheid policies.

The Assembly, at the same time, deplored the total disregard by the South African Government of United Nations resolutions, as well as that Government's determined aggravation of racial issues by more discriminatory laws and measures and their enforcement, accompanied by violence and bloodshed. It recalled that the Security Council had, on 1 April 1960, "recognized that the situation in South Africa was one that had led to international friction and, if continued, might endanger international peace and security." For the first time, it called the Council's attention to Article 11, paragraph 3, of the Charter. This Article provides that "the General Assembly may call the attention of the Security Council to situations which are likely to endanger international peace and security."

The Assembly's two resolutions, in 1961, on race conflict were adopted soon after the Council was first seized in 1960 with the item on the racial situation in South Africa. Although the Council had recognized in resolution 134 (1960) that the continuation of the situation "might endanger international peace and security," the Assembly now went further in noting that the continuance of apartheid policies "endangers international peace and security." In fact, in resolution 1663 (XVI), the Assembly said that the continuance of those policies "seriously" endangered international peace and security.

Until 1961, therefore, the Assembly did not regard the racial situation of South Africa as a threat to international peace. It viewed that situation as one impairing friendly relations between nations, as a grave threat to peaceful relations between ethnic groups in the world, and as prejudicial to international harmony. Only after the Council began to consider the racial situation of South Africa did the Assembly begin to see it as a danger to international peace. The Assembly would assert that view in stronger terms in connection with the combined item after 1962.

Nevertheless, it may safely be said that both items were dealt with by the Assembly from 1946 to 1961 mainly as a matter of human rights, based on the human rights standards of the United Nations, and not on the existence of a threat to international peace and security. During that period, in each resolution that it adopted on any of the two items the Assembly either made a reference to the human rights provisions of the Charter and/or the Universal Declaration or recalled its earlier resolutions containing such references. The Assembly then considered South Africa's racial situation within its purview as an issue of internal peaceful change and a question of human rights.

The Policies of Apartheid of the Government of the Republic of South Africa (1962-80)

After 1961 the Assembly requested Member States to take specific measures, separately or collectively, to help bring about the abandonment of apartheid. It requested the Security Council to take measures, including mandatory sanctions, to secure South Africa's compliance with United Nations resolutions. It also requested the Council to consider the expulsion of South Africa from membership. It recognized the legitimacy of the struggle of the oppressed people of South Africa for the attainment of their human rights and self-determination, condemned apartheid as a crime against humanity, and branded the Government of South Africa as racist. It also adopted the International Convention on the Suppression and Punishment of the Crime of Apartheid.

Faced with South Africa's defiance and expansion of its racist legislation, the Assembly's recommendations became increasingly severe after 1961. In 1962, the Assembly reaffirmed that the continuance of apartheid policies "seriously" endangered international peace and security, and requested the Council to take appropriate measures, including sanctions. For the first time, the Assembly suggested specific measures of diplomatic and economic nature to be taken by Member States, separately or collectively, such as breaking off diplomatic relations, closing their ports to South African vessels, and boycotting all South African goods. It recalled the Council's resolution of 1960 which had asked the Government of South Africa to take measures aimed at bringing about racial harmony based on equality.[294]

In 1963, the Assembly took up the plight of political prisoners, detainees and restrictees in South Africa and considered humanitarian assistance to persecuted people and their families. It spoke of the harsh repressive measures taken by the Government of South Africa, the trial of a large number of political prisoners under arbitrary laws, and the serious hardship faced by the families of persons persecuted for opposition to apartheid. It recommended that the international community provide the people concerned with humanitarian assistance and requested the Secretary-General to seek ways and means therefor. It foresaw that the trials then in progress would inevitably lead to further deterioration of the situation, and further disturb international peace.[295] Resolutions adopted by the Assembly on political prisoners and detainees essentially dealt with humanitarian matters.[296]

It was in 1965, however, that the Assembly asked the Council for the first time to take action against South Africa under Chapter VII of the Charter on the grounds that "the situation in South Africa constitutes a threat to international peace and security."[297] The Assembly reached this conclusion apparently on the basis of its consideration, as expressed in the preamble of the resolution, "that prompt and effective international action is imperative in order to avert the grave danger of a violent racial conflict in Africa, which would inevitably have grave repercussions throughout the world." The Assembly repeated its request to the Council for the adoption of mandatory sanctions many times thereafter.[298] In 1965, the Assembly also expressed its grave concern at the explosive situation in South Africa as a result of apartheid which violated South Africa's obligations under the Charter, and expressed dismay that South Africa's racial policies were aggravating the situation in neighbouring territories in southern Africa.

Continuing its pressure on South Africa, the Assembly time and again appealed to Member States to comply with Security Council resolution (1963) on the voluntary arms embargo.[299] In 1968, it requested all states and organizations to suspend cultural, educational, sporting, and other exchanges with South Africa.[300] Many times thereafter, the Assembly urged all states and organizations to do so.[301]

In 1966, for the first time, the Assembly condemned the policies of apartheid practiced by the Government of South Africa as a crime against humanity, and repeated that condemnation in a number of subsequent resolutions.[302] It also reaffirmed that the situation in South Africa continued to pose a grave threat to international peace. Broadening its focus, the Assembly deplored "the attitude of the main trading partners of South Africa, including three permanent members of the Security Council, which, by their failure to co-operate in implementing resolutions of the General Assembly, by their refusal to join the Special Committee on the Policies of Apartheid of the Government of the Republic of South Africa and by their increasing collaboration with the Government of South Africa, have encouraged the latter to persist in its racial policies." It again appealed to all states for contributions to humanitarian programmes and for asylum, travel facilities, and educational and employment opportunities to refugees from South Africa.

The following year, the Assembly requested all states to commemorate 21 March, the International Day for the Elimination of Racial Discrimination, anniversary of the killing of peaceful African demonstrators against "pass laws" at Sharpeville, South Africa, in 1960.[303] It declared that freedom fighters against apartheid should be treated, when arrested, as prisoners of war under international law, particularly the Geneva Convention relative to the Treatment of Prisoners of War of 12 August 1949.[304]

In 1969, the Assembly noted with grave concern the brutal treatment of political detainees and the death of some of them because of inhuman treatment, and expressed solidarity with all those persecuted for opposing apartheid. It also condemned the Government of South Africa for its enactment of the Terrorism Act of 1967.[305] It further expressed the conviction that the policies and actions of the Government of South Africa "constitute a grave threat to international peace and security."[306] The following year, it noted with indignation the continued persecution and torture of African patriots and other opponents of apartheid under the Terrorism Act, and called upon the South African Government to end all such repressive measures.[307]

In 1971, the Assembly took note of the report of the Ad Hoc Working Group of Experts on the Treatment of Political Prisoners in South Africa, established under resolution 2 (XXIII) of the Commission on Human Rights of 6 March 1967, and expressed grave concern at reports of ill-treatment, torture, and death of opponents of apartheid in detention in South Africa. It called again on all states to do everything in their power to exert their influence to secure the repeal of all oppressive legislation in South Africa and the liberation of all persons imprisoned, detained, or banned for their opposition to apartheid. It also noted the deportations, bannings, detentions, and trials of a number of religious leaders in South Africa.[308]

That same year, the Assembly reaffirmed the determination of the United Nations to intensify its efforts to remedy the grave situation in southern Africa and to ensure the achievement of the legitimate rights of all the inhabitants of that area, irrespective of race, color, or creed.[309]

Subsequently, in 1972, the Assembly called upon the Government of South Africa to put an immediate end to all forms of physical and mental torture and other acts of terror against opponents of apartheid under detention or imprisonment and to punish the perpetrators of such criminal acts. It requested the Secretary-General to publicize the report of the Special Committee on Apartheid on maltreatment and torture of prisoners and detainees. It also requested the Secretary-General to transmit the report of the Special Committee to the Commission on Human Rights.[310] At the same time, it demanded the repeal of all repressive laws, regulations, and proclamations used to persecute opponents of apartheid, and invited a world-wide collection of contributions for assistance to the victims of apartheid.[311]

In another effort to strengthen its action against South Africa, the Assembly in 1973 adopted the International Convention on the Suppression and Punishment of the Crime of Apartheid, in the conviction that it would be an important step towards the eradication of the policies and practices of apartheid.[312] That same year, the Assembly took note of the report of the Secretary-General on the International Conference of Experts for the Support of Victims of Colonialism and Apartheid in Southern Africa, and reaffirmed "that the policies and actions of the South African régime have created and continue to pose a serious threat to international peace and security."[313]

The Assembly then called upon the Government of South Africa to repeal all repressive laws including the Unlawful Organizations Act of 1960 which had declared the ANC, PAC, and other organizations unlawful.[314] It also expressed deep concern "over the grave situation in South Africa, which constitutes a threat to international peace and security," and requested all governments to sign and ratify the International Convention on the Suppression and Punishment of the Crime of Apartheid.[315]

In 1975, the Assembly expressed deep concern "over the grave situation in South Africa, which constitutes an affront to human dignity and a threat to international peace and security."[316] Obviously, here the Assembly described in one breath the situation in South Africa both as a matter of human rights and as a threat to international peace.

Continuing to denounce what it called inhuman and criminal policies, the Assembly in 1976 strongly condemned "the establishment of bantustans as designed to consolidate the inhuman policies of apartheid, to destroy the territorial integrity of the country, to perpetuate white minority domination and to dispossess the African people of South Africa of their inalienable rights."[317] It also condemned the "racist régime of South Africa for its ruthless repression of the oppressed people of South Africa and other opponents of apartheid," while demanding the immediate and unconditional release of all political prisoners and restrictees and proclaiming 11 October the Day of Solidarity with South African Political Prisoners.[318]

The Assembly further expressed deep concern over "the explosive situation in South Africa resulting from the wanton killings by the racist régime of hundreds of peaceful demonstrators against apartheid and racial discrimination, including many school children."[319] This was a reference to the incidents at Soweto and other black townships on 16 June 1976. Again, the Assembly noted with grave concern that some governments continued to collaborate with the South African régime, in pursuit of their strategic, economic, and other interests, and thus encouraged that régime to persist in its "criminal policies."[320]

In another action, the Assembly took note in 1976 of the national uprising of the oppressed people of South Africa against the apartheid régime and expressed outrage at the continuing massacres and other atrocities by that régime against school children and other peaceful demonstrators. It welcomed the coming into force of the International Convention on the Suppression and Punishment of the Crime of Apartheid, and proclaimed 16

June the International Day of Solidarity with the Struggling People of South Africa.[321]

The Assembly continued to express itself against South Africa in ever stronger terms. In 1977, it called upon all states to co-operate fully in effective international action, in accordance with Chapter VII of the Charter, "to avert the grave menace to the peace resulting from the policies and actions of the racist régime of South Africa."[322] The call was made soon after the Council had adopted the mandatory arms embargo. The Assembly noted "that the racist régime of South Africa has further aggravated racial discrimination, domination and exploitation of the great majority of the people of South Africa and has intensified ruthless repression in order to enforce its criminal policy."[323] It also noted that the racist régime of South Africa continued its policy of apartheid, repression, bantustanization, and aggression and aggravated the threat to international peace and security, and condemned the "illegitimate minority racist régime of South Africa for its criminal policies and actions."[324]

Later, the Assembly reaffirmed that humanitarian assistance to those persecuted under repressive and discriminatory legislation in South Africa, Namibia, and Southern Rhodesia was appropriate and essential. It expressed grave concern over the continued and increased repression against all opponents of apartheid and racial discrimination in South Africa, Namibia, and Southern Rhodesia.[325] It further reaffirmed "its full commitment to the eradication of apartheid and the elimination of the threat to international peace and security caused by the apartheid régime" and that apartheid was a crime against the conscience and dignity of mankind.[326] It also spoke of the necessity of "the elimination of the inhuman and criminal system of apartheid."[327]

In 1980, the Assembly reiterated its earlier calls on the South African Government and Member States. It reaffirmed that apartheid was a crime against humanity. It also reaffirmed the legitimacy of the struggle of the oppressed people of South Africa and their national liberation movement by all available means, including armed struggle. In another action, it urged the Security Council to determine that the situation in South Africa constituted a threat to international peace and security and to impose effective mandatory sanctions, including an oil embargo, against South Africa, under Chapter VII of the Charter. It also condemned the collaboration of "certain Western and other States, as well as those transnational corporations and other organizations" which maintained collaboration with the "racist régime" in the political, economic, military and nuclear and other fields.[328]

In the same year, the Assembly condemned the violence and repression practiced by the apartheid régime against all opponents of apartheid.[329] It noted with grave concern the intensified repression of the opponents of apartheid through detention, torture and killing, and the institution of political trials under arbitrary laws providing for death and other inhuman sentences. It called again for the release of political prisoners,[330] and requested the Commission on Human Rights to investigate crimes against women and children in South Africa.[331] It recalled its resolution 34/93C of 1979 on an international conference on sanctions against South Africa, and authorized the Special Committee against Apartheid to take all necessary steps, in co-operation with the Organization of African Unity, for the organization of the conference in 1981.[332]

In May 1981, the Conference on Sanctions against South Africa was held at the UNESCO House, Paris. It was attended by 124 Governments, United Nations organs, Organization of African Unity, Movement of Non-Aligned Countries, specialized agencies of the United Nations, intergovernmental organizations, national liberation movements, national and international non-governmental organizations and a number of experts and statesmen. The Conference adopted a declaration in which it expressed its deep conviction that the situation in South Africa, as well as in southern Africa, was of deep concern to all governments and organizations and to humanity as a whole. It affirmed that the sanctions provided under Chapter VII of the United Nations Charter, if universally applied, were the most appropriate and effective means to ensure South Africa's compliance with the decisions of the United Nations. It also expressed its conviction that South Africa was vulnerable to sanctions, and that sanctions under Chapter VII were feasible and would be effective.

Thus, on the combined item, that is, from 1962 to 1980, inclusive, the Assembly has increasingly spoken of the human rights of the oppressed people of South Africa and their right to self-determination and majority rule. It has described the South African Government's policies as inhuman, criminal, and aggressive, and has spoken of the need to speedily eliminate those policies.

Almost every Assembly resolution on South Africa's racial situation contains a reference to human rights. But, since 1962, the Assembly has increasingly considered South Africa's racial situation on the double-track of human rights and threat to international peace. It has also increasingly strengthened its tone both on the substance of apartheid as a matter of human rights and the nature of the threat posed by apartheid against international peace. With regard to the latter point, it has stated that it was mindful of the primary responsibility of the Council for the maintenance of international peace and security.[333] Apparently, the Assembly has been aware not only of the growing likelihood of violent racial conflict in South Africa, and perhaps even in southern Africa, but also of the fact that dealing with the matter primarily as one of human rights had been subjected to the limitations of domestic jurisdiction clause and that therefore emphasizing the threat to international peace might be a more effective way of dealing with it.

Because of the powers vested by the Charter in the Council to adopt mandatory sanctions, the Assembly has increasingly turned to it for effective action. But the Council would not adopt mandatory sanctions unless it first determined that there was a threat to international peace and security. Mindful of the need for such a prior determination, the Assembly increasingly spoke of the existence of a threat in the South African situation to international peace and security. Whether the Council determined the existence of such a threat is a matter which will be seen presently.

Security Council

On 1 April 1960, the Council adopted its first resolution on South Africa's racialized legal order.[334] The resolution was the outcome of a complaint concerning ''the situation arising out of the large-scale killings of unarmed and peaceful demonstrators against racial discrimination and segregation in the Union of South Africa.'' The Council recognized that such a situation had been brought about by the racial policies of the Government of South Africa and deplored the disturbances that had led to the loss of life of so many Africans as well as the policies and actions of the Government of South Africa. It called upon that Government ''to initiate measures aimed at bringing about racial harmony based on equality'' and to abandon its policies of apartheid and racial discrimination. It also recognized that the situation in South Africa was one ''that has led to international friction and if continued might endanger international peace and security.''

The Council did not then regard the racial situation in South Africa as a threat to international peace and security. In fact, it considered the matter mainly because of the Sharpeville incidents of 21 March 1960, when about 69 Africans were shot dead and 200 injured by the police at one place alone. The Council's motivation was mainly humanitarian at that point in time.

In 1963, the Council again considered the matter and adopted a resolution in which it took note of world public opinion as had been reflected in Assembly resolution 1761 (XVII) of 1962.[335] It also regretted that some states were indirectly providing encouragement to the Government of South Africa to perpetuate, by force, its policy of apartheid. It adopted a non-mandatory arms embargo against South Africa. The reason for adopting that embargo can be seen in two preambular paragraphs of the resolution. In those paragraphs, the Council noted with concern the arms build-up in South Africa and said that some of those arms were being used in furtherance of racial policies. It expressed its conviction that the situation in South Africa was ''seriously disturbing international peace and security.'' Still, it did not at that point regard the situation as a ''threat'' to international peace. The Council's action was not, indeed, prompted by the existence of a threat to international peace but by humanitarian considerations and as a matter of human rights and fundamental freedoms which ought to be observed, it believed, in accordance with the Charter.

In another resolution adopted in 1963, the Council recalled its previous resolutions on the matter and repeated its previous statements concerning the racial policies of South Africa and the "disturbance" caused to international peace.[336] Also, the Council said that it took into account the serious concern of Member States with regard to the policy of apartheid, as expressed in the general debate in the Assembly as well as in the discussions in the Special Political Committee. It recognized the need to eliminate discrimination in regard to basic human rights and fundamental freedoms for all in South Africa. It expressed its firm conviction that "the policies of apartheid and racial discrimination as practised by the Government of the Republic of South Africa are abhorrent to the conscience of mankind and that therefore a positive alternative to these policies must be found through peaceful means." It noted with deep satisfaction the overwhelming support for Assembly resolution 1881 (XVIII) of 1963, on political prisoners, which was of a humanitarian character.

In that resolution the Assembly emphasized the need to change the racialized legal order, because it was an evil per se. The Council did not mention the existence of any threat to international peace because either it did not believe that such threat existed or it did not want to do so in order not to feel constrained to adopt mandatory sanctions.

In 1964, the Council adopted two resolutions on South Africa's racial situation. The one dealt entirely with political prisoners and the Rivonia trial then in progress. The Council said that the Rivonia trial was "instituted within the framework of arbitrary laws of *apartheid*."[337] It was humanitarian in content and made no reference at all to any disturbance of, or threat to, international peace. In the other resolution, the Council expressed its conviction that the situation in South Africa was "continuing seriously to disturb international peace and security."[338] It also repeated many of its earlier calls of a humanitarian nature, and invited the Secretary-General to establish a program for the education and training abroad of South Africans. There was no mention of a threat to international peace, only a disturbance. Unless the Council was prepared to take action against South Africa under Chapter VII of the Charter, it could not speak explicitly of the existence of a threat to international peace.

It was not until 1970 that the Council concerned itself again with the situation in South Africa. At that point, it again condemned the evil and abhorrent policies of apartheid and expressed its total opposition to those policies.[339] It referred to human and political rights as set forth in the Charter and the Universal Declaration, and suggested certain measures to be implemented by all states in order to strengthen the voluntary arms embargo against South Africa. The justification for strengthening the arms embargo can be seen in the preambular paragraph of the resolution which expressed the Council's conviction that "the situation resulting from the continued application of the policies of *apartheid* and the constant build-up of the South African military and police forces . . . constitutes a potential threat to international peace and security." The Council also stated that "the extensive arms build-up of the military forces of South Africa poses a real threat to the security and sovereignty of independent African States opposed to the racial policies of the Government of South Africa, in particular the neighbouring States."

The Council thus simultaneously spoke of a potential threat to international peace and of a real threat to the security and sovereignty of African states opposed to apartheid. As far as the potential threat was concerned, the Council did not feel constrained to take action under Chapter VII of the Charter. But, one might ask, is not a "real threat to the security and sovereignty of independent African States" tantamount to a threat to international peace and security, as provided for under the Charter? On the other hand, is not the extensive arms build-up of most states a threat to other states?

Nevertheless, the Council evaded again an outright statement that the situation was a threat to international peace. Apparently, it wished to strengthen the arms embargo against South Africa but felt constrained by, or took shelter behind, the humanitarian nature of the matter and did not feel free to express the existence of a threat to international peace. The Council would repeat, however, the point regarding the real threat to African states in its subsequent resolutions. One can already see a change taking place in the Council's concept of a threat to international peace.

In its subsequent resolution, two years later, the Council repeated a number of humanitarian aspects which it had expressed earlier.[340] However, it regressed to expressing only grave concern that the South African situation "seriously disturbs international peace and security in southern Africa." It did not mention the existence of any threat, real or potential, to international peace.

The Council next dealt with the South African problem in 1976, after an interval of four years. It adopted a resolution by consensus, soon after the uprising and large-scale killings in Soweto and other African townships on 16 June.[341] It was motivated largely by humanitarian considerations. It again referred to the serious disturbance caused by South Africa's situation to international peace and security. It expressed its deep shock over large-scale killings and wounding of Africans in South Africa, as well as its sympathy to the victims. It also expressed its conviction that the situation had been brought about by the policies of apartheid in South Africa.

In October 1977, the Council was again motivated by humanitarian considerations to consider the situation in South Africa. Local opposition against the South African regime was continuing and the Government had instituted a massive crack-down on political opponents, including the banning of numerous individuals, organizations, and news media in October

1977. In September, Steve Biko, leader of the Black Consciousness Movement, had died in detention. The Council adopted a resolution in which it recalled its earlier resolutions "calling upon the South African racist regime urgently to end violence against the African people and take urgent steps to eliminate *apartheid* and racial discrimination."[342] It expressed grave concern over reports of torture of political prisoners and the deaths of a number of detainees, as well as the mounting wave of repression against individuals, organizations, and news media. It also expressed its conviction that the violence and repression by the South African regime had greatly aggravated the situation and would "certainly lead to violent conflict and racial conflagration with serious international repercussions." It did not say outright that there existed any threat to international peace. The import of the resolution was again humanitarian.

Significantly, in November 1977, for the first time in United Nations history, the Council adopted mandatory sanctions against a Member State.[343] Acting under Chapter VII of the Charter, the Council determined "that the acquisition by South Africa of arms and related materiél constitutes a threat to the maintenance of international peace and security" and imposed a mandatory arms embargo on South Africa. In the preambular part of its resolution, the Council recalled its resolution 392 (1976) and recognized that the military build-up and persistent acts of aggression by South Africa against the neighbouring states seriously disturbed the security of those states. It also strongly condemned the South African Government for its acts of repression, its defiant continuance of the system of apartheid, and its attacks against neighbouring independent states.

Thus, the imposition of the mandatory arms embargo was linked by the Council to a threat to international peace, which threat was in turn linked to the acquisition by South Africa of arms and related materiél, but not directly to the apartheid policy. The Council did not establish a direct link between apartheid and international peace or between apartheid and the full implementation of the Charter provisions in good faith.

In December 1977, the Council decided to establish a committee, consisting of all its members, to examine the progress of the mandatory arms embargo which it had called for.[344]

Until November 1977, the Western permanent members of the Council had resisted the adoption of mandatory measures against South Africa. Once South Africa was adequately armed, however, Western members went along with the partial embargo, but resisted total sanctions including economic sanctions. The increased reaction by the black people and some guerrilla action in South Africa, world public opinion, the human rights policies of some Western leaders, and the reconsideration by Western states of their interest in Africa all led to the adoption of the mandatory arms embargo. It would have been quite hypocritical of those governments to be lecturing to the world on human rights while closing their eyes to apartheid and increasing repression in South Africa.

Whatever the phraseology used by the Council in imposing the mandatory arms embargo against South Africa, the action of the Council seems to have been motivated by the racialized legal order and the consequent repressive measures in South Africa rather than its belief in an imminent, or even potential, threat to international peace and security. An examination of the discussions and debates held during the adoption of the resolution on arms embargo will testify to that effect. For example, the representative of the United States at the Council linked the repressive measures of October 1977 of the Government of South Africa directly with the Council's action. He said that the Council had "just sent a clear message to the Government of South Africa that the measures which were announced on 19 October have created a new situation in South Africa's relationship with the rest of the world."[345] This meant that such repressive measures as then practiced by South Africa would not be tolerated by the Council.

At the same meeting, the representative of the United Kingdom put it quite explicitly:

> We have made clear our view, which is reflected in the first operative paragraph, as to the nature of the threat to international peace and security. We do not interpret the reference in the preamble to "acts of aggression" as being used in the technical sense of Article 39 of the Charter.[346]

The representative of France said that the message was clear and that South Africa ought to understand that it would have to come to its senses and rapidly put an end to its policy of apartheid. Earlier, on 31 October 1977, the representative of France had said that his Government had decided to vote in favor of a mandatory embargo on arms shipments to South Africa, on the clear understanding that, in strictly legal terms, there could be no question of denying any country the right of self-defence under Article 51 of the Charter. He considered the Council action a protest against the stockpiling of weapons intended for purposes of internal repression.[347] In other words, France voted for the arms embargo mainly on humanitarian grounds, not because of a threat to international peace.

The representative of the Federal Republic of Germany on the Council said that his Government considered the decision of the Council, which had "been reached after intensive consultations, conducted by all parties with a strong sense of responsibility, to be a necessary and adequate response to the challenging action taken by the Government of South Africa on 19 October."[348]

Speaking after the adoption of resolution 418 (1977), the Secretary-General said:

> However, it is abundantly clear that the policy of *apartheid* as well as the measures taken by the South African Government to implement this policy are such a gross violation of human rights and so fraught with danger to international peace and security that a response commensurate with the gravity of the situation was required.

It is, of course, unfortunate that the situation in South Africa should have deteriorated to such a point that the Council felt compelled to take this extraordinary measure. However, this should come as no surprise to the Government of South Africa when it considers how long the world has appealed in vain for the abandonment of its *apartheid* policies.

We can only hope that the gravity of the Council's decision will be fully recognized by the Government of South Africa and that it will therefore begin, without delay, the process of restoring fundamental human rights to all people in South Africa, without which there can be no peace.[349]

On 4 November 1977, the South African Minister of Foreign Affairs protested in the strongest terms against the Council's action imposing the mandatory arms embargo. He maintained that Article 51 of the Charter affords the right of self-defence to every Member State and regarded the Council's action as an incitement to violence. He also said that "no action can be taken against any person in South Africa who criticises the Government or wishes to bring about a change of government by constitutional means."[350] He said that the South African Government was in favor of, and supported, the preservation of fundamental human rights and that "the invocation of high principles of moral rectitude and human rights serves merely as a pretext to hide a motley variety of less worthy motivations."[351]

On 21 September 1979, the Council issued a statement condemning the "independence" of Venda, proclaimed by South Africa, and declared it "totally invalid." The Council said that the creation of Bantustans was designed to divide and dispossess the African people and establish client states under South Africa's domination in order to perpetuate apartheid.[352] Apparently, the Council regarded the matter primarily as one of human rights. Three days later, in a letter to the President of the Council, the South African representative said that the Council had "no authority or jurisdiction in this matter" and that the Council's condemnation was an attempt to deny to the people of Venda their right to self-determination.[353]

In 1980, the Security Council unanimously adopted its last resolution during the period under review, motivated again mainly by humanitarian considerations.[354] It reaffirmed "that the policy of *apartheid* is a crime against the conscience and dignity of mankind and is incompatible with the rights and dignity of man, the Charter of the United Nations and the Universal Declaration of Human Rights, and seriously disturbs international peace and security." It recognized "the legitimacy of the struggle of the South African people for the elimination of *apartheid* and for the establishment of a democratic society in which all the people of South Africa as a whole, irrespective of race, colour or creed, will enjoy equal and full political and other rights and participate freely in the determination of their destiny." It expressed grave concern over the repression and the killings of school children protesting against apartheid, as well as the repression against churchmen and workers. Indeed, the resolution was adopted in the wake of country-wide school boycotts by black schoolchildren, strikes by black workers, and a series of repressive measures by the South African Government.

In sum, one can see that the Council believed that the tension in South Africa was the direct result of the Government's apartheid policies. The main thrust of the Council's resolutions between 1960 and 1980 was humanitarian. Generally, stronger repressive measures in South Africa brought about stronger action by the Council. Both the resolutions of the Council and the discussions in that organ indicate that the Council's main objective was to achieve racial equality in South Africa, in conformity with the standards of the United Nations. That the Council did not feel competent to adopt mandatory measures against South Africa sooner, because of grave and outrageous violations of the Organization's human rights standards, without first having to perceive a threat to international peace, is not much to the credit of the Organization insofar as the general cause of human rights is concerned. However, the adoption of the mandatory arms embargo is a step forward with regard to the principle of racial non-discrimination, and may prove a valuable precedent in the future in that respect.

V. THE DOMESTIC JURISDICTION CLAUSE OF THE CHARTER

General Assembly

Discussions of Substance

Invocation by South Africa of the Domestic Jurisdiction Clause

From the beginning, South Africa invoked the Charter's domestic jurisdiction clause, Article 2 (7), and objected to the Assembly's considering South Africa's racial situation.

At its first, second, third, and fifth sessions, the Assembly decided, without a vote, to include the item concerning the treatment of the people of Indian origin in its agenda. There was no formal objections to those decisions. The following years, invoking the domestic jurisdiction clause of the Charter, the representative of South Africa repeatedly objected to including the item in the agenda, but to no avail. On the same grounds, South Africa also opposed all the substantive draft resolutions on the item.[355]

On 24 October 1946, the South African representative argued in the General Committee that the matter under consideration involved not "Indian nationals," but Indians who were "nationals of South Africa." In accordance with the domestic jurisdiction clause of the Charter, he contended, the question was essentially within South Africa's domestic jurisdiction and should be deleted from the agenda. The General Committee, which proposes to the General Assembly the agenda for the session, did not share these views and the item was not removed.[356] The Assembly then referred the matter to the First and Sixth Committees, where it was considered jointly.[357]

In the joint committee meeting in November 1946, the representatives of both India and South Africa expounded their views. India maintained that the South African Government had violated an agreement between the British Government and India to the effect that Indians emigrating to South Africa would not be subjected to any special laws, different from those applicable to Europeans. India also held that the Government of the Union of South Africa violated the Smuts-Gandhi agreement, reached as a result of Gandhi's passive resistance campaigns in 1907 and 1913, as well as the Cape Town Agreement of 1932 between India and South Africa. Specifically, the South African Government was charged with having passed in 1946 the Asiatic Land Tenure and Indian Representation Act completely segregating Indians in residence and trade. India further maintained that South Africa had unilaterally repudiated the Cape Town Agreement and also violated the human rights provisions of the Charter.[358]

The representative of South Africa, in turn, maintained that the urban Indian influx and the growing commercial success of Indian traders was threatening the future of the Europeans (whites) and that, as a result of such threat and the failure of repatriation, public opinion had compelled the Government to pass the "Pegging Act" and the Asiatic Land Tenure and Indian Representation Act. He said that an agreement which had been reached with regard to a reduction of the Indian population by voluntary and assisted repatriation had failed. He further maintained that in regulating its domestic affairs a state was not subject to outside control or interference and its actions could not be called into question by any other state. With regard to the Cape Town Agreement of 1927 and the Joint Communiqué of 1932, he held that these instruments did not give rise to treaty obligations.[359]

In 1947, South Africa repeated in the First Committee its contention that the domestic jurisdiction clause of the Charter excluded the matter from United Nations competence.[360] In the plenary meeting of the Assembly, the South African representative objected again to the Assembly's consideration of the matter. He pointed out that according to the Cape Town Agreement India was to encourage repatriation of Indians and that South Africa had undertaken to provide free passage and a bonus to all those who would return to India.[361]

The arguments advanced in the Assembly in favor and against the applicability of the domestic jurisdiction clause up to the eighth session revolved around the following questions:

(a) The meaning of the term "intervention" and whether a recommendation constitutes intervention;
(b) The meaning of the expression "matters which are essentially within the domestic jurisdiction of any State;"
(c) Whether a matter governed by international agreements can fall essentially within domestic jurisdiction;
(d) Whether a matter governed by the Charter in general, or by the Charter provisions on human rights, or by the Charter provisions on the maintenance of international peace can fall essentially within domestic jurisdiction.[362]

Even while discussing these constitutional questions, the Assembly did not refrain from making recommendations to indicate the way to a settlement of the dispute. In its first resolution on the item, the Assembly stated that because of the treatment accorded to the people of Indian origin in South Africa "friendly relations" between the two Member States had been impaired and that, unless a satisfactory settlement was reached, those relations were likely to be further impaired.[363] That language implicitly referred to Article 14 of the Charter which uses similar phraseology, and was the apparent basis for the Assembly's competence. In other words, the Assembly was recommending, under Article 14, that a peaceful settlement should be reached.

At its seventh session in 1952, the Assembly included in the agenda and discussed the new item on race conflict in South Africa. During the discussion on the adoption of the agenda as well as during the discussion in the Committee, the representative of South Africa once more invoked the domestic jurisdiction clause, but in vain.[364] In addition to the arguments advanced earlier in connection with the item on people of Indian origin, delegates debated whether the Assembly's establishing a commission to study the racial situation prevailing in a Member State constituted intervention.[365] At the tenth session of the Assembly, in 1955, delegates debated whether just including an item in the agenda constituted intervention.[366]

From the mid-1950s, South Africa did not participate in the discussions on the item relating to the treatment of people of Indian origin in South Africa. Also from 1958 to 1961, the Assembly repeatedly called on the parties concerned to enter into negotiations with regard to that item, without prejudice to their positions on the question of domestic jurisdiction. The call was accepted by India and Pakistan, but not by South Africa.

From 1959 to 1966, despite South Africa's repeated objections, the Assembly continued discussing the racial situation in South Africa. Some states who favored including the item (two items from 1959 to 1961, inclusive, namely, the item on the people of Indian origin and the item on race conflict) in the agenda maintained that the matter did not fall essentially within domestic jurisdiction and that to include an item in the agenda or to discuss it did not constitute intervention within the meaning of Article 2 (7). Some states held that "matters which were the subject of international law and international obligations could not fall within the ambit of Article 2 (7)." Others said that "questions involving the peace and security of the world or a situation which had international repercussions or was likely to cause international friction or endanger international peace could not fall essentially within domestic jurisdiction." Still others contended that in South Africa no danger to peace existed. During this period, the delegations of South Africa seldom participated in the debates.[367]

The overwhelming majority of the Member States clearly regarded the Organization as competent to deal with the racialized legal order in South Africa because of the flagrant violation of the Charter and of the principle of racial non-discrimination. No Member State condoned South Africa's racial policies. On the other hand, because some Member States maintained that issues of human rights fell essentially within domestic jurisdiction, no unanimity existed regarding the jurisdiction of the United Nations in the matter or on the action it could take.

Among the strict constructionists of the domestic jurisdiction clause were some Member States who were also permanent members of the Security Council and whose veto power on the Council would become important after 1960 when the Council began considering the racial policies of South Africa. It may be useful, therefore, to look separately at the positions of the Big Five on the question of competence in the Assembly debates on the racial situation in South Africa, both before and after 1960.

In 1946, while discussing the item on the treatment of people of Indian origin in the Joint Committee, the representative of China said that South Africa's laws were discriminatory not only against Indians but also against all Asiatics and were based on differences of color and race. He appealed to the Committee "to consider the question from the point of view of preserving international peace." He also stressed the particular interest that China had in the question because of the Chinese community in South Africa.[368] China later said in the Assembly's plenary meeting that it regarded the matter essentially as a political one.[369]

The Soviet delegation believed that the United Nations was competent to examine the question, in terms of Articles 10 and 14 of the Charter, and that the question was one of international importance because of Member States' obligations under the Charter. It regarded the matter essentially as political and was opposed to referring the matter to the International Court of Justice.[370] France said that South Africa's laws did not seem to be in accordance with the Cape Town Agreement and that the measures of 1943 revealed a spirit of discrimination.[371] The United Kingdom and the United States supported South Africa's proposal to refer the issue of competence to the International Court of Justice.[372] Earlier in the General Committee, the Soviet delegation had maintained that the matter did not fall within domestic jurisdiction because it constituted a breach of agreements between India and South Africa concerning the status of Indian immigrants into South Africa.[373]

In 1947, China said in the First Committee that the Assembly was fully competent to determine its own jurisdiction.[374] France said that it did not ignore the difficulties facing South Africa, which had to deal with races in various stages of evolution, and noted South Africa's statement that its legislation was in a state of evolution towards equality. France said further that it did not believe that there was any question of racial persecution in South Africa.[375] The Soviet delegation considered the matter within United Nations jurisdiction because the situation had acquired international proportions, as it had led to a rupture of relations between the two states and had been made the subject of a recommendation by the Assembly.[376] The United States representative said that whatever its legal aspects the problem was moral and political in nature and that to reach a peaceful solution account should be taken of the domestic jurisdiction clause without, however, infringing fundamental human rights.[377] In the Assembly's plenary meeting, the United States said that the matter under discussion was essentially within South Africa's domestic jurisdiction and therefore beyond the Assembly's competence.[378]

In 1952, on the item on race conflict, China said that, under Article 10, the Assembly could discuss any questions on matters within the scope of the Charter. Article 2 (7) could not be isolated from Articles 13 and 56 whereby the Assembly could initiate studies, the Chinese representative said, and added that respect for human rights was clearly a question of both national competence and international cooperation. He concluded that a narrow interpretation of Article 2 (7) would make it impossible for the Assembly to initiate studies and make recommendations and would prevent Member States from taking joint action in economic and social matters.[379] France considered the discussion of the item to be a clear case of intervention in the internal affairs of a Member State and in direct contravention of Article 2 (7).[380] The United Kingdom believed that the question of race conflict in South Africa was within South Africa's domestic jurisdiction.[381] The United States said that it ''wished to avoid both excess of zeal and timid legalism in dealing with the South African racial problem.'' The United States thought that the exercise of the right of discussion did not contravene Article 2 (7) and that ''the legal restriction contained in that Article should not prevent adequate consideration of the vital question of human rights in a dynamic world. On the other hand, it would be unwise to leave the door open to every kind of proposal.''[382] The Soviet delegation expressed its conviction that ''the General Assembly was fully competent, indeed, obliged to put an end to the violation of the purposes and principles of the Charter implicit in South Africa's racial policies.''[383] From 1952 through 1957, the United States voted with the majority on the Indian question while abstaining on the question of race conflict in South Africa. Only in 1958 did the United States shift position and begin voting against South Africa's racial policies.[384]

By 1961, however, the position of the United Kingdom had changed. In that year, the representative of the United Kingdom on the Special Political Committee said that ''while the importance the United Kingdom attached to the proper observance of Article 2, paragraph 7, of the Charter remained undiminished, it regarded *apartheid* as being now so exceptional as to be *sui generis*.''[385] In the same year, at the Assembly's sixteenth session, the United Kingdom representative said in the Special Political Committee that the United Kingdom had voted for resolution 1598 (XV) on the item on race conflict because it had been convinced that apartheid had international repercussions which lifted the matter from the limitations of Article 2 (7). He added, however, that international repercussions were not the same as a threat to international peace and security. He, therefore, opposed proposals made by some delegations to adopt sanctions against South Africa under Chapter VII or to expel South Africa from United Nations membership.[386] Three years earlier, in the same Committee, the United Kingdom had said that the Assembly was not competent to discuss the race conflict in South Africa, let alone to adopt a resolution on the subject.[387]

Several reasons can be suggested for the change of the United Kingdom's position. First, South Africa withdrew from the British Commonwealth in 1961, so that London felt free to castigate Pretoria and avoid turmoil within the Commonwealth. Second, the United Kingdom Government was exposed to greater pressure from newly independent African states, not only within the Commonwealth but also within the United Nations. Third, the United Kingdom Government might have wished to co-ordinate its policies on this subject with those of the United States Government which, since 1958, had been voting against apartheid. Fourth, the Security Council had already adopted a resolution on the matter, and by so doing it had already established a link between South Africa's racial situation and international peace.

By 1962, when the two items were combined, the discussion of United Nations competence to consider the matter had lost much of its fervor and the arguments began centering on the action to be taken against South Africa. That year, in the Special Political Committee, China said nothing new in substance.[388] The Soviet Union supported a proposal to expel South Africa from United Nations membership or to impose mandatory sanctions on South Africa.[389] The United States recommended that the Assembly reaffirm its condemnation of apartheid, urge South Africa to meet its Charter obligations, and perhaps request the Security Council to maintain a close watch on the situation, as one that might lead to a threat to world peace. It opposed the proposal to expel South Africa from United Nations membership or to impose mandatory sanctions on it.[390] France and the United Kingdom took positions similar to that of the United States.[391]

The People's Republic of China came into the United Nations late in 1971 and indicated its position on domestic jurisdiction in the Assembly debates in 1972. Speaking in the Special Political Committee, the Chinese representative said that the United Nations "must severely condemn the white South African authorities and the imperialistic Powers which were supporting them and it should strengthen the worldwide sanctions against the South African authorities."[392]

Gradually, there was a softening of position by the Western permanent members of the Security Council with regard to domestic jurisdiction. It took long years for them to agree with the overwhelming majority that the Organization was competent to deal with the matter.[393]

Although all United Nations Members regarded the racial situation in South Africa as inconsistent with the Charter, some of them, particularly the Western permanent members of the Council, who were South Africa's traditional trade partners and military friends, relied heavily on the domestic jurisdiction clause of the Charter in voting on the issues. On the one hand, several Western states admitted that the racial situation in South Africa was a flagrant violation of the Charter and inconsistent with human rights and fundamental freedoms. On the other hand, they held that the Assembly was incompetent to deal with the matter on the grounds of domestic jurisdiction. Although their positions did not serve the cause of human rights, their resistance in the Assembly did not significantly affect the vote.

As noted earlier, the Assembly in its first resolution (1946) implicitly referred to Article 14. It apparently based its authority to act on this Article. Under Article 14, the Assembly is empowered to consider and recommend such action as it deems fit when it determines that friendly relations are impaired by any situation, irrespective of its origin. Despite some states' objections on the basis of Article 2 (7), the Assembly found itself competent in this matter from the very beginning. Some governments, which earlier objected to the Assembly's competence, later changed their opinion because of the unique case of apartheid. It is generally accepted that the Assembly is competent to consider, study, investigate, and make recommendations on human rights, and that if international peace is endangered, then the Security Council may consider the matter for action including the adoption of mandatory sanctions under Chapter VII.[394]

South Africa's Contention that the Rights in Question Were Non-fundamental

In November 1946, South Africa maintained that it had not violated any human rights and fundamental freedoms such as the right to exist, the right to freedom of conscience and freedom of speech, and the right of free access to the courts. It argued that "there did not exist any internationally recognized formulation of such rights, and the Charter itself did not define them. Member States, therefore, did not have any specific obligations under the Charter, whatever other moral obligations might rest upon them."[395]

The following year, the representative of South Africa maintained similar views, asserting that "the Charter prohibited racial discrimination only when the matter involved fundamental human rights" and that the "South African legislation did not in any case infringe those fundamental rights." He added that "the existing racial distinctions ought perhaps to be modified, but such modifications could be made only by the Government of the Union of South Africa, for it was a question which fell essentially within the competence of a State, inasmuch as there was no infringement of the fundamental rights prescribed in the Charter."[396] In other words, South Africa was saying that the matter fell within domestic jurisdiction because the violated human rights were not fundamental. The United Nations, however, has held all along that the violated rights in South Africa were fundamental, and therefore of international concern and outside domestic jurisdiction.

True, the Charter did not define "human rights and fundamental freedoms," and the Universal Declaration which did define rights and freedoms, had not yet been adopted when the South African representative made these statements. On the other hand, even after the Universal Declaration was adopted, in addition to the controversy over its binding character, the fundamental character of some of those rights and freedoms have still not been universally accepted.

The European Convention for the Protection of Human Rights and Fundamental Freedoms (1950) contains most of the civil and political rights of the Universal Declaration and proclaims in its preamble that the States Parties are thus taking the first steps to enforce certain of the rights contained in the Universal Declaration. Obviously, all rights and freedoms of the Universal Declaration are not regarded as fundamental by the European Convention. Furthermore, the Charter speaks of "human rights and fundamental freedoms" whereas most authors usually refer to them as *fundamental* human rights. Rights and freedoms are generally used interchangeably, and the adjective "fundamental" is often used to qualify both rights and freedoms. Also, the rights of the Universal Declaration have not been uniformly categorized.[397]

No doubt, the South African racial legislation violates almost all the human rights and fundamental freedoms contained in the Universal Declaration. Moreover, the gross and systematic violation of those rights in South Africa under the unique system of apartheid violates human dignity itself. Human equality is a fundamental right. Racial non-discrimination is specifically and repeatedly emphasized in the Charter. It is one of the fundamental themes of the Charter, basic to the observance of other human rights and fundamental freedoms. The Minorities Treaties under the League, and even the precarious doctrine of humanitarian intervention, were necessitated as a result of practices of racial discrimination. The principle of non-discrimination is contained in the Charter with sufficient precision. The Charter prohibits racial discrimination. This prohibition is unequivocal and requires no further elaboration.[398]

The absence of a precise definition of human rights does not render the relevant provisions of the Charter devoid of legal character. The adoption of the Universal Declaration in 1948 provided the definition and the internationally recognized formulation of those rights. The first report (3 October 1953) of the Commission on the Racial Situation in the Union of South Africa stated that other terms of the Charter such as "international peace and security," "threats to the peace," "breaches of the peace," and "acts of aggression," were not defined but yet, certainly, they imposed obligations on Member States. It also stated that the notion of "human rights and fundamental freedoms" was sufficiently familiar in 1945 dating back at least to the French Declaration of 1789 and the American Declaration of Independence.[399]

Member States clearly have obligations under the Charter in the field of human rights, notwithstanding their obligation under the specific provisions on non-discrimination. Lauterpacht has written that the fact that an obligation cannot be enforced does not alter its legal nature, that the legal nature of those provisions cannot be decisively influenced by the Charter's failure to define them, that United Nations Members are not, in law, entitled to ignore or violate the human rights provisions, and that to maintain such an argument would destroy both the legal and the moral authority of the Charter as a whole and run counter to the "cardinal principle of construction according to which treaties must be interpreted in good faith."[400]

This good faith principle may be seen in Article 2, paragraph 2, of the Charter whereby "all Members, in order to ensure to all of them the rights and benefits resulting from membership, shall fulfil in good faith the obligations assumed by them in accordance with the present Charter." Also Article 55 (c) imposes a legal obligation upon Member States and the Organization itself by saying that the United Nations "shall" promote universal respect for, and observance of, human rights and fundamental freedoms for all without distinction as to race, sex, language, or religion.

Political rights, which are gravely violated in South Africa, are generally regarded as having to do with the right to enjoy government by consent. These active rights complement and guarantee personal freedom and equality before the law by enabling a person to elect his rulers, to be elected himself, and to participate in government. These rights normally apply to citizens and not to aliens. By denying the political right of participation in government to the majority of the citizens of South Africa, that Government implies that those people are aliens. The Minority Treaties concluded after the First World War recognized not only religious and cultural rights, but also the political rights of minorities. The political rights of citizens are considered fundamental in all civilized societies. No state except South Africa denies political rights, by law, to the majority of its citizens.

Furthermore, political rights are regarded as fundamental in Western, liberal democracies. The South African Government boasts of being an ally and a bastion of Western democracy and a bulwark against communism.[401] Yet, in South Africa political rights have been outrageously violated. As late as 1979, the South African Government was still expressing the conviction that political rights were not fundamental rights. The South African Ambassador to the United States, Donald Sole, was reported to have said at a meeting in Washington, D.C., that the basic human rights

are the right to be properly fed, the right to be decently clothed, the right to be adequately housed, to receive elementary medical care, the right to remunerative employment and the right to make sure one's children receive better education and training than one received oneself.

These are the priorities of my part of the world; not the political rights which are so stressed by American moralists.[402]

It is unnecessary here to show in detail the condition of the African population of South Africa in each aspect of life that the Ambassador mentioned. Their conditions in general were seen earlier, and there are many United Nations reports on each aspect of their lives. It should be pointed out, however, that Ambassador Sole's statement glosses over the main point: that political rights are fundamental because they are the best possible assurance for attaining all the other rights that he cites. Statements implying that some people have no right to demand anything beyond material existence vitiates the political theory which has all through centuries concerned itself with man's position in the society and state. Political thinkers for centuries have been concerned with man's development and happiness both as an individual and as part of society as a whole. Apparently, such concerns have not preoccupied the Government of South Africa. The situation in South Africa is, indeed, unique in the whole world, and Sole's statement cunningly avoids mentioning the relative condition of the black and white populations in South Africa.

Even if man were to live by bread alone, it must be noted that malnutrition among blacks, particularly Africans, arising out of poor hygiene and sanitation and poverty, especially among those who have no land, is widespread in South Africa. The severest forms of malnutrition, protein deficiency (Kwashiorkor) and starvation (Marasmus), are rampant in a country that boasts of food exports worth $2 billion a year. Although mortality rates based on malnutrition are very high in South Africa, overall official statistics are not available because, since 1967, kwashiorkor has been dropped from the list of notifiable diseases, in order not to offend the Government's sensitivity.[403] Moreover, if political rights are not fundamental, then why has the South African Government recently begun talking of the political rights of the Coloreds and Indians?[404] If the Coloreds' political rights are now considered important, how can that Government logically deny those same rights to Africans?

On 1 May 1945, at the sixth plenary session of the San Francisco Conference, Field Marshall Jan Smuts of South Africa said:

> The new Charter should not be a mere legalistic document for the prevention of war. I would suggest that the Charter should contain at its very outset and in its preamble, a declaration of human rights and of the common faith which has sustained the Allied peoples in their bitter and prolonged struggle for the vindication of those rights and that faith. This war has not been an ordinary war of the old type. It has been a war of ideologies, of conflicting philosophies of life and conflicting faiths. In the deepest sense it has been a war of religion perhaps more so than any other war in history. We have fought for justice and decency and for the fundamental freedoms of man, which are basic to all human advancement and progress and peace. Let us, in this new Charter of humanity give expression to this faith in us, and thus proclaim to the world and to posterity, that this was not a mere brute struggle of force between the nations but that for us, behind the mortal struggle, was the moral struggle, was the

vision of the ideal, the faith in justice and the resolve to vindicate the fundamental rights of man, and on that basis to found a better, freer world for the
future.[405]

Despite those inspiring words on the fundamental rights of man, by
a former South African leader, the African population of South Africa,
which constitutes the overwhelming majority in the country, is deprived of
the first tenet of democracy, namely, equality. Africans are deprived not
only of political and juridical equality, but also of economic and social
equality. Also, as the majority of the South African population is prevented
from sharing political power, another condition of democracy, namely,
majority will is violated. The political right to participate in government is
fundamental in order to achieve political, juridical, economic, social and
cultural equality and equal opportunity in all walks of life, as distinct from
equality of condition. The political right to participate in government means
also to participate, directly or through representation, in making the laws
of the country. In South Africa, where is the morality, the justice, or the
fundamental rights of man, which Field Marshall Smuts mentioned?

Lauterpacht has noted that "the Stoics envisaged the common law of
humanity based on the most fundamental of all human rights, the principle
of equality."[406] Fundamental rights have, during the last two centuries,
become part of the constitutions of most countries in the world, even those
of totalitarian states. They are a fundamental theme of the United Nations
Charter. With the entry into force of the two International Covenants on
human rights, which have defined and given legal force to the relevant
Charter provisions, human rights have properly become part of international
law. The Universal Declaration and the Covenants took the place of the
International Bill of Human Rights envisioned at the San Francisco Conference. As Lauterpacht wrote in 1950, long before the adoption of the
Covenants on human rights:

> The International Bill of Human Rights, when adopted as an effective and
> enforceable instrument, will complete the historic achievement of the Charter
> in the sphere of human rights and fundamental freedoms. Pending that con-
> sumption, the Charter, when interpreted in good faith and acted upon by the
> Members of the United Nations and its organs, is a potent instrument for
> fulfilling a task which—alongside of that of the preservation of peace—constitutes
> the crucial purpose of the United Nations and of international law. These tasks
> are complementary and, upon final analysis, identical.[407]

South Africa's black population enjoys no equality with whites in the
mainstream of political, economic, and social life in South Africa.[408] As the
majority in South Africa have been kept in an awkward relationship with
the state, they have also been denied the political equality emphasized by
J. J. Rousseau's concept of "general will." Consequently, without the
democratic tenets of equality and majority will, the four fifths of South

Africa's population view the state as an oppressor, disconnected from the main body of the society.

For the liberation movements and other people, mainly blacks, who decided to resort to armed struggle, the South African Government has no legitimacy. These people do not feel obliged to obey laws which they or their representatives had no role in making. As stated by Alfred Nzo, Secretary-General of the ANC, at a meeting in London on 26 June 1980, the "campaign inside South Africa for the unconditional release of Nelson Mandela and all other political prisoners is indicative of the fact that the present régime has no legitimacy to govern South Africa." He added that that point was articulated in the Freedom Charter, which stated twenty-five years ago that "no government can justly claim authority unless it is based on the will of the people."[409]

The South African Government could not deny in good faith that its apartheid policy violated the Charter provisions on human rights and fundamental freedoms, no matter how general a view it took of human rights and freedoms. In fact, there was no need for the Assembly to argue on the basis of the general provisions for human rights contained in the Charter. The Charter specifically provides for racial equality as one of the foundations for the enjoyment of human rights and fundamental freedoms, as is evident from so many provisions prohibiting racial discrimination.

By violating this foundation, the South African Government has hindered the observance of human rights and fundamental freedoms in South Africa, and violated the Charter. It has, in fact, violated the foundation of human rights and fundamental freedoms. Racial non-discrimination is essential for the full observance of human rights and fundamental freedoms in accordance with the Charter; it cannot be practiced as a legal and official policy without violating the Charter. The international community has been unanimous in asserting that the Government of South Africa has violated the human rights and fundamental freedoms of its population as well as the Charter. Arguments have only taken place about what measures the United Nations should take against the South African Government, or about the Organization's competence.

In brief, whether one looks at human rights and fundamental freedoms in general, or at the principle of non-discrimination in particular, the South African Government has violated both the Charter and the human rights and fundamental freedoms of the great majority of its population. It has attempted to evade its obligations under the Charter by speaking not about the Charter term "human rights and fundamental freedoms," but of "fundamental human rights" in an extremely restrictive sense. The restrictive interpretation that the South African Government has accepted, and would have liked others to accept, has resulted in a system of apartheid that is close to slavery. Indeed, some United Nations resolutions and reports have referred to aspects of apartheid as practices or institutions similar to slavery, or as a collective form of slavery.[410]

Discussions on Procedure

South Africa's Motion to Refer the Question of Domestic Jurisdiction to the International Court of Justice

In 1946, while the joint First and Sixth Committees were considering the item on the people of Indian origin, the representative of South Africa submitted a draft resolution proposing that the Assembly seek an advisory opinion from the International Court of Justice as to whether the matter was, under Article 2 (7) of the Charter, essentially within domestic jurisdiction. The delegation of Colombia submitted another draft resolution which would ask the Court for an advisory opinion. The first paragraph of the Colombian draft proposed:

> To request the International Court of Justice to give an advisory opinion on the following legal questions:
> (a) Whether the Members of the United Nations, in accordance with the Preamble and Article 1, paragraph 3 of the Charter, are under obligation to amend immediately their internal legislation when it establishes racial discrimination incompatible with the text of the Charter.
> (b) Whether the Members of the United Nations are entitled in the future to enact internal legislation embodying racial discrimination.
> (c) Whether laws of racial discrimination constitute, or may be alleged by States to constitute, matters of internal jurisdiction on which the General Assembly is debarred from making recommendations to the State or States concerned, to the Security Council or to the Economic and Social Council.[411]

As the majority of the Member States believed that the political aspects of the question far outweighed its legal aspects and that the Assembly was competent to consider the matter, the South African draft was strongly opposed and was ultimately withdrawn without having been put to vote at the Committee stage. It was later defeated when reintroduced at the plenary meeting of the Assembly.[412] Similarly, the Colombian draft was also withdrawn. The Colombian draft explicitly referred to "racial discrimination" as distinct from the more general issue of human rights. As already seen, in 1971, in the case of Namibia, the Court advised that to establish and to enforce distinctions, exclusions, restrictions, and limitations exclusively based on grounds of race, color, descent or national or ethnic origin which constitute a denial of fundamental human rights was a flagrant violation of the purposes and principles of the Charter. That opinion also constituted a reply to the South African Government's argument that it had not discriminated in respect of *fundamental* human rights. Most probably, the Court would have advised similarly had it been asked in 1946 on the same question.

The racial policies of the Government of South Africa have been considered mainly in political organs, rather than in legal ones such as the Sixth (Legal) Committee. Apparently, the intention was to put political pressure on that Government. In retrospect, it might have been more effective to have had the legal opinion of the Court to strengthen the position of the Assembly in the matter. As early as 1950, Lauterpacht weighed the advantages and disadvantages of referring the matter to the Court for an opinion as to competence, and concluded that such referral would have been desirable in order to remove a disturbing source of confusion.[413] It seems unfortunate that the opportunity was missed.

Security Council

In general, the domestic jurisdiction clause of the Charter, which applies to all organs of the United Nations, constitutes a limitation not only on the Assembly but also on the Council. It may be noted, however, that "it was emphasized in the discussions of the San Francisco Conference that there was no intention of defining the scope of domestic jurisdiction by any rigid or legal formula. The intention was to state a general principle."[414] The Council, in particular, is not subject to this limitation in one case: whenever it determines the existence of any threat to the peace, breach of the peace, or act of aggression and decides to apply enforcement measures under Chapter VII, to maintain or restore international peace and security.

In 1960, the representative of South Africa objected on the grounds of domestic jurisdiction to the Council's considering the situation in South Africa. However, most speakers maintained that Article 2, paragraph 7, did not apply and that the Council was competent in the matter. The arguments related to (a) the meaning of the term "to intervene," (b) whether a matter dealt with by the Charter can fall essentially within domestic jurisdiction, (c) whether a matter governed by the Charter provisions on human rights can fall essentially within domestic jurisdiction, (d) whether a matter governed by the Charter provisions on the maintenance of international peace can fall essentially within domestic jurisdiction, and (e) the effect of previous decisions of the Assembly or the Council to deal with the matter.[415]

While the South African Government was interpreting the domestic jurisdiction clause very rigidly and arguing that the Sharpeville incidents of March 1960 did not constitute a situation which might lead to international friction or endanger international peace, the representatives of France, the United Kingdom, and the United States were willing to have the Council consider the matter and make recommendations thereon. France and the

United Kingdom, which abstained on the resolution adopted in 1960, had expressed doubts as to the competence of the Council to take any measures. Against the Western members' conservative position, the representative of the Soviet Union asserted that the Council should take measures to put an end to acts of violence against the black people in South Africa.[416]

In 1963, in the discussions relating to the two resolutions which were adopted by the Council in that year on the situation in South Africa, references were made to South Africa's objections, but the majority upheld the Council's competence on the grounds that the situation involved the violation of fundamental principles of the Charter. The provisions of Articles 1(3), 13, 55, 56, and 62 on human rights were invoked during discussions and the domestic jurisdiction clause was considered non-applicable since both the Assembly and the Council had previously adopted resolutions on the matter.[417] The arguments on domestic jurisdiction related to the same points as discussed in 1960.

The Government of South Africa did not participate in the discussions. The Foreign Minister of South Africa, in reply to the Council's decision to invite South Africa to participate in the consideration of the question in July 1963, wrote that his Government had decided not to participate because its policies fell "solely" within the domestic jurisdiction of a Member State.[418] It is interesting to note that the South African Government then spoke of a policy which fell "solely" within domestic jurisdiction instead of using the Charter terminology of "essentially" which connotes a wider scope of exception.

On 2 August 1963, during the Council's discussions, the United States representative said that a fundamental principle on which there was general agreement was that all Member States had pledged themselves to take action, in co-operation with the United Nations, to promote observance of human rights, without distinction as to race. He expressed the belief that the matter was of proper and legitimate concern to the United Nations and that, moreover, the apartheid policy had clearly led to a situation the continuance of which was likely to endanger international peace and security.[419]

On 5 August, China's representative, regretting that South Africa had invoked the domestic jurisdiction clause, said that the promotion of human rights and fundamental freedoms was a paramount purpose of the United Nations, no less important than maintaining international peace and security. He also said that it served no useful purpose then to re-open the debate on domestic jurisdiction as that issue had long been settled by an impressive number of precedents.[420] Apparently, he was referring to previous discussions of domestic jurisdiction both in the Assembly and in the Council.

The next day, the United Kingdom representative repeated his Government's view, as stated in 1961, that the case of apartheid was *sui generis* and could, therefore, be considered and treated differently. France expressed the opinion that the measures proposed in the resolution would, juridically speaking, constitute direct interference in the domestic jurisdiction of a Member State, but that, on the question of apartheid, the French Government had no hesitation about approving the agenda, although France could only condemn racial discrimination.[421] However, both France and the United Kingdom abstained on resolution 181 of 7 August 1963.

On 27 November, when the Council resumed its consideration of the matter, before the unanimous adoption of its resolution 182 of 4 December 1963, it was seized with a report submitted by the Secretary-General, containing the reply of the Foreign Minister of South Africa. The Foreign Minister said:

> The South African Government's attitude has often been stated and is well known. In this connexion it must be emphasized that the South African Government has never recognized the right of the United Nations to discuss or consider a matter which falls solely within the jurisdiction of a Member State . . .
>
> While the South African Government entered into consultations with the then Secretary-General in 1960 this was on the basis of the authority of the Secretary-General under the Charter of the United Nations and on prior agreement that the consent of the South African Government to discuss the Security Council's resolution of 1 April 1960 would not require prior recognition from the South African Government of the United Nations authority.
>
> The present request from the Secretary-General is, however, based on a Security Council resolution which violates the provisions of Article 2 (7) of the Charter of the United Nations. It would be appreciated that in the circumstances it is impossible for the South African Government to comment on the matters raised by the Secretary-General since by doing so it would by implication recognize the right of the United Nations to intervene in South Africa's domestic affairs.[422]

In 1963, the three Western members of the Council again would not consent to measures under Chapter VII of the Charter; they only went so far as to recommend voluntary measures.[423] In connection with the two resolutions adopted by the Council on 9 and 18 June 1964, South Africa objected to the competence of the Council, through a communication addressed to the President of the Council, and held that the Report of the Group of Experts covered matters essentially within the domestic jurisdiction of the Republic of South Africa. The Council believed, however, that apartheid affected the implementation of fundamental principles of the Charter and the Universal Declaration and that, in subscribing to the Charter, the South African Government had accepted the obligation to have its racial policies accord with the standards set by the world Organization.[424]

On 19 November 1964, the Government of South Africa replied as follows to the Secretary-General's letter of 19 June 1964 transmitting the text of the Council resolution of 18 June 1964:

> It is difficult for the South African Government to conceive of a more far-reaching example of attempted intervention in matters falling within the do-

mestic jurisdiction of a sovereign Member of the United Nations than is represented in the terms of the resolution in question. What is in effect sought is that a Member State should abdicate its sovereignty in favour of the United Nations.[425]

The South African Government thus held firmly to the domestic jurisdiction clause of the Charter, while ignoring other fundamental principles and purposes of the same Charter. It invoked one provision of the Charter against other provisions on fundamental principles such as the provisions on racial equality. Yet, if the domestic jurisdiction clause were to be given a rigid interpretation, then the repeated and consistent references to human rights and fundamental freedoms, including racial equality, would be rendered superfluous and even meaningless. The domestic jurisdiction clause seems to make sense only when considered in counter-balance to other fundamental principles of the Charter. A broad interpretation of "intervention" and "domestic jurisdiction" would make virtually the whole Charter, except Article 2, paragraph 7, a waste of words, as has been noted by one writer, and governments do not commit themselves to collaborative effort to promote the universal enjoyment of human rights if they adhere to the belief that every state has the sovereign right to treat its citizens as arbitrarily as it pleases.[426] In becoming a Member of the United Nations and a party to its Charter, however, the South African state assumed certain international obligations, including the obligations imposed by the Charter provisions on human rights. By virtue of its membership in the United Nations, a state voluntarily gives up part of its sovereignty, of which domestic jurisdiction is a corollary. Article 103 of the Charter, for example, provides that "in the event of a conflict between the obligations of the Members of the United Nations under the present Charter and their obligations under any other international agreement, their obligations under the present Charter shall prevail."

In abstaining on both resolutions of the Council in 1964, the representative of France maintained that, in his Government's opinion, "the United Nations was not entitled to intervene so directly in the domestic affairs of a Member State." The representatives of Czechoslovakia and the Soviet Union, on the other hand, explained their abstention on resolution 191 of 18 June 1964 on the grounds that "the resolution offered only inadequate, ineffective measures."[427]

From 1964 to 1970, the Council did not discuss the racial situation in South Africa. During the discussions in the Council in July 1970, the representatives of France, the United Kingdom, and the United States again took a position against mandatory sanctions under Chapter VII.[428] During the rest of the period under review, no new substantial argument was made in the Council discussions on domestic jurisdiction with regard to South Africa's racial legislation other than those already made in the Council and Assembly.

Over the years, the Western permanent members of the Security Council softened their position on the domestic jurisdiction issue to accept the competence of the United Nations. At first, they only went so far as to agree to include the issue on the agenda, to discuss it, and make recommendations. However, after repeated appeals to the Government of South Africa went unheeded, during which time that Government was speedily implementing and entrenching apartheid through bantustanization and other repressive measures, even the Western permanent members of the Council became aware that more effective action was needed, and that they might have to soften their position on domestic jurisdiction still further.

At the Council meeting on 28 October 1977, discussion focused on adopting mandatory sanctions against South Africa under Chapter VII of the Charter—an action which would affect the domestic jurisdiction position of the Western permanent members. At that meeting, the Council, under rule 39 of its provisional rules of procedure, heard a statement by Horst Gerhard Kleinschmidt, external representative of the Christian Institute of Southern Africa.[429] He said that on 19 October his organization had been "banned" together with seventeen other organizations in South Africa, and that the advocates of dialogue and reform had seen that every voice of opposition would be punished in South Africa. Yet, he went on, "allies of *apartheid*," who benefited economically from the system in South Africa, were prepared only for the most cautious of measures. He requested the Council not to debate the question of whether economic sanctions would hit the poorest people worst, because, he said, the poor people wanted to know when apartheid would end, not when would it become more endurable. Measures such as codes of employment practices had provided no hope, would never end apartheid, and had not benefited those affected, he said.[430]

At a meeting of the Council on 31 October 1977, the representative of France said that the question of apartheid was no longer the internal affair of an individual state, but a matter of legitimate concern to the entire international community which ought to take measures for putting an end to apartheid practices that were both reprehensible and dangerous.[431]

In the afternoon meeting of the Council on that same day, the Council voted unanimously to condemn South Africa for resorting to massive violence and repression, but did not adopt three other draft resolutions, including one on economic sanctions, because of the negative votes of three permanent members of the Council—France, the United Kingdom, and the United States. In explaining his vote, the Soviet representative said that his country had supported mandatory sanctions against South Africa because the situation there was the result of years of connivance by certain Western countries. He regretted that the veto of the Western Powers had prevented the United Nations from adopting sanctions proposed by African states.[432]

The adoption of the mandatory sanctions against South Africa on 4 November 1977 indicated a clear shift in the position of the Western permanent members of the Council with regard to domestic jurisdiction. As

seen earlier, the ultimate action was taken primarily on humanitarian
grounds; not because of an imminent threat posed by apartheid to international peace and security. In essence, it was an action taken against the
racial legislation in South Africa. Speaking at the invitation of the Council
after it adopted the mandatory arms embargo, the representative of the Pan
Africanist Congress of Azania described the Council's action as a symbolic
gesture arriving seventeen years late. He said that if such action had been
taken in 1960, several thousands of lives would have been saved and the
bitterness felt in the country would have been avoided. He expressed the
conviction that Western countries had for too long given a lease of political
life to the South African Government for their own economic interests, and
he rejected the reasons given by them to justify their support for the racist
and oppressive régime.[433]

At the same meeting, the representative of the African National Congress said that the triple veto had confirmed that whatever the Western
Powers pretended to be doing in support of the struggle against apartheid
was calculated only in terms of pounds, dollars, francs, and Deutschmarks,
and not based on principles. Moreover, he said, the Council's action was
too little, too late. The situation in South Africa, he continued, was characterized by expropriation, hunger, super-exploitation, and social depriva-
tion, maintained by the ever-escalating reign of terror and aggression, and
called for comprehensive mandatory sanctions under Chapter VII of the
Charter.[434]

On 26 January 1978, the Council invited Donald Woods, former Editor
of the South African *Daily Dispatch*, to address it. He was among those
"banned" by the South African Government on 19 October 1977, and had
escaped from South Africa. He told the Council that although race prejudice
existed in many parts of the world, the unique affront which apartheid
represented to all mankind was the fact that it was only in South Africa that
racism was institutionalized through actual statute law. He said that the
United Nations had already agreed that apartheid was a threat to world
peace, but he was more concerned with its disastrous effects within his
country.[435] He pleaded for positive, constructive, non-violent, practical, and
effective United Nations action against apartheid. He said that, to save South
Africa from a racial civil war, the Western Powers should reassess their
position and reconsider the institution of economic sanctions, keeping in
mind that the most authentic black spokesmen in South Africa, including
Nelson Mandela and Steve Biko, had repeatedly and consistently stated that
they would prefer any economic hardship to a continuation of a policy which
they regarded as a negation of their humanity in every facet of their lives.
He challenged the Western Powers never again to condemn the South African
Government if the basis of their reluctance to bring any pressure against
that Government was their own self-interest.

Explaining that Prime Minister Vorster had gained many votes by defying the world to "do your damnest" [sic], Mr. Woods said that it would be a mistake to believe that Vorster or his followers did not care about world opinion. The only reason why so far world opinion had not been effective, he said, was that it was merely vocal. For thirty years in South Africa, he continued, the United Nations censure had been regarded as a joke, but if concerted international action, based on moral force backed by practical action, was adopted to bring the South African Government to the negotiating table, the dawn of liberty would be seen in that unhappy land. In response to a question whether the Western support for the South African Government stemmed from a policy of containing communism and protecting the important sea routes of the Indian Ocean, he replied in the negative and said that in fact the actions of the Pretoria Government had done more to promote the communist belief in South Africa than anything else.[436]

According to two observers, "with the United Nations Security Council resolution of 4 November 1977, terming the export of arms to South Africa a threat to the peace and imposing a mandatory arms embargo, the domestic jurisdiction argument has been significantly eroded."[437] At the same time, while it is true that the domestic jurisdiction argument in respect of apartheid has been significantly eroded, its significance with regard to human rights violations in general should not be overemphasized. Even in the case of apartheid, the Council could not bring itself to determine that apartheid itself constituted a threat to international peace and security, and felt the need to establish a link between the acquisition of arms by South Africa and international peace.

South African liberation movements and many United Nations members have said that certain members of the Council used the domestic jurisdiction argument as a pretext to further their economic, military, and other interests and to prevent the United Nations from adopting effective measures against South Africa.[438] The Western permanent members of the Council argued that their attitude was prompted by genuine belief in the legal considerations surrounding domestic jurisdiction, adding that mandatory sanctions would not be effective anyhow and would most hurt the poor majority people of South Africa. Whatever the different arguments on the point of domestic jurisdiction, the position of the Western permanent members was not consistent and kept changing. Because of the position of those members, the Council adopted the mandatory arms embargo against South Africa as late as more than three decades after the Assembly first considered the matter. In general, the Council ultimately followed the course of action recommended by the Assembly, although slowly, reluctantly, and only partially.

In brief, for an unduly long period of time, the Western permanent members of the Council did not support measures beyond discussion and recommendation, using the argument that human rights were matters within domestic jurisdiction. This position of the powerful members of the Organization did, in effect, strengthen South Africa's defiant position. It also nullified the understanding reached at the San Francisco Conference with regard to outrageous violations of human rights, which endanger international peace or obstruct the application of the Charter.

As already seen, France linked the mandatory arms embargo with the use of imported weapons for internal repression, a matter of human rights. The United Kingdom dissociated its vote from the technical meaning of the term ''act of aggression'' in Chapter VII of the Charter. The Council thus adopted an embargo mainly on humanitarian grounds, though formally based its action on a threat posed by South Africa's import of arms. The Council's practice in this matter does not allow one to draw a clear-cut conclusion as to how it justified its action in regard to the domestic jurisdiction clause. The Council has vacillated on the question of domestic jurisdiction. It has not determined that the racial situation, that is, apartheid, itself is a threat to international peace, although it has repeatedly said that the race conflict in South Africa resulted from the policies of apartheid.

PART III

EFFECT

VI. UNITED NATIONS IMPACT ON SOUTH AFRICA

Pressures by the United Nations

General

The United Nations has persistently called on South Africa to revise its racialized legal order. Its efforts reached a climax when it adopted the mandatory arms embargo. Since then, the General Assembly has strengthened its calls for mandatory economic sanctions in order to make it clear to South Africa that it has to abandon apartheid peacefully.

Unfortunately, the United Nations has not yet achieved its objective in South Africa. The South African Government has not yet effected the necessary changes. On the contrary, it has stated that it would disregard the Organization's action and other external pressures. It has, however, said that hurtful discrimination would be eliminated. As the South African Government has become more isolated, it has resorted to some tactics, propaganda, and minor changes in its apartheid policies. In the 1960s, South Africa began feeling pressure in international sports competitions. Since 1974, it has been suspended from participation in the work of the General Assembly and has confronted growing demands for expulsion from membership. As seen earlier, it has already been expelled from a number of specialized agencies.[439] It has been greatly isolated inside as well as outside the United Nations "family." Certainly, no country finds large-scale isolation comfortable in this increasingly interdependent world.

In addition to the efforts of the Assembly and the Council, other United Nations organs and bodies have adopted many resolutions and decisions denouncing apartheid. They have published studies of the harmful effects of apartheid on almost all aspects of life. The Centre against Apartheid, acting as the secretariat of the Special Committee against Apartheid, has widely publicized United Nations resolutions, decisions, studies, conferences, seminars, and meetings on apartheid, as has the United Nations Department of Public Information.

The Special Committee against Apartheid, in co-operation with governments and intergovernmental and non-governmental organizations (NGOs), has made world public opinion increasingly aware of the nature and consequences of apartheid.[440] It has co-operated with, and has had increasing response from, national and international trade unions, student and youth organizations, women's organizations, churches, and anti-apartheid and solidarity movements. These organizations have demonstrated and protested against apartheid, against investments in and loans to South Africa, and against imports from South Africa. Some of these groups, such as the British, Irish, and Dutch anti-apartheid movements and the International Defence and Aid Fund (London) have helped conduct quite active campaigns against apartheid including campaigns against sporting links with South Africa, and have helped to raise funds for the victims of apartheid. These organizations have aroused public opinion which has then put pressure on governments. The most active of these organizations have been operating in Western countries, as the governments of those countries have the closest links with South Africa. The Centre against Apartheid lists hundreds of organizations around the world working towards the elimination of apartheid.

The United Nations, as the center of global pressure against South Africa's policies, has had a three-fold impact: (a) it has isolated South Africa within the United Nations; (b) it pressured South Africa's friends within United Nations organs, which in turn have pressured South Africa; and (c) it has exerted pressure through world public opinion, working with NGOs and other groups. How much of the external pressure put on South Africa has emanated directly from the United Nations cannot be determined. However, it can generally be said that almost all the external pressure against South Africa has originated from United Nations efforts. Virtually all governments, intergovernmental organizations, and NGOs which have made any effort against apartheid have usually done so either in co-operation with the United Nations or have followed United Nations recommendations.

The role played by NGOs and other groups in putting pressure on governments may be exemplified from a statement by Patricia M. Derian, U.S. Assistant Secretary for Human Rights and Humanitarian Affairs:

> Private groups also have called upon the US Government to disassociate itself more clearly from the South African Government through our trade and investment policies. Specifically, they have urged the US Government to curtail or halt private trade and investment to South Africa. They have called upon corporations to withdraw from South Africa. In at least two cases, corporations have done so. It might be useful for this subcommittee to review these recommendations too. Private groups have also urged the US to consider if there are any circumstances whereby it could support economic sanctions against South Africa in the United Nations. To date, the US has limited its support of sanctions to our expanded arms embargo.[441]

At the same time, it has also been written:

> In effect, the lesson learned from the international anti-apartheid movement of the last decades is that the movement resulted in some loosening of the apartheid system, and that South Africa is shifting away from the rigid implementation of the separate development plans. Whatever the evidence cited, there is no clear link of causation between whatever liberalization has occurred and the international movement that has developed.[442]

Certainly a clear causal link cannot be established, because the minor liberalization that has occurred in South Africa has resulted not only from external pressures but also under internal pressures. Moreover, it is impossible to apportion the external pressure on South Africa as between the United Nations, South Africa's allies, NGOs, and world public opinion. It may be said, however, that United Nations discussions and decisions have generally influenced governments' policies with regard to apartheid. The same holds true with groups which have co-operated with the United Nations in their efforts against apartheid. Even the change in the positions of some of the Western Member States on apartheid has been brought about by the persistent efforts of the rest of the United Nations Member States.

In the late 1970s, world public opinion, organizations, and groups urged Western Governments to have United States and Common Market corporations operating in South Africa adopt the "Sullivan Principles" and the EEC "Code of Conduct" in order to improve the conditions of black workers. Conceived in 1977 by the Reverend Leon Sullivan, the Sullivan Principles aim at desegregating the workplace, establishing fair employment practices and equal pay for equal work, creating job training and advancement programs, and improving the quality of workers' lives. The aim of the Common Market's "Code of Conduct" is similar.[443]

Foreign corporations in South Africa have greatly benefited from the cheap labor market. These corporations are generally capital-intensive and employ only a fraction of the black force. Not all foreign corporations have signed the codes of conduct, and those which have signed have not all carried out the principles fully, because no sanctions for enforcement exist. In October 1979, 71 percent of the black workers were still employed in segregated job categories. Irrespective of the assertions of these companies and their governments that the increased national wealth in South Africa will ultimately reach the general population, the foreign-based corporations undoubtedly help sustain the apartheid system. Therefore, black leaders outside the system who oppose apartheid generally regard the codes of conduct as helping to prolong the sufferings of South Africa's blacks.[444]

Moreover, close observers of the scene have said that despite the good intentions behind them, they are based on illusions, and although they may ease the consciences of some Americans and Europeans, these codes in fact accomplish little of significance in the real world of South Africa. They have also said that the presence of Western business is enormously important to white South Africans, psychologically as well as economically, and whereas South Africans talk about standing alone against the world, they are desperate for links, especially with the United States.[445]

The External Pressure and South Africa's Response

Whenever South Africa has felt strong external pressure, it has made a token move to alter local conditions, albeit a cosmetic change. As has been said by Sonny Leon, a veteran Colored politician, "when racial tension peaked and overseas pressures increased, the Government reacted by promises and undertakings" and created expectations which it could not carry out because of the right-wing resistance in the National Party.[446] An interesting study in this regard has attempted to show "how an ethnic oligarchy, as presently mobilized, hardly anticipates the rising costs to its rule but instead mostly reacts to pressure only."[447]

In the late 1960s, when South Africa was becoming isolated in international sports, it started to seek better relations with neighbouring states by offering them economic advantages as a "carrot" in exchange for their acquiescence to its internal racial policies. In resolution 2775F (XXVI) of 29 November 1971, the Assembly characterized South Africa's "outward policy" tactics as designed primarily to obtain acquiescence for its racial policies, confuse world public opinion, counter international isolation, hinder assistance to the liberation movements by the international community, and consolidate white minority rule in southern Africa. Similarly, in resolution 3411G (XXX) of 10 December 1975, the Assembly denounced the "manoeuvres of the racist régime of South Africa" on the same grounds.[448]

On 24 October 1974, the year when South Africa was suspended from participating in the Assembly's work and when the Council was being pressed to expel South Africa from United Nations membership, the South African representative said at a Council meeting that his country would do everything in its power to move away from discrimination based on race and color.[449] He also said that South Africa had not changed its position on domestic jurisdiction, but was willing to discuss its differences with other countries, particularly African countries. He denied that South Africa had adopted "a provocative and challenging attitude towards the world body" and urged that the United Nations should keep open the channels of communication instead of expelling South Africa, adding that the situation in South Africa was changing peacefully.[450]

One day earlier, Prime Minister Vorster had said that southern Africa had come to a crossroads and ought to choose between peace and escalation of violence.[451] South Africans' claim that the racial situation was changing provided support for the position of its Western allies on the Council, whose votes were later to save South Africa from expulsion. Much later, during the 1978 House of Assembly debates in South Africa, a Member of the South African Party reminded the House of the promise which the Foreign Minister had earlier made to the world that discrimination based on color would become a thing of the past.[452]

With regard to South Africa's claim that the United Nations and others have no influence in its internal policies, the *Economist* (London) has reported that "although the South African whites present a confident face to the world, many of them have secret doubts" and that "this is strikingly revealed by the number of prosecutions for smuggling money out of the country," especially after the Soweto incidents of 1976.[453] Also, a report tabled in the South African Parliament on 1 May 1979 stated that "it would be naive to deny or ignore the effect of international attempts to influence labour and other policies in South Africa."[454]

On 10 February 1978, in connection with a proposal to repeal the Prohibition of Mixed Marriages Act and Section 16 of the Immorality Act in the House of Assembly, members of the Progressive Federal Party and the New Republic Party, two of the Opposition parties, spoke of the embarrassment to South Africa, the country's image in the outside world, and the notoriety and unfavorable publicity caused against South Africa as well as the harm done to the country by these laws.[455]

On 20 April 1978, the Minister of Sport and Recreation said in the House that while the Opposition members were creating the impression abroad that he was lying about the sports policy in South Africa, the Western countries were conferring in Paris to decide on South African sport and to consider whether they should adopt a formula similar to the Gleneagles Agreement. He quoted from a telegram from Washington telling him that South African policy caused a collision of principle and practice. He complained against Opposition efforts to discredit the nation's sports policy just one week before South Africa "had to try to convince the Western countries that everything which had happened in South Africa as far as sport was concerned would justify the Western countries not applying a Gleneagles agreement in regard to South Africa." He further said that the application of such an agreement would embarrass South Africa.[456]

In the House debates over the Advocate-General Bill, proposed in May 1979 to further restrict the freedom of the press in South Africa, a Member of the Progressive Federal Party opposed the Bill saying that South African representatives, ambassadors and information officials abroad would be kept busy trying to erase and gloss over the bad image of South Africa that would be created by attacks on the freedom of the press. He also said that there were two matters which influenced the attitudes of governments in the Free World most—human rights and freedom of the press. Other Opposition members made similar statements in that debate.[457]

International pressure on South Africa increased especially after the

Soweto incidents of June 1976. The *Economist* reports that there were growing pressures from labor, church, and student groups, and even the attitudes of banks were changing.[458] By 1977, some major American banks and corporations were persuaded to limit their operations in South Africa. Among these were the Chase Manhattan Bank, General Motors, Control Data, and Polaroid.[459] On 15 December 1977, it was reported that the Barclays Bank of South Africa withdrew $11.5 million from Government defence bonds in South Africa after a year of pressure from Barclays International, the British parent company.[460] In January 1978, Canada was reported to have withdrawn all Canadian trade officials from South Africa.[461]

In February 1978, Common Market Ministers were weighing pressures against South Africa while the British Foreign Secretary "warned that it would be premature to take fresh action [alluding to the mandatory arms embargo adopted by the United Nations in November 1977] against South Africa until the problems of Rhodesia and South-West Africa were dealt with."[462]

The same argument has been made informally in the United Nations by Western members of the Council to explain their opposition to the adoption of comprehensive and mandatory sanctions against South Africa. Zimbabwe has, in the meantime, achieved independence. When Namibia attains independence, the Western members will have one less reason for opposing comprehensive sanctions against South Africa.

Pressures against investing in and granting loans to South Africa have come not only from labor, church and student groups but also from teacher and investor groups. Under pressure, Citibank decided not to make loans to the Government of South Africa or to Government-owned manufacturing and utility enterprises.[463] There have also been protests against the sale of South Africa's gold coins, especially the Krugerrand, in the United States.

Pressures against collaborating with South Africa came from too many sources and countries to be included in this book. It should be noted, however, that the United Kingdom and the United States are the two biggest trade partners of South Africa. The significance of United States capital and loans in supporting the apartheid system is contained in a 231-page report on "U.S. Corporate Interests in South Africa" prepared by the Subcommittee on African Affairs of the Senate Foreign Relations Committee. That report concluded that United States corporate interests had strengthened the apartheid régime economically and militarily and undermined the "fundamental goals and objectives of U.S. foreign policy."[464]

Even Afrikaner newspapers have acknowledged the impact of external pressures. Referring to United States Ambassador Donald Mc Henry's statement that relations between South Africa and America would deteriorate further if no rapid progress was made towards meaningful participation for all South Africans in government, Afrikaner newspaper *Beeld* wrote that that kind of threat could not be lightly shaken off, because America had enormous power which it could use to make things very difficult for South Africa diplomatically and economically.[465] There is no doubt that "South Africans are extremely sensitive to American views, economically and psychologically," a *New York Times* columnist has commented.[466]

After the Security Council imposed a mandatory arms embargo on South Africa in 1977, the pace of change in that country, however slow, accelerated. As South Africa is known to be well-armed, the arms embargo has never been considered fully effective. But the 1977 embargo gave the signal that comprehensive and mandatory sanctions, including economic measures, were a possibility. Some Western reporters say that black people in South Africa generally favor sanctions against South Africa. A *New York Times* reporter wrote, before the imposition of the 1977 arms embargo, that blacks generally believed that whites, particularly Afrikaners, were not expected to yield otherwise and that "sanctions may well be indispensable to change, however retrogressive their immediate effect."[467]

One of the arguments usually advanced by Western governments against the imposition of mandatory sanctions on South Africa has been that such sanctions are never effective. If so, how did these same governments expect sanctions imposed early in 1980 to be effective against Iran and the Soviet Union? If they count on the psychological effect of sanctions, why should they ignore that effect in the case of South Africa?

As the momentum has gained for increasing international pressure on South Africa to eliminate apartheid, a new United States Administration has elaborated a new policy towards South Africa. This new policy apparently gives priority to economic and strategic interests over human rights considerations. It holds that United States concerns with southern Africa are linked to the United States recognition of the strategic, political, and economic importance of that region to the United States and the Western world. It is designed to seek to promote peace and regional security and deny opportunities to those who seek contrary objectives, to support proven friends and negotiated solutions to the problems of southern Africa, and to do its best to foster basic human liberties in keeping with both United States principles and United States interests. This new policy was well expounded in a paper presented to a conference in June 1981 by United States Assistant Secretary of State for African Affairs, Chester A. Crocker.[468]

Known as "constructive engagement," the new policy aims at keeping closer ties with the South African Government and gives priority to the settlement of the Namibian problem rather than the elimination of apartheid. It is also based on the premise that the South African society is going through some changes and that closer relationship will encourage further changes. In line with this policy, the United States has accepted South Africa's request to train coast guard personnel, and to authorize South African honorary consuls in additional cities. Recently, on 31 August 1981, the United States vetoed a resolution in the Security Council, which would have strongly condemned South Africa for its massive invasion deep into Angola's territory, destroying towns and killing more than 600 people. Also, on 3 September, at the beginning of the emergency special session of the General Assembly on the Question of Namibia, the only vote cast in the Credentials Committee against the rejection of the credentials of the South African delegation came from the United States.

While the new United States policy toward South Africa may please Pretoria, a recent report by the Study Commission on U.S. Policy Toward Southern Africa certainly can not.[469] In its comprehensive report, titled *South Africa: Time Running Out*, the Commission concludes that blacks in South Africa will eventually alter the status quo and that fundamental political change without sustained, large-scale violence is still possible, although time is running out. It finds that the active collaboration of the South African Government is not an important factor in the protection of the Cape sea route, that white intransigence, growing political instability, rising levels of racial violence and armed conflict promote the growth of the Soviet influence in the region, and that should South Africa hold back the supply of key minerals, such stoppages would most likely be short term.

The Commission makes some policy recommendations intended to serve as a framework for action by the U.S. Government and private organizations. Among other things, it recommends that genuine political power-sharing in South Africa should be promoted with a minimum of violence, by systematically exerting influence on the South African Government. It also recommends that the U.S. Government should encourage its allies to adopt similar policies. It does not support trade embargoes against South Africa, or the withdrawal of U.S. investment, but it recommends a freeze on U.S. investment in South Africa. Thus the report is at variance with some of the premises on which the new U.S. policy is based.

Evidently, the South African Government is not invulnerable to international pressure. Under both internal and external pressures, that Government has made some changes and proposed some others in its domestic politics. It is not feasible to classify changes as those effected under internal pressure and those under external pressure. The changes have been brought about by a combination of internal and external pressures.

Internal Changes

Sports Policies

The United Nations General Assembly has repeatedly called on states to end sports links with South Africa, because racial segregation violates the Olympic principle of non-segregation.

In 1964, South Africa was not allowed to participate in the Olympic

Games in Tokyo. It was provisionally accepted for the 1968 Olympics, pending changes in its sports policies. It promised the International Olympic Committee in Teheran in 1967 that it would send a mixed team to the forthcoming Olympics and that all members of the team would wear the same colors and march under the same flag. These changes did not alter the segregationist sports policies within South Africa.[470] Therefore, in 1968, again South Africa was refused participation in the Olympics.

In 1970, South Africa was expelled from the Olympic movement. It has also been expelled from a number of international sport associations. In 1976, because of a trip to South Africa by a New Zealand rugby team, black African nations withdrew from the Summer Olympics in Montreal in protest against New Zealand's participation. In June 1977, the Commonwealth Conference in Gleneagles, Scotland, agreed to take every practicable step to discourage sporting links with South Africa because of that country's official policy of apartheid. The Commonwealth felt the necessity of such an agreement in order to avoid a boycott of the 1978 Commonwealth Games.[471]

In September 1976, South Africa announced a new sports policy which brought about some minor internal changes by extending South Africa's "multinational" sports policy to allow black club teams to play white club teams under special circumstances. The new policy did not bring about nonracial sport. Members of each population group still had to join the clubs of their own racial group.[472] The change did bring about competition between black and white teams, but there were no mixed, non-racial team events.

In February 1978, Sports Minister Piet Koornhof "clarified" the 1976 sports policy. He said that no legal permission was necessary for racially mixed clubs or games. He also said that he would undertake changes in liquor laws to allow sports clubs to integrate their bars and restaurants by applying for "international status". Although the assertion that no legal permission was necessary for racially mixed clubs or games seems correct, the Group Areas Act (1950), the Liquors Act, and the Reservation of Separate Amenities Act (1953), have a prohibitory effect. For example, it was reported that the same day that Minister Koornhof was stating on television that racially mixed sports were not illegal in South Africa, "six policemen swooped [down] on a soccer team near Pretoria threatening its eight white and six black members with arrest for breaking the law by playing together."[473]

At the same time, it was reported that "South Africa, facing demands for its expulsion from international Tennis, today [12 February 1978] named an 18-year-old player of mixed race, Peter Lamb, to the Davis Cup team."[474] That team played the United States in Nashville, Tennessee, in March 1978, against great public pressure from the American Coordinating Committee for Equality in Sport and Society (ACCESS), other organizations, and individuals.

In April 1979, a South African English newspaper, *The Star* (Johannesburg), pointed out, in connection with the cancelled tour of a French rugby team, that South Africa needed more than a sporting gesture. It said that the problem arose because South Africa did not heed threats, made twenty years ago, that it would be expelled from international sports if South African sports bodies did not become multiracial. It also said that the countries most friendly to South Africa, such as Britain, New Zealand, Australia, and France, could no longer accept South Africa's empty promises "because pressure was on them, too, from an anti-apartheid world."[475]

In December 1979, the head of the South African Council on Sport (black), Hassan Howa, described the changes in sports in South Africa as cosmetic, saying that permits were still required to play non-racial sport. At the same time, the Supreme Council of Sport in Africa decided that African athletes would boycott the Olympic events in which Britain would participate if a Springbok rugby team of South Africa was allowed to tour Britain in 1980. But the cosmetic changes made in sports policies in South Africa were best verified by the statement of a Nationalist member of Parliament in South Africa who, in May 1979, said that "integrated clubs and integrated sport constituted far less than one per cent of the sports activities in South Africa."[476]

An editorial in the *Rand Daily Mail*, a newspaper of the English-speaking population, has recently taken a position against the isolation of South Africa in international sports, but at the same time had this to say:

> One cannot state such an attitude, however, without also taking note of the cogency of the arguments used by the isolationists. They say bluntly that white South Africans refuse to change until they are forced to do so; that our white sportsmen were quite happy to go on playing apartheid sport and isolating their black fellow-countrymen without raising a word of protest against such a violation of the spirit of sportsmanship—not even in the gross case of Basil D'Olivera—until they themselves suddenly felt the sting of isolation. Then, suddenly and miraculously, their consciences were awakened.
> There can be no doubt that this is true. . . .[477]

Despite some changes made in South Africa's sports policies, the criterion in the formulation of these policies is still race, not merit. Non-racial sport at club level is discretionary; integration at that level depends on the goodwill of the white sports clubs, which is not forthcoming. In their international teams the South African Government now includes some blacks, but when in July 1980 two blacks were included in a high school team in Pretoria, the right-wing Nationalists made such a big fuss that Prime Minister Botha could not dare confront the challenge. The minor changes brought about have resulted from international pressure to isolate South Africa in an area where it hurts. White South Africans are great sports fans. As noted by a South African newspaper, "there can be little doubt that pressure has played a significant role in bringing about change in the sports front."[478]

South Africa is still a member of several international sports federations, mainly because of the constitutions of these federations. Some of these constitutions entail a weighted voting system that enables South Africa's Western friends to protect it from expulsion, while others require a two-thirds or sometimes a three-quarters majority vote for expulsion, again with the same protective effect for South Africa.

South Africa's Western friends have all along maintained that sports and politics should not be mixed. It is strange that this argument should be used to the benefit of a state which has created a problem by just doing that—mixing sports and politics. It is also ironic that some of the Western countries holding that view chose to boycott the 1980 Summer Olympics in Moscow because of the Soviet invasion of Afghanistan. In that case, apparently, it was permissible to mix politics with sports.

Because of its racial segregation in sports, South Africa's teams in international sports events are increasingly confronting difficulties even in countries which have traditionally been its sports partners. In September 1981, for example, South Africa's national Springboks rugby team met so much opposition and violence in the United States that some events were cancelled by local authorities while others had to be played secretly.

Labor Policies

Just before the imposition of the mandatory arms embargo on South Africa in November 1977, the South African Government began considering changes in the field of labor. In August 1977, it appointed Nicolas Wiehahn as the chairman of a commission to make suggestions for the improvement of the labor situation. On 25 April 1978, the Minister of Labor said in the House that pressure had been exerted on South Africa by the outside world to influence the labor situation by drawing up codes, and referred to the Sullivan and EEC codes. After playing down the significance of those codes, he said:

> I do want to concede, though, that we in South Africa take cognizance of and are sensitive to how the outside world feels about these matters. When all is said and done, industrialists from overseas are investing in our country and are employing people here, and because the world has become a small place to live in, the situation has simply developed in such a way that what happens in one country also affects other countries.[479]

The new labor legislation was enacted in 1979 pursuant to the reports of the Wiehahn Commission (Commission of Inquiry into Labor Legislation) and the Riekert Commission (Commission of Inquiry into Legislation Affecting the Utilization of Manpower). It gave trade union rights to African workers and did away with some of the "job reservation" categories. The formation of racially-mixed trade unions was to be granted only in exceptional circumstances. The Industrial Conciliation Amendment Act, which entered into force on 1 October 1979, established the National Manpower Commission and the Industrial Court. The Commission is to determine the negotiating rights and working conditions of African workers as well as the political activities of trade unions. It is also to make suggestions as to the termination of a union's registration, and to exercise control over industrial training. The Industrial Court is to determine unfair labor practices and see about the administration of labor laws. It can decide not only on disputes of right (about the interpretation of laws) but also on disputes of interest (such as wage negotiations). There is no appeal from the Court's decision.[480]

In the words of one British journalist, the Wiehahn Commission's proposal to give trade union rights to Africans was prompted by the realization that, if allowed to continue to operate unregistered and uncontrolled, African unions "would come under foreign influence and might undermine the statutory conciliation procedures by setting up alternative negotiating channels at plant level. In addition, the illegality of black [African] unionism was placing foreign companies under intense pressure back at home, as a result of which they were setting up their own channels of communication with their black [African] workers."[481]

The new legislation that followed the Wiehahn proposals aims at controlling the political activities of African workers through unionization. It is designed to keep black unions racially segregated, thus preventing them from becoming a united front. It gives excessive power to administrators to grant or deny registration to African unions.

The new legislation enacted upon the Riekert Commission's proposals strengthened the "influx control" rather than weakening or eliminating it. The requirements for African residence in urban (white) areas are the availability of accommodation and suitable employment, both verified by white authorities. Employers who ignore these criteria face the increased fine of R500. African workers without verified accommodation and employment are "endorsed out" to homelands.[482]

In July 1979, the so-called "illegal" African workers in urban areas were given time until the end of October 1979 to register; otherwise, they would have to leave the urban areas. To register, they had to have secured approved accommodation and to have worked for one employer for more than one year, or for a number of employers for more than three years. After October 1979, the South African authorities cracked down on the "illegal" African workers, "endorsing out" a huge number of them.[483]

To forestall the establishment of independent African trade unions, white unions have resorted to the device of setting up "parallel" African unions in each industry or firm under the umbrella of the white-dominated Trade Union Council of South Africa (TUCSA). These unions have enabled transnational corporations, such as Siemens, GEC and British Leyland, to ignore the Sullivan Principles and the EEC Code of Conduct and to obstruct, at the same time, the setting up of genuinely independent African trade unions.[484]

The new labor legislation was necessitated by the growing demand for skilled black labor, the insecurity created by increasing black unemployment, the international pressure against South Africa's labor practices and the pressure by foreign capital on the Government to provide favorable conditions for continued investment. It is also in line with the Government's intention to create a black middle class that would have an interest in maintaining the system. According to one South African black newspaper, it is designed to make the system more acceptable both internally and internationally.[485]

At the time of writing, there was a new Labor Relations Amendment Bill before the House, maintaining restrictions on unregistered unions and illegal strikes. The Bill envisaged the establishment of work councils with a view to better controlling trade unions, and prohibited unions from having their main offices in the homelands. Unions are also restricted in raising funds, a limitation which hampers their ability to sustain strikes.

Petty Apartheid

Petty apartheid refers to the system of laws concerning the social segregation of blacks and whites in South Africa in public places such as restaurants, public toilets, theatres, public parks, benches, bars, and hotels. It is segregation achieved by the enforcement of laws, not merely through custom. For the purpose of making the system more acceptable both internally and internationally, the South African Government has recently made some changes in petty apartheid, too.

In the mid-1960s, B. John Vorster assumed the premiership with promises of reforms and of eliminating petty apartheid within two years. It has been reported, however, that as a result of the mixing of the races in a few public places, some conservative Afrikaners then broke away from the National Party and formed the Herstigte Nationale Party.[486]

In 1977, an American reporter wrote that "some Government officials favor easing 'unnecessary' discrimination as a means of blunting black protest and regaining a measure of international respectability."[487] In 1978, another correspondent reported that some reforms were suggested including the easing of petty apartheid, but that those reforms would not weaken the white-power structure.[488]

Since P. W. Botha assumed the premiership, more public places have been opened to all races. In September 1979, the Government modified the permit system for admission of blacks into white restaurants. Restaurant owners may now apply for permission to admit members of all racial groups for all times, not only for once. But, time will show what percentage of the Afrikaner restaurateurs will take such voluntary action.

In recent years, certain hotels and other public places in South Africa have been desegregated. But despite so much talk about moving away from apartheid, even petty apartheid has not been eliminated. Although public parks are open to all races, their toilets are still segregated. Some hotels are open to Africans. In the words of one commentator, ''in some they can eat and sleep but are subject to restrictions on drinking, dancing or swimming. Multi-racial audiences watch biting avant-garde satire in Johannesburg's 'off-Broadway' market Theatre, but the city's cinemas remain strictly segregated.''[489] In any case, the elimination of petty apartheid will not, by itself, end the ''grand apartheid'' (Grand Design) that entails the white-power structure and that is the cause of the problem.

Constitutional Proposals and Changes

In 1977, a ''new deal'' was brought forth proposing constitutional changes which would offer some limited political role to Coloreds and Indians, in a Cabinet of Councils, ''without in any way jeopardizing the interests and sovereignty of the white nation.''[490] These proposals, made under the premiership of B. J. Vorster, were not accepted by the Coloreds and the Indians, because the Africans were excluded. The Africans living in white areas were not included because they were, unrealistically, supposed to exercise their political rights through the homelands to which they belonged.

After October 1978, when P. W. Botha ascended to the premiership, he commissioned reviews of the political rights of Africans living in white-designated areas and of the size and design of the fragmented homelands with a view to consolidating those territories, if necessary. A parliamentary select committee was appointed, under the chairmanship of the Minister of Justice and the Interior, Alwyn L. Schlebusch, to hear more evidence from all those who could contribute to the finding of a new political dispensation. The Schlebusch Commission of Inquiry into the Constitution did not include leaders of all races.

The Schlebusch Commission's proposals, submitted to Parliament and accepted as an interim report in May 1980, envisaged a President's Council which would include sixty appointed white, Colored, Indian, and Chinese members, and which would have advisory functions to the Parliament (white). Another council would be set up for Africans. This council would be in advisory capacity to the President's Council; in other words, the Africans' council would be an advisory council to another advisory council. This proposed segregation of the Africans was said by a Cabinet minister to be necessitated by the Africans' ''slower thought processes.''[491] The proposals were soon turned down both by the Africans and by the true representatives of Coloreds and Asians. The proposals also envisaged the abolition of the Senate and the election of a vice-president to act as chairman of the President's Council which would replace the Senate.

On 1 August 1980, the Republic of South Africa Constitution Fifth Amendment Act amended the Constitution Act of 1961. It established the office of Vice State President, defined his functions, provided for an increase in the number of Ministers, abolished the Senate, prescribed afresh the composition of the House of Assembly, and established a President's Council and defined its functions.[492] One of the major functions of the Council is to formulate recommendations for a new constitutional dispensation for the various population groups.

As the members of the President's Council would be appointed, not elected, the Government could not fail to find Colored and Asian persons to serve on the President's Council which excluded the Africans. And, as the Africans vehemently rejected the advisory council designed for them, the Government withdrew its proposal to that effect but went ahead with the President's Council, which began functioning officially on 3 February 1981.

According to a South African reporter, at a hearing before the Schlebush Commission in 1979, two leading Afrikaner academics, Marinus Wiechers and David van Wyk, warned that the attempt to draw up a constitution acceptable to all South Africans "would not succeed unless its base was widened to include leaders of all races." That view was shared by David Welsh, head of Comparative African Government and Law at the University of Cape Town, and Harold Rudolph, a senior lecturer in constitutional and administrative law at the University of Witwatersrand. Welsh and Rudolph supported the idea of "government by consensus in a *federal framework* based on the voluntary group association with the protection of minorities." Rudolph believed that blacks calling for simple majority rule in a unitary system could be persuaded to compromise. At the same time, he warned that "blacks could not be expected to trust and support a system of government from which they were excluded." Welsh, for his part, said that "he did not believe that the ANC was irrevocably *committed to violence*" and that "they had opted for armed struggle with great reluctance in the aftermath of Sharpeville and the banning of their organization."[493]

Four members of the Progressive Federal Party, the main parliamentary opposition party, composed mostly of English-speaking whites, dissented from the recommendations of the Schlebusch Commission with regard to Africans. They argued that the constitutional future of the country should be negotiated with the Africans rather than be imposed on them.

The constitutional proposals are linked to Prime Minister P. W. Botha's "national strategy," based on his twelve-point plan of August 1979. Under that plan South Africa is a multinational society; various peoples should have self-determination in "vertical differentiation;" the territories of the homelands should be consolidated; Coloreds and Indians should be consulted in matters of common concern; schools and amenities should be kept separate; unnecessary discrimination should be eliminated; the country should be defended against foreign intervention; a more neutral position should be adopted in international affairs; defence should be strengthened; the free enterprise system should be preserved and promoted; the economic interdependence of the various peoples of South Africa should be recognised and a constellation of southern African states should be formed.[494]

In November 1979, the Prime Minister addressed a conference of business leaders in Johannesburg. He said that the constellation of southern African states could include any country in the sub-continent which would co-operate in a regional context. It would include the so-called independent homelands. The constellation might take the form of a confederation of states linked by a council of states. Self-governing homelands could be given associate membership or observer status at the council. Urban Africans might be represented on the council by their original homelands or a way might be devised for them to be represented by their community councils.[495]

It is clear that all internal changes made or proposed so far by the South African Government aim at keeping the white-power structure intact. There is no move toward political power-sharing. As long-time students of South African affairs have noted, these constitutional proposals do "not indicate an attitude change but, above all, more sophisticated co-optation tactics."[496]

Yet, the Government of South Africa, some news media and others have publicised these cosmetic shifts as substantive changes. They have heralded them as the beginning of positive change in South Africa. On 17 June 1981, for example, in his testimony to the Subcommittee on Africa of the Foreign Affairs Committee of the House of Representatives, Assistant Secretary of State Crocker said that the United States Government was convinced that a process of change was under way in South Africa.

South Africa's Propaganda Efforts

In 1972, the South African Government began allocating secret funds to the Department of Information, without the knowledge of the Parliament, to publicize South Africa's good intentions towards change.[497] Since then the South African Government has increasingly resorted to propaganda to appease world public opinion and lessen international pressure. The South African Department of Public Information has maintained offices in many countries, and kept close contact with opinion-makers in the news media, parliaments, and other institutions, organizations, and individuals. In cooperation with other agencies, such as the South African Foundation, it has invited influential people to South Africa to impress them with South Africa's progress and "good intentions."

After the Soweto incidents in 1976 and Steve Biko's death in detention from torture in 1977, international pressure on South Africa increased, culminating in the imposition of a mandatory arms embargo in November 1977. Foreign investment began to decline. To sustain its economic growth at a level high enough to absorb the annual population increase and the new entrants into the labor market, South Africa desperately needed continued investment. But, for that purpose, it had to retain foreign confidence. It, therefore, undertook publicity efforts to emphasize the economic and strategic importance of South Africa to Western countries.

The South African Government also emphasized its policy of "plural development" or "plural democracy," which are euphemisms for apartheid. It attempted to convince the world that there are many nations in South Africa and that that country is, therefore, a multi-national one. Each nation, according to that view, exercises its own independence and self-determination, and the Africans of each nation have that nation's citizenship, instead of South African citizenship.

The propaganda campaign was managed by the Department of Information until 1978 when it was disbanded because of the Department of Information scandal, also known as the Info Scandal, Muldergate, or Rhoodiegate. The Info Scandal involved the misuse of public funds to influence opinion-makers both at home and abroad. The former Secretary of Information, Eschel Rhoodie, indicated that a cabinet committee of three persons had approved of the Department's secret activities.[498]

The Info Scandal resulted from the attempts that had been made to bribe or influence politicians and trade unions in Africa, Europe, and North America, as well as the international press, to take a favorable stand towards South Africa. As aptly stated by Amnesty International, "to some extent, the revelations about the Information Department indicated the government's sensitivity to international criticism of *apartheid* and human rights violations."[499] In fact, the disclosures further indicated the Government's lack of confidence in the strength of the policies of apartheid.

Internal Opposition

Even internal opposition to apartheid has been influenced by the United Nations. In recognizing the legitimacy of the struggle by the oppressed people of South Africa for the elimination of apartheid, the United Nations has called for moral, political, and material assistance to the victims of apartheid, has established funds for the training of blacks from South Africa, has involved the South African liberation movements in its work, has acknowledged its own special responsibility for the elimination of apartheid, and has encouraged the struggle of South Africa's blacks through a host of efforts. Adam and Giliomee have observed that outside pressures "operate in conjunction with the crucial internal events. African morale draws partly from the international constellation. Black perceptions in turn affect forms and frequency of resistance, as highlighted in the township upheavals of 1976 or the ever threatening strikes of unorganized frustration."[500]

What changes South Africa has made have been in response to pressure from both inside and outside. In a message written by Nelson Mandela, and smuggled out of Robben Island, which took about two years to reach ANC leaders, Mandela, a leader of the African population of South Africa, stressed the importance of external pressures by saying: "The world is on our side. The OAU, the United Nations and the Anti-Apartheid movement continue to put pressure on the racist rulers of our country. Every effort to isolate South Africa adds strength to our struggle."[501]

The same point was made by Dr. Nthato Motlana, a well-known African leader and Chairman of the Committee of Ten of Soweto, who said at a public meeting in October 1979: "The few concessions [made by the South African Government] were the result of external pressure as well as pressure from local blacks working outside the system."[502] However, the growing internal opposition seems to be of immediate and greater concern to the Government of South Africa. The most troublesome opposition, of course, is the growing armed struggle and radical opposition by blacks.

Armed Struggle and Radical Opposition

After the South African Government banned the two liberation movements, ANC and PAC, in 1960, and adopted more repressive legislation directed at freedom of the press and expression, all avenues of peaceful change in South Africa were virtually closed. As a result, the liberation movements went underground and decided to resort to armed struggle. Since then, and particularly after the Soweto incidents of 1976, there has been a gradual intensification of the armed struggle against apartheid. The then Minister of Justice, James T. Kruger, was reported to have said on 8 December 1976 that "an explosion in a crowded Johannesburg restaurant might have signalled the beginning of urban guerrilla warfare by anti-government militants."[503] From 1977 to 1979, police and cabinet ministers warned of an increase in the "terror" campaign against South Africa, saying that the campaign had reached the stage where well-armed gangs equipped with sophisticated weapons had tried to reach South Africa's urban areas.[504]

In November 1979, Col. J. C. Prinsloo, senior staff officer at Civil Defence Headquarters, was reported to have said that more effective action by "terrorists" could be expected in the foreseeable future. He also said that although PAC had declined as an organization it remained a potential threat and should not be taken lightly. He added that the ANC had regional headquarters in Gaborone and Botswana, four more in Maputo, and an escape and infiltration route through Lesotho.[505]

According to news reports, about 8,000 South African refugees are now being trained in camps in Angola, Botswana, and Swaziland. Many are said to be Soweto students who fled the country after the uprising in June 1976.[506] Since the Soweto incidents of 1976, political trials have changed significantly. The captured freedom fighters, whom the Government calls terrorists, have been attacking police stations, carrying guns illegally and training for guerrilla activities.[507] Previously, political trials usually involved distribution of political leaflets and incitement to racial hatred. In January 1980, a bank was placed under siege by ANC's military men in Silverton in broad daylight.[508] On 1 June 1980, ANC's men set two of the SASOL (petroleum from coal) plants ablaze causing an estimated $8 million damage.[509]

From June 1976 to July 1979, about 44,300 people were convicted of charges of riotous assembly, public violence, sabotage, inciting or promoting unrest, arson, and malicious damage to property. At least 965 people were detained in 1980. In the same year, there were 31 political trials held under security laws, most of them under the Terrorism Act. Most of the accused were between 18 and 25 years of age. Over 1,400 people have been banned or banished since 1961. As of June 1981, there were 161 people banned and 152 detained under security laws, without trial. In April 1979, Solomon Mahlangu was hanged because of guerrilla activities. In November 1979, James Mange, another freedom fighter, was given the death sentence, which was later converted to life imprisonment. In November 1980, three other freedom fighters were sentenced to death. At the time of this writing they were awaiting appeal. In August 1981, three more freedom fighters were sentenced to death. In recent years, many freedom fighters have been given long prison terms in South Africa.

In addition to the growing armed struggle in South Africa, there have been country-wide strikes and school-boycotts. Blacks in South Africa have become conscious of their inferior status and, therefore, restive. School-boycotts and strikes from April to June 1980 have given cause to the police to shoot and kill scores of blacks in just one weekend.[510]

Some whites have also taken part in the radical opposition to apartheid. The most recent example is that of Renfrew Christie who was sentenced in June 1980 to ten years' jail term for having conspired to gather information on the strategic material of energy in South Africa and having attempted to pass the information on to the ANC with the intent to endanger the maintenance of "law and order."[511] The term "law and order" is asserted frequently in political trials in South Africa. Yet, "law and order" in South Africa does not reflect a moral consensus. It does not reflect the common denominator of the moral values of society as four fifths of the population cannot participate in the law-making process. In South Africa, there is no linkage between law and moral consensus through the public opinion. As there is no law in its proper sense in that country, it is not law but dictate that endeavors to keep the imposed order. Out of desperation, the South African Government confuses the law, which is the means, with order, which is the objective.

Moderate Opposition

Moderate opposition in South Africa generally comes from those Africans, Coloreds, and Asians who work within the system, as well as from some whites. Many blacks agree that they are born into the system and work in it, but they have strong disagreements as to what constitutes collaboration with the Government. Chief Gatsha Buthelezi, for example, who is the KwaZulu leader and heads the Inkatha (cultural) movement, is in favor of peaceful change and against the use of violence. He favors a unitary state. He has not accepted independence for KwaZulu but, as the Chief minister of KwaZulu, he believes that he is using his position to thwart the "Balkanization" of South Africa into mini-states, subvert apartheid, and advance black emancipation. On the other hand, Dr. Ntatho Motlana, chairman of the Committee of Ten of Soweto, regards acceptance of the homelands policy as collaboration.[512]

With regard to moderate opposition from among the Coloreds, the Labor Party of the Colored Persons' Representative Council was a moderate opponent of apartheid. It was the majority party in that Council. It was a co-founder, together with the Inkatha movement of Chief Buthelezi, of the South African Black Alliance. The Labor Party was against violent change, and demanded "one-man, one vote" solution to the constitutional problem. It opposed Coloreds' participation in the Defence Force, and refused to take part in celebrations commemorating the establishment of the Republic. It also declined to give its views to the Schlebusch Commission (all-white) investigating constitutional change, because it wanted to deal directly with the Prime Minister.[513] In April 1980, the Colored Representative Council was abolished because of disagreements between the Government and the Colored Labor Party, the dominant party in that Council.[514] The Council had been composed of twelve elected and fifteen nominated members.

The Asians are mainly people of Indian origin. Like the Coloreds, the great majority of Indians are against apartheid and do not seem to be willing to consent to any constitutional changes that would be unacceptable to the Africans. The Reform Party of the South African Indian Council (SAIC) is a member of the Black Alliance, as is the Colored Labor Party. As reported by a South African newspaper, both parties support universal franchise in a unitary state and a national convention to decide on an agreed constitution. As a member of the Black Alliance, the Reform Party is trying to effect change in South Africa from within the system.[515]

Both the Indian and the Colored youths, however, have a more radical position with regard to change. Reportedly, they identify more closely with the black consciousness movement and with Africans who reject negotiation with the Government unless the elimination of apartheid is the item on the agenda. In any case, many Coloreds and Indians are aware that since they themselves are discriminated against, they are duty-bound to support the Africans. Many also realize that majority rule is inevitable, and they do not wish to be on the losing side.[516]

The whites in South Africa consist of the Afrikaners, who have been in power since 1948, and the English-speaking people. The apartheid policy is the creation of the Afrikaners, particularly the ruling National Party and it is they who have the greatest resistance to change. The Nationalists are composed of two factions, namely the "verkramptes" (hardliners, right wing) and the "verligtes" (enlightened, moderate). The Verkramptes do not want to make any concessions to blacks because, they say, there will then be no end to concessions. The Verligtes, who are outnumbered in the party caucus, would like to make some concessions but they are not prepared to grant full equality. They would like to be able to re-enter the community of nations.[517]

After Prime Minister Botha took office, he indicated his intention to effect some reforms by declaring that whites would have to "adapt or die."[518] But he soon had to confront the leader of the Party's right wing, Dr. Andries Treurnicht. Dr. Treurnicht, who is known also as "Dr. No," forced Prime Minister Botha to say that his much-publicized twelve-point plan was no more than "a reaffirmation of the basic principles of the National Party."[519] Nevertheless, one American political scientist has said that "Botha's reformism, totally unexpected of the former Defense Minister with a reputation as a hardliner, seemed calculated both to defuse the continuing potential for major black unrest inside South Africa and to improve the country's badly tarnished image abroad so that it might regain acceptance in the West as an ally."[520]

As against the Nationalists, the Progressive Federal Party, official opposition, advocates a policy of power sharing with the blacks through negotiation and agreement through a national convention. It is not, however, prepared to accept unqualified majority rule. It advocates full citizenship rights to all South Africans, including the right of all citizens to participate in the government. It stands for universal franchise and a federal system, with constitutional safeguards—that is, a veto—on certain minority rights in the federal parliament. The New Republic Party, Afrikaner opposition party in Parliament, is in favor of four separate racial political units representing each race group. Each unit would have its own constitutional body with jurisdiction over its own domestic affairs. It proposes a federation between these four units, in a federal council with jurisdiction over matters of common interest. It further proposes a confederation between the four-unit federation and the three independent and seven non-independent homelands.[521]

All Afrikaner parties still stick to the main elements of the policy of "grand apartheid" and maintain that the whites must decide themselves on the political dispensation. As of February 1981, the National Party occupied 132 seats in the House, as against 18 for the Progressive Federal Party, 8 for the New Republic Party, and 1 independent. In the elections held in April 1981, the PFP raised its seats from 18 to 26. Although the ultra-conservative HNP did not win a seat, its share of the poll increased more than threefold over the previous election. NP won 131 of the elected seats, which was 3 seats short of the 1977 elections. There are also 12 seats which are filled by nomination and through election by members of the House.

Recently, some Afrikaners, mostly journalists and academics, have begun speaking out against apartheid. As reported by a *New York Times* columnist, a group of influential Afrikaner journalists in Johannesburg said in December 1978 that it was vital that a visible and irreversible process of change should be underway within two or three years if blacks were to be expected to believe that peaceful change was possible.[522] On 13 January 1980, Willem de Klerk, editor of *Die Transvaler*, reportedly became the first Afrikaner Nationalist to call publicly for a revision of laws enforcing race separation. He warned whites against drawing up proposals unilaterally and trying to impose them on blacks.[523]

Willie Esterhuyse, an eminent academic of the Stellenbosch University (Afrikaner), was reported by a South African journalist to have concluded in his new book, *Farewell to Apartheid*, "that apartheid has become the greatest threat to the survival of the Afrikaner in South Africa." "Apart from claiming that race discrimination will have to go if the Afrikaner hopes to survive," it was reported, "Esterhuyse asks whether the Afrikaner has a moral right to survive if he can only do so through discrimination." The report cited other Afrikaners who have questioned the policy of apartheid. It referred to Erica Theron, a leading academic, who questioned the necessity of the Group Areas Act; Floors van Jaarsveld, an eminent historian, who has attacked apartheid as an invalid ideology; Hennie Coetzee, editor of the Calvinist monthly *Woord en Daad*, who has called for the repeal of section 16 of the Immorality Act; Marinus Wiechers, a prominent constitutional lawyer, who has called for the revision of the political system culminating in national convention; Justice Victor Hiemstra, a pillar of the Afrikaner intellectual establishment, who has called for a system of power sharing; and the Afrikaanse Studente Bond which has recognized the permanence of blacks in white areas and said that apartheid cannot provide a complete solution to the country's problems.[524]

Another South African reporter has said that, as a result of the defeat of Bishop Abel Muzorewa at the polls in Zimbabwe, the Afrikaner newspaper *Die Vaderland* called for consultation in South Africa with "real leaders."[525] This meant consultation for an agreed solution, not the imposition of solutions decided unilaterally. It also meant consultation with real black leaders such as Nelson Mandela, Govan Mbeke, and other leaders serving life sentences in prison, as well as with leaders such as Gatsha Buthelezi, Dr. Nthato Motlana, and Bishop Desmond Tutu.

Professor van Jaarsveld, already mentioned, was reported to have said in forceful terms that the Afrikaners were confronted with the choice of substantial constitutional reforms or war. In the long run, he said, Afrikaners would be forced to share power with other races for the sake of survival.[526]

Among the whites, English-speaking people have generally shown some opposition to apartheid, or at least to the most repressive and repugnant aspects and policies of apartheid. Alan Paton, whose novel *Cry, the Beloved Country* has won world-wide acclaim, has said that "if people intended staying here the only hope was to hasten efforts to achieve a just order of society in which every child of all races had security and a future."[527] He is reported also to have said that the fall from power of Marcelo Caetano of Portugal in April 1974 and the Soweto incidents of June 1976 were turning points in the 1970s for South Africa. These events, he said, sent the message to white South Africa that the age of domination was over and to black South Africa that the age of freedom had begun.[528]

Also from among the whites, a voice of opposition to apartheid has recently been heard from a small but influential community. Apparently for the first time, South Africa's Jewish Community spoke out at the end of May 1980 on the fundamental problems of South Africa. In a resolution unanimously adopted by the congress of the South African Jewish Board of Deputies, the community welcomed recent reforms, but expressed its belief that unless more meaningful and more significant changes in the social, economic, and political structure of South Africa were initiated, the ever-mounting external and internal pressures might well erupt into violence and bloodshed.[529] That community ought to know well the consequences of racial discrimination.

Since the mid-1970s, the South African Government has begun feeling the squeeze on several fronts. First, there was the liberation of Angola and Mozambique. Those events could not but influence the black population of South Africa and encourage their own aspirations. Second, in the wake of those "winds of change," came the Soweto atrocities with considerable bloodshed, making world opinion aware of the inherent danger of civil war. Third, South Afica entered into a stage of isolation by being expelled from a number of international organizations, and by being confronted with the threat of mandatory and comprehensive sanctions by the United Nations, partially imposed in 1977. Fourth, the Western members of the Security

Council began to recognize the untenability of the policy of apartheid, with its inherent dangers of violence and bloodshed, and to reassess their own interests in Africa.[530] Fifth, in view of its human rights policies, the Carter administration in the United States was obligated to exert some pressure on South Africa.

While the goals desired by the United Nations and the international community have not been achieved in South Africa, there have been some changes which are important for what they portend. Their importance emanates from the fact that a growing section of the white population of South Africa, including the Afrikaners, are becoming increasingly aware of the necessity for, and even the inevitability of, change. One writer reported that in South Africa "privately, moderate ministers speak of a federal solution, similar to that advocated by the parliamentary opposition [PFP] under which the 8.7 million blacks living outside the tribal homelands would be drawn into regional and national governments with whites, Asians and Coloreds," but that "it could take as long as 20 years to convert Afrikaner voters from their commitment to white supremacy."[531] Fundamental change in South Africa then is a matter of time.

Prospects for Internal Peaceful Change

It has been seen that any reforms made so far, as well as those proposed, do not substantively affect the structure of white power, and have not eliminated or even weakened apartheid. The pace towards change is extremely slow. The opposition within the ruling National Party is too strong to permit any meaningful change in the near future. Unless the Afrikaners are confronted with greater internal and external pressure, they do not seem interested in eliminating apartheid. Their powers and privileges, as well as their historical and cultural perceptions, have been shaped too strongly for any such meaningful change. As one South African newspaper has pointed out, "tragically, we cannot anticipate any fundamental change in the immediate future. There is still only tentative recognition among only some Nationalists of the need to face up to reality."[532]

On the other hand, it has been noted that both external and internal pressures on South Africa have been growing. Therefore, the Government of South Africa has increasingly felt the need to get the support of a segment of the black population in order to maintain its monopoly of power. It is trying to enlist the black moderates in a new system which will give the blacks living in "white" areas a semblance of power sharing in the decision-making process at the national level. It is also trying to draw the blacks of the "white" areas into the economic system, thereby creating a black middle class with a stake in the system. A South African journalist has remarked that "a growing ground-swell inside the National Party is moving toward a climate of joint decision-making with South Africa's blacks."[533]

In the election campaign in 1977, as reported in the *New York Times*, Prime Minister Vorster vowed that his party (Nationalists) would never share political power with Africans.[534] In the meantime, he himself, however, fell from political power because of the Department of Information scandal, and the new Prime Minister made some changes. Nevertheless, Afrikaner unity, both within and outside the National Party, seems to be the foremost requirement among Afrikaners, a requirement that makes fundamental change almost impossible. The reason Prime Minister Botha failed to keep up to his promises of reform has apparently been this requirement of unity. To cause a split in the Party is the last thing that any Afrikaner politician would want to do.

But, in drawing an analogy to the situations in Zimbabwe and Namibia, a journalist of the *Rand Daily Mail* suggested that "the assumption of a likely split in the ruling group in a crunch situation in South Africa does not seem far-fetched" and that "ruling groups, composed of divergent interests, will split over the strategies and tactics best suited to preserve their position."[535] Two seasoned observers of the scene believe that, faced with an escalating cost crisis, the South African régime has no strategies to follow other than abdication, coercion, and co-optation. They predict that the South African régime will most likely follow "the simultaneous strategy of co-optation by manipulation and, above all, fragmenting the challenge."[536]

Militarily, South Africa is very strong, and faces no threat from its neighbours in the foreseeable future. In the last ten years, South Africa's defence budget has gone up perhaps ten times. Also, South Africa's military contingents have reportedly encircled black townships, keeping them under control. Yet, even Prime Minister Vorster, who had initiated some minor changes, spoke of "ghastly alternative" for South Africa, in comparison later to Prime Minister Botha's "total strategy."[537] P. W. Botha's "total strategy" is designed to confront the "total onslaught" against South Africa. That onslaught is perceived in the form of attacks against South Africa from both inside and outside including communist agitation against South Africa. Prime Minister Botha's proposal for setting up a "constellation of southern African States" is designed as part of the "total strategy."

Despite South Africa's military strength, both internal and external pressure on the Government of South Africa is increasing. Internal pressure is growing in the form of armed guerrilla struggle, while external pressure is growing towards the adoption by the United Nations and the international community of stronger action against South Africa. Governments and organizations have been increasing their pressure on South Africa, both unilaterally and multilaterally.

In June 1980, the Dutch Parliament decided in favor of a unilateral oil embargo on South Africa. That same month, the United Nations Environment Programme Governing Council voted to cease all co-operation with

South Africa because the policy of apartheid violated the right to a wholesome and peaceful life and an environment unfettered by inhuman restrictions. At the same time, the Norwegian Government refused to grant a visa to the South African Minister of Interior and Justice, Alwyn Schlebusch, to visit Norway. Again in June 1980, the International Labor Conference endorsed the report of its Committee on Apartheid which proposes important recommendations and practical action by Governments, employers and workers, and by ILO in the struggle against apartheid.[538]

On 20 June 1980, the European Parliament stated that it deplored the continued imprisonment of Nelson Mandela and other leaders of the African people, called for their release, and condemned the persistent refusal of the South African Government to extend the most elementary political and human rights to all the people of South Africa. In September 1981, the World Council of Churches announced that it was breaking off links with two Swiss banks and one in the Federal Republic of Germany because of their loans to South Africa. At the same time, the Council announced grants to ANC, PAC, SWAPO and the South African Congress of Trade Unions.

There is no question that major change in South Africa is inevitable. No order that has been universally condemned for so long and that creates so much internal opposition can survive much longer. The question becomes then, what kind of change and when? The South African Government does not seem prepared to effect the fundamental change which will be acceptable to blacks, with full racial equality and power sharing in the political system. It may choose to follow the path of Zimbabwe where a seven-year war has left thousands dead and crippled. Thousands of war invalids can be seen on the streets in Zimbabwe today. Of course, that kind of change in South Africa will not be a peaceful change.

At what point pressure will force the South African Government to negotiate with black representatives cannot be foreseen. In 1978, there were black leaders in South Africa who believed that common sense among the whites might ultimately prevail, and that whites and blacks could find a political accommodation without the horrible violence that many had foreseen. Dr. Nthato Motlana, an influential African leader, was reported to have predicted that "external pressures, including an economic squeeze, eventually would bring to power 'an Afrikaner de Gaulle' who will lead a reluctant white community into granting full political rights to blacks."[539] He was said to have based his evaluation on the conviction that people would prefer to share the rich land rather than die.

Former Prime Minister Vorster was reported in 1977 to have said that he did not "foresee a racial war in South Africa now or in the future."[540] Certainly, he is in the minority in his opinion with regard to the prospects of a racial war. In December 1979, Helen Suzman, veteran Member of Parliament of the Progressive Federal Party, predicted civil disobedience in the 1980s because of "ridiculous" South African laws.[541] Also, in an interview in London, Donald Woods was reported to have said that, unless the Government revised its racial policies, "there will be a bloody civil war in which young South African blacks would have the support of Communist countries."[542] One may go on listing such predictions. Many resolutions of the United Nations and statements made at the world Organization on the subject of apartheid have asserted the same point of view as did Donald Woods. That there is reaction where there is pressure is a law of nature as well as common sense.

Despite all its repressive legislation, restrictions on the freedom of the press, and military capability, the South African Government is apparently going to be confronted with the increased determination of its black people to change the racialized legal order. More significantly, the black population is expected to double in twenty years. Thus, by the end of the century, that population will increase from about twenty-two million to about forty-four million. One may speculate that the white-power structure in South Africa is destined to collapse within ten or fifteen years. One would also hope that the whites will be sensible enough to negotiate an agreed solution as soon as possible. Delay, protracted armed struggle, and bloodshed, with concomitant racial hatred, will only make things worse for the future of everyone, including the whites, in South Africa.

Unless wisdom prevails on the part of the Afrikaners, which does not appear likely now, it seems that fundamental change in South Africa will come mainly through internal armed struggle. It is only the unity of purpose, strong determination, and spirit of sacrifice of the black people which will bring about the change of the racialized legal order in South Africa. As has been aptly said by a student of international relations, "change in South Africa will be primarily an internal matter" and "the onus of change is on black and white South Africans, and the onus of pressure is on the West."[543]

Pressures from the United Nations and the international community, which have been limited, are helpful, but marginal. Such pressures have provided great moral support to those opposing apartheid and have isolated South Africa, but, ultimately, the problem will be settled according to the power relationships within the country. Should the United Nations impose comprehensive and mandatory sanctions on South Africa, it might induce that Government to hasten the process of change.

VII. CONCLUSIONS

Beginning in 1946, and growing more intensive particularly after 1948 when apartheid became the official policy of the Government of South Africa, the United Nations membership has regarded South Africa's statutory racial discrimination as a violation of the human rights standards of the United Nations Charter, the Universal Declaration of Human Rights and other international human rights instruments. It has not accepted the arguments of the Government of South Africa that racial segregation is necessitated by the structure of the South African society, that segregation does not entail discrimination against the fundamental human rights of the black population, and that racial segregation will lead to separate development. The United Nations and the international community have adopted increasingly strong standards against racial segregation and discrimination.

Persistent calls by the United Nations to the South African Government over three decades to revise its policies, as well as the advisory opinions of the International Court of Justice and the work of the International Law Commission, have made it clear beyond dispute that South Africa has violated the human rights standards of the international Organization. South Africa's racial legislation and its persistent defiance of the United Nations calls have also violated the "good faith" Article of the Charter (Article 2, paragraph 2). The great number of United Nations resolutions on South Africa's racial situation, adopted over thirty-five years, is a very good indication of the international community's evaluation of that situation.

The United Nations first aimed at achieving racial equality and then self-determination and majority rule in South Africa. Both the General Assembly and the Security Council have sought these objectives, although the Council has followed the Assembly with some delay and hesitation. In its pursuit of self-determination and majority rule in South Africa, the United Nations appears to have been inconsistent in its goals in view of other decolonization processes or cases of majority-minority conflicts where it has not supported the right of self-determination or majority rule. By adding the right of self-determination and majority rule to its pursuit of racial equality in the case of South Africa, the United Nations has somewhat shifted from its earlier position on the need to change the legal order. It has put emphasis on the need to change the political order and the political system, which in any case would have changed if racial equality had been achieved.

Both the Assembly and the Council have branded the South African Government as racist. Both organs have recognized the legitimacy of the struggle of the black people of South Africa, but the Council to date has stopped short of mentioning the armed struggle. The Council has characterized apartheid as a crime against the conscience and dignity of mankind, but not as a crime against humanity as the Assembly has. While both organs have considered the matter mainly a human rights issue, each has increasingly seen in the situation a threat to international peace. Again, the Council followed the Assembly with some reluctance insofar as the threat to peace was concerned. Despite the Assembly's legitimization of the armed struggle, both organs have urged peaceful change in South Africa and have resorted to such peaceful means as recommendations, appeals, consultations, demands, deplorations, condemnations, and voluntary and mandatory sanctions. Indeed, the Assembly has recommended sanctions as one of the essential means for achieving a peaceful solution. The United Nations has used the Secretary-General, the Good Offices Commission, the Committee on Racial Situation, a Group of Experts, a Committee of Experts, and a Security Council committee on the implementation of the arms embargo as executive bodies.

The Assembly did not adopt South Africa's 1946 motion to refer the domestic jurisdiction issue to the International Court of Justice for resolution. Instead, it has referred the issue to political bodies, and ultimately considered it in plenary meetings. Especially since 1961, with the influx of new members from the third world, the Assembly's efforts against apartheid have intensified. It has aimed at making world public opinion aware of the nature and implications of apartheid by disseminating information. It has pressured South Africa's Western friends which, in turn, pressured South Africa. As a unique case in United Nations history, it has suspended South Africa from participation in its work, has caused South Africa's withdrawal or expulsion from a number of specialized agencies and sports organizations, and has greatly isolated South Africa within and outside the United Nations system. It has also activated many non-governmental organizations and other groups against apartheid.

The United Nations has, apparently, attached more attention to racial discrimination than to discrimination on the other grounds set out in the Charter. It has seen a threat to international peace in human rights violations, particularly in South Africa's racial situation. The Charter, the Universal Declaration, and a number of human rights instruments, drawn up by the international organization, have recognized the link between the observance of human rights and the maintenance of international peace. The Organization has considered the matter increasingly on the double track of human rights violations and threat to international peace.

As early as 1946, when it first considered the matter, the United Nations regarded South Africa's racialized legal order as impairing "friendly relations" between states. Encouraging friendly relations is a task entrusted to the Assembly under Article 14, although its resolutions are only recommendatory. The maintenance of international peace and security is a task entrusted primarily, not exclusively, to the Security Council. Since the early 1960s, both the Assembly and the Council have increasingly seen a threat to international peace in the racial situation of South Africa. The Council first considered the matter in 1960, fourteen years after the Assembly. The Council's consideration of a matter implies the possible existence of a dispute or situation, the continuance of which is likely to endanger the maintenance of international peace and security.

For some time, certain members of the United Nations objected to consideration of the matter by the Organization because of the domestic jurisdiction clause, although there has always been a consensus regarding South Africa's violation of the Charter provisions on human rights. Those same members, who were South Africa's closest economic partners, objected to the adoption of any measures against South Africa, again because of the domestic jurisdiction clause. Eventually, those members also came to criticize South Africa's racial policies strongly enough to drop their objections against the adoption of partial mandatory measures, a fact which does not lend much credibility to their earlier arguments on domestic jurisdiction.

From material presented herein, it is obvious that the Charter provisions on human rights vis-à-vis the domestic jurisdiction clause are ambiguous. Nevertheless, if the spirit, the principles, the purposes, the good faith Article (Article 2), and the human rights provisions of the Charter are taken into account, together with the San Francisco understanding about grievously outraged human rights, the domestic jurisdiction defense becomes only nominally significant. South Africa's argument that it had not violated any fundamental rights within the terms of the Charter was tantamount to saying that unless it was established that South Africa violated the fundamental rights of the black population the matter would be one of domestic jurisdiction and the United Nations would have no legitimate concern about it. This position conveniently ignored the fact that the United Nations did, indeed, consider from the very beginning that South Africa had violated fundamental human rights.

Although both the Assembly and the Council have considered South Africa's racial legislation a violation of the Charter, the resolutions of the two organs have not been parallel or synchronized. From the very first, the Assembly has given a dynamic interpretation to the domestic jursidiction clause. The Council, on the other hand, was reluctant to take any meaningful action until November 1977, allegedly because of that clause.

The Assembly repeatedly urged the Council to adopt mandatory sanctions against South Africa. It also asked the Council to consider the expulsion of South Africa from United Nations membership, but without result. Only the Council can impose mandatory sanctions, and, under Article 6, only upon the recommendation of the Council can the Assembly expel a Member State which has persistently violated Charter principles. When verbal denunciation proved insufficient to eliminate apartheid, the Assembly by 1962 began linking South Africa's racial situation with international peace. By 1965, it began urging the Council to adopt mandatory sanctions against South Africa. By the late 1960s the Assembly began recognizing the legitimacy of the struggle of the opponents of apartheid in South Africa, while at the same time continuing to pressure the Council to take more effective action. By 1962, when the Assembly began to intensify its action against apartheid, United Nations membership had considerably increased, mostly with members from the third world.

In adopting the mandatory arms embargo, on 4 November 1977, the Council followed a course of action long recommended by the Assembly. It has not, however, followed the Assembly's repeated recommendations to impose on South Africa mandatory and comprehensive sanctions, including an economic embargo, because of the objections and the veto power of the three Western permanent members, namely, France, the United Kingdom, and the United States. Those Member States had long held that, in the absence of a threat to international peace, the Council was not competent to deal with the matter, while admitting that South Africa's racial legislation violated the Charter. Persistent violation of the Charter, regrettably, was not regarded by those states as justifying effective action against South Africa to compel it to comply with its obligations under the Charter. Nevertheless, with the adoption of the mandatory arms embargo against South Africa, the United Nations has greatly eroded the domestic jurisdiction clause, or has established concurrent jurisdiction with Member States, in cases of persistent and gross racial discrimination such as apartheid.

A mandatory arms embargo was imposed on South Africa because of the inherent injustices of the unique system of apartheid along with a determination reached by the Security Council that the purchase of arms by South Africa constituted a "threat to international peace." The Western permanent members of the Council had all along contended that apartheid, as a matter of human rights, was a matter within domestic jurisdiction. The Council debates during the adoption of the embargo made it clear that the reasoning for, and the objectives of, the embargo were mainly humanitarian; but a threat to international peace had to be determined by the Council so that it might take mandatory measures.

The Council's position has been different from that of the Assembly. Not only did it begin to consider the matter much later than the Assembly, but there were also long intervals during which it did not discuss or consider the matter at all. It usually followed the Assembly and hesitated in taking action against South Africa. The requirement for great power unanimity in the Council has been an obstacle to dealing with South Africa effectively. As evidenced from the position of the Western permanent members of the Council, principles were compelled to yield to economic interests. It was not the vital interests of those permanent members which constituted an obstacle to more effective action, but mainly their economic interests. Security Council action in the matter was brought about by conflicting interests and power configurations rather than by adherence to principles. Under Article 24, in discharging its duties, the Council is required to act in accordance with the Purposes and Principles of the United Nations. Even if it is granted that power and responsibility should go hand in hand and that, therefore, the veto power enjoyed by the permanent members of the Council is essential, it would be extremely difficult to justify the ineffective action taken by the Council and to maintain that the Council has carried out its responsibilities properly in the case of South Africa, unless one believes that the Council has no say in human rights matters, no matter how grave human rights violations.

Obviously, had the Assembly had the authority to take mandatory measures against South Africa, all things being equal, it would have done so long ago. The Assembly has been adamant in urging the Council to take effective action against South Africa. It can, therefore, be said that the United Nations action against South Africa has been shaped within the legal limitations of the domestic jurisdiction clause and the unequal distribution of powers between the two of the principal organs as well as under political considerations relating to the national interests of certain permanent members of the Council. While the Assembly appears to have viewed the situation in South Africa as persistent aggression, the Council seems to have dealt with the matter with gradualism and to have been less dynamic.

Western permanent members of the Council have argued against mandatory sanctions on the grounds of domestic jurisdiction; they have maintained that economic sanctions would not be effective against South Africa and that such action would hurt the black people of that country most. In the case of South Africa, the domestic jurisdiction argument is not valid any more, after the imposition of the arms embargo in 1977; the other arguments are highly questionable. Most black leaders have said that the black people are willing to make that sacrifice to live in dignity eventually. With regard to the effectiveness of sanctions, the position that sanctions are not effective is debatable. Such an assertion does not take into account the psychological effect of mandatory sanctions, and the isolation that it brings to the country concerned.

Evidently, when South Africa felt pressure it made some moves towards change, even though the changes have been minor. So long as the United Nations action consisted of mere recommendations, appeals, requests, condemnations, and similar verbal action, South Africa did not feel the necessity to change its racial policies. But, when it felt the pressure in the field of sports, when it was suspended from participating in the Assembly's work, when its expulsion from United Nations membership was being discussed in the Council, and when the mandatory arms embargo was imposed, it began making some minor changes and trying to convince the world that racial discrimination in South Africa was being eliminated.

Obviously, South Africa cares about world opinion and especially about the positions of its Western friends, but so long as its position in the United Nations was protected by its friends, who were permanent members of the Council, it did not feel the need to make any move towards change and thus give up its privileges.

The South African minority Government has pursued "possession goals" to preserve what it considers valuable for the ruling minority, regardless of the cost to others. Its interests have prevailed over its obligations under the Charter, over its pledge under the "good faith" Article, and over international norms and morality. Although it has verbally defied the United Nations' repeated recommendations for over three decades, it has ultimately made some changes, under both internal and external pressures, and is in the process of making some others. It has revised its sports and labor policies and petty apartheid, and is in the process of bringing about some constitutional changes. All these changes, however, fall far short of the aspirations of the black people of South Africa and of the United Nations. All these changes are adjustments within the system of apartheid, preserving the essential pillars of apartheid and keeping the white power structure intact.

Aside from these minor changes, South Africa has resorted increasingly to propaganda, with secret funds, to convince world public opinion, and mainly its traditional Western friends of the soundness of apartheid. The South African Government has sought to buy influence through newsmedia, parliaments, organizations, and influential individuals, as has been revealed in its Department of Information scandal. As international action against South Africa has increased, so has South Africa's propaganda efforts. But, its relationship with the United Nations has been one of conflict, rather than one of co-operation, as pledged by each Member State under Article 56.

The means used by the United Nations for its objectives in South Africa have been inadequate. The white minority Government of South Africa deems the whites' interests and privileges too good to be given up just because of recommendations, appeals, condemnations, and the partial embargo that came too late and is being circumvented. The United Nations has taken only limited action against South Africa. Apart from the fact that it has not taken, and apparently cannot take, "action by air, sea or land forces," as provided under Article 42—mainly because of the non-existence of the special agreements envisaged under Article 43, if not because of the non-existence of the political will to do so—the United Nations has also failed to adopt comprehensive measures to enforce its decisions, as provided in Article 41. Nor has it expelled South Africa from membership. Nevertheless, even limited United Nations action has had some effect on the South African Government, which has also had to cope with the rising internal protests of its own black population.

Internal opposition to apartheid has shown a steady growth through demonstrations by black students against inferior education, protests and strikes by black workers against discrimination in the field of labor, pronouncements by Church leaders against apartheid, and various actions by other segments of the population. In South Africa, there is both radical opposition to apartheid and moderate opposition from those who would like to change the system from within. United Nations efforts have encouraged internal opposition to apartheid. In fact, the United Nations has long recognized the legitimacy of the struggle against apartheid. That struggle, especially as waged by the national liberation movement of South Africa, has grown to such an extent as to be recognized as the beginning of an armed struggle. The liberation of Angola, Mozambique, and Zimbabwe has strengthened the spirit of the blacks and given a message to the whites of South Africa that apartheid has to go.

Although South Africa is strong militarily, there is a growing awareness even among the Afrikaners that the internal struggle is bound to become intolerable. They have also realized that their Western friends cannot condone apartheid forever and that fundamental changes will have to be made. Prime Minister P. W. Botha's announcement, soon after he came to power, that whites should have to "adapt or die" should be seen in that light. So far, the whites have not sufficiently adapted themselves nor does it seem that they are prepared to do so soon. On the other hand, the black population is showing a determination to fight. That population, it is estimated, will double in twenty years. It seems that South Africa will follow the path of Zimbabwe and that real change in South Africa will come mainly through internal armed struggle, within perhaps ten to fifteen years, unless the whites bring about peaceful change within a few years. Apartheid, a universally condemned system, cannot be maintained forever against the will of the great majority of South Africa's population.

United Nations action has not proved effective enough to bring about peaceful change in South Africa. The limited action, which has been taken under legal limitations and political considerations, has only had marginal effect. The consideration of the matter primarily as one of human rights has proved detrimental to the pursuit of internal peaceful change because of the domestic jurisdiction clause. Emphasis was not put on the violation of the specific Charter provisions on racial non-discrimination, but rather on human rights violations in general. That kind of treatment has obscured the consistent and gross violations of human rights in South Africa and confused that situation with other human rights violations in other parts of the world. It has also necessitated the need to determine the existence of a threat to international peace before meaningful action could be taken. Nevertheless, in future cases of racial legislation in any Member State the consideration of the domestic jurisdiction clause may not prove so restrictive after the precedent established with South Africa.

The South African case is one where the United Nations has failed to mobilize all potential resources and power to bring an end to the persistent violation of the Charter by a Member State. The domestic jurisdiction clause of the Charter has been utilized by some permanent members of the Council to protect their short-term interests rather than to accede to the long-term and wider interests of the international community, while the Assembly is constitutionally unable to go beyond verbal action. Neither the principles and purposes of the Charter nor the growing interdependence among Member States have prevailed over the self-interests of a few powerful Member States.

As an international system, the United Nations is an institutionalized pattern of relations among its members. As a process of international politics, it is part of international relations. As such, it is subject to institutional and political weaknesses. Apartheid has been condemned not only by consensus within the United Nations, but also by state practice. No state, other than South Africa, practices apartheid. The reason why there has been consensus for condemnation but not for action against apartheid in the United Nations is because of both the constitutional structure of the Organization and the power relationships inside and outside the Organization.

The South African case suggests that so long as any recalcitrant Member State has significant common interests with any of the permanent members of the Security Council that member is likely to be shielded against expulsion from United Nations membership or against any strong action by the United Nations, a situation that may further erode the credibility of the Organization.

The requirement for unanimity among the permanent members of the Council has, in the case of South Africa, served to perpetuate the violation of Charter provisions on human rights in general, and the principle of racial non-discrimination in particular. Although the United Nations has so far failed to bring about meaningful peaceful change in South Africa, or to induce the South African Government to co-operate with it, the Organization's action on South Africa has not yet ended. There are still efforts to make the Security Council adopt mandatory and comprehensive sanctions against South Africa. Regardless of whether change in South Africa will ultimately be peaceful or violent, the United Nations can take pride in having contributed towards peaceful change in South Africa, mainly on the basis of its human rights standards, and despite the Organization's constitutional and political constraints.

In sum, in examining the only case where the United Nations has persistently endeavored to change the internal legal order of a Member State, one can conclude that the Organization's action against South Africa has had the following major facets:

(a) It has sought internal peaceful change by trying to alter the racialized legal order of South Africa;

(b) It has sought internal peaceful change on the basis of the Organization's human rights standards, although because of the Charter's domestic jurisdiction clause it has increasingly linked South Africa's racial situation to the question of a threat to international peace and security;

(c) It has greatly eroded the domestic jurisdiction clause with regard to any future case of persistent, gross and legalized racial discrimination, by adopting the mandatory arms embargo against South Africa;

(d) It has encouraged internal and external opposition to apartheid, and caused the South African Government to make changes in its racial legislation, albeit minor changes, as attested to by both black and white South Africans and international observers; and

(e) It has had an impact on South Africa although such impact cannot be precisely determined because of the nature of international relations that does not render possible an exact causal link owing to the innumerable variables involved.

APPENDICES

Appendix I

LIST OF GENERAL ASSEMBLY RESOLUTIONS ON THE RACIAL POLICIES OF THE GOVERNMENT OF SOUTH AFRICA

No. of resolution	Title of resolution	Date adopted	Vote
44 (I)	Treatment of Indians in the Union of South Africa	8 Dec. 1946	32-15-7
265 (III)	Treatment of People of Indian origin in the Union of South Africa	14 May 1949	47-1-10
395 (V)	-do-	2 Dec. 1950	46-3-10
511 (VI)	-do-	12 Jan. 1952	44-0-14
615 (VII)	-do-	5 Dec. 1952	41-1-15
616 A and B (VII)	The question of race conflict in South Africa resulting from the policies of apartheid of the Government of the Union of South Africa	-do-	35-1-23 (616 A) 24-1-34 (616 B)
719 (VIII)	Treatment of People of Indian origin . . .	11 Nov. 1952	42-1-17
721 (VIII)	Question of race conflict in South Africa . . .	8 Dec. 1953	38-11-11
816 (IX)	Treatment of People of Indian origin . . .	4 Nov. 1954	45-1-11
820 (IX)	Question of race conflict in South Africa . . .	14 Dec. 1954	40-10-10
917 (X)	-do-	6 Dec. 1955	41-6-8
919 (X)	Treatment of People of Indian origin . . .	14 Dec. 1955	46-0-8

171

No. of resolution	Title of resolution	Date adopted	Vote
1015 (XI)	Treatment of People of Indian origin . . .	30 Jan. 1957	42-0-12
1016 (XI)	Question of race conflict in South Africa . . .	-do-	56-5-12
1178 (XII)	-do-	26 Nov. 1957	59-6-14
1179 (XII)	Treatment of People of Indian origin . . .	-do-	64-0-15
1248 (XIII)	Question of race conflict in South Africa . . .	30 Oct. 1958	70-5-4
1302 (XIII)	Treatment of People of Indian origin . . .	10 Dec. 1958	69-0-10
1375 (XIV)	Question of race conflict in South Africa . . .	17 Nov. 1959	62-3-7
1460 (XIV)	Treatment of People of Indian origin . . .	10 Dec. 1959	66-0-12
1597 (XV)	Treatment of People of Indo-Pakistan origin in the Union of South Africa	13 Apr. 1961	78-0-2
1598 (XV)	Question of race conflict in South Africa . . .	-do-	95-1-0
1662 (XVI)	Treatment of People of Indo-Pakistan origin . . .	28 Nov. 1961	Unanimous
1663 (XVI)	The question of race conflict in South Africa . . .	-do-	97-2-1
1761 (XVII)	The policies of apartheid of the Government of the Republic of South Africa	6 Nov. 1962	67-16-23
1881 (XVIII)	-do-	11 Oct. 1963	106-1-0
1978 A and B (XVIII)	-do-	16 Dec. 1963	100-2-1 (A) 92-2-0 (B)
2054A and B (XX)	The policies of apartheid of . . .	22 Dec. 1965	87-1-5 (A) 93-1-7 (B)

No. of resolution	Title of resolution	Date adopted	Vote
2202 A and B (XXI)	The policies of apartheid of . . .	16 Dec. 1966	84-2-13 (A) 99-1-1 (B)
2307 (XXII)	-do-	13 Dec. 1967	89-2-12
2396 (XXIII)	-do-	2 Dec. 1968	85-2-14
2506 A and B (XXIV)	The policies of apartheid of the Government of South Africa	21 Nov. 1969	101-2-6 (A) 80-5-23 (B)
2624 (XXV)	-do-	13 Oct. 1970	98-2-9
2671 A, B, C, D, E, F (XXV)	-do-	8 Dec. 1970	105-2-6 (A) 111-2-1 (B) 107-2-6 (C) 106-2-7 (D) 111-2-1 (E) 91-6-16 (F)
2764 (XXVI)	-do-	9 Nov. 1971	109-2-0
2774 (XXVI)	United Nations Trust Fund for South Africa	29 Nov. 1971	110-1-1
2775 (XXVI)	The policies of apartheid of . . .		
A	—Arms Embargo	29 Nov. 1971	107-2-5
B	—Educational material on apartheid	-do-	112-1-3
C	—Programme of Work of the Special Committee on Apartheid	-do-	108-1-5
D	—Apartheid in Sports	-do-	106-2-7
E	—Establishment of Bantustans	-do-	110-2-2
F	—Situation in South Africa resulting from the policies of apartheid	-do-	86-6-22
G	—Dissemination of information on apartheid	-do-	108-2-6
H	—Trade union activities against apartheid	-do-	104-1-9
2923 (XXVII)	The policies of apartheid of . . .		
A	—Maltreatment and torture of prisoners and detainees	15 Nov. 1972	121-1-1

No. of resolution	Title of resolution	Date adopted	Vote
	B —United Nations Trust Fund for South Africa	15 Nov. 1972	122-1-1
	C —Programme of Work of the Special Committee on Apartheid	-do-	115-2-8
	D —Dissemination of information on apartheid	-do-	119-1-5
	E —Situation in South Africa resulting from the policies of apartheid	-do-	100-4-21
	F —International Conference of Trade Unions against Apartheid	13 Dec. 1972	105-2-6
3055 (XXVIII)	Political Prisoners in South Africa	26 Oct. 1973	112-1-2
3068 (XXVIII)	International Convention on the Suppression and Punishment of the Crime of Apartheid	30 Nov. 1973	91-4-26
3151 (XXVIII)	The policies of apartheid of . . .		
	A —Trade union action against Apartheid	14 Dec. 1973	107-1-12
	B —Programme of Work of the Special Committee on Apartheid	-do-	119-2-4
	C —Dissemination of Information on Apartheid	-do-	123-1-3
	D —Intensification and Co-ordination of United Nations action against Apartheid	-do-	121-2-5
	E —Action by Intergovernmental and non-governmental organizations	-do-	117-1-10
	F —United Nations Trust Fund for South Africa	-do-	125-1-1
	G —Situation in South Africa resulting from the policies of Apartheid	-do-	88-7-28
3324 (XXIX)	Policies of apartheid of . . .		
	A —United Nations Trust Fund for South Africa	16 Dec. 1974	Adopted without objection
	B —Arms Embargo against South Africa	-do-	109-1-9
	C —Release of political prisoners	-do-	118-0-2
	D —Programme of Work of the Special Committee on Apartheid	-do-	111-0-10
	E —Situation in South Africa	-do-	95-13-14

No. of resolution	Title of resolution	Date adopted	Vote
3411 (XXX)	Policies of apartheid of . . .		
	A —United Nations Trust Fund for South Africa	28 Nov. 1975	Adopted without objection
	B —Solidarity with the South African political prisoners	-do-	-do-
	C —Special responsibility of the United Nations and the international community towards the oppressed people of South Africa	-do-	97-0-9
	D —Bantustans	-do-	99-0-8
	E —Apartheid in sports	-do-	Adopted without objection
	F —Programme of Work of the Special Committee against Apartheid	-do-	103-0-7
	G —Situation in South Africa	10 Dec. 1975	101-15-16
31/6	Policies of apartheid of . . .		
	A —The so-called independent Transkei and other bantustans	26 Oct. 1976	134-0-1
	B —United Nations Trust Fund for South Africa	9 Nov. 1976	Adopted without vote*
	C —Solidarity with South African prisoners	-do-	-do-
	D —Arms embargo against South Africa	-do-	110-8- 20
	E —Relations between Israel and South Africa	-do-	91-20-28
	F —Apartheid in sports	-do-	128-0-12
	G —Programme of work of the Special Committee against Apartheid	-do-	133 0 8
	H —Economic Collaboration with South Africa	-do-	110-6-24
	I —Situation in South Africa	-do-	108 11 22
	J —Programme of Action against Apartheid	-do-	105-0-27
	K —Investments in South Africa	-do-	124-0-16
32/105	Policies of apartheid of . . .		
	A —United Nations Trust Fund for South Africa	14 Dec. 1977	Adopted without vote
	B —International Anti-Apartheid Year	-do-	141-0-0
	C —Trade Union Action against Apartheid	-do-	138-0-0

No. of resolution	Title of resolution	Date adopted	Vote
	D —Relations Between Israel and South Africa	-do-	88-19-30
	E —Political Prisoners in South Africa	-do-	Adopted without vote
	F —Military and Nuclear Collaboration with South Africa	-do-	113-7-17
	G —Economic Collaboration with South Africa	-do-	111-7-22
	H —Dissemination on Information on Apartheid	-do-	140-0-0
	I —Programme of Work of the Special Committee against Apartheid	-do-	136-0-4
	J —Assistance to the National Liberation Movement of South Africa	-do-	112-9-17
	K —Situation in South Africa	-do-	113-0-27
	L —World Conference for Action against Apartheid	-do-	140-0-0
	M —International Declaration against Apartheid in Sports	-do-	125-0-14
	N —Bantustans	-do-	140-0-0
	O —Investments in South Africa	16 Dec. 1977	120-0-5
33/183	Policies of Apartheid of . . .		
	A —United Nations Trust Fund for South Africa	24 Jan. 1979	Adopted without vote
	B —International Mobilization against Apartheid	-do-	122-4-0
	C —Tributes to the Memory of Leaders and Outstanding Personalities Who Have Made Significant Contributions to the Struggles of the Oppressed Peoples	-do-	129-0-0
	D —Relations Between Israel and South Africa	-do-	82-18-28
	E —Oil Embargo against South Africa	-do-	105-6-16
	F —Political Prisoners in South Africa	-do-	Adopted without vote
	G —Nuclear Collaboration with South Africa	-do-	96-5-23
	H —Economic Collaboration with South Africa	-do-	98-10-20
	I —Dissemination of Information on Apartheid	-do-	130-0-0
	J —Programme of Work of the Special Committee against Apartheid	-do-	124-0-4

No. of resolution	Title of resolution	Date adopted	Vote
	K —Assistance to the Oppressed People of South Africa and their National Liberation Movement	24 Jan. 1979	115-0-12
	L —Situation in South Africa	-do-	103-9-17
	M —Military Collaboration with South Africa	-do-	113-3-13
	N —Apartheid in Sports	-do-	112-0-15
	O —Investments in South Africa	-do-	117-0-10
34/93	Policies of Apartheid of . . .		
	A —Situation in South Africa	12 Dec. 1979	109-12-21
	B —United Nations Trust Fund for South Africa	-do-	Adopted without vote
	C —International Conference for Sanctions against South Africa	-do-	125-7-12
	D —Arms Embargo against South Africa	-do-	132-3-9
	E —Nuclear Collaboration with South Africa	-do-	119-4-18
	F —Oil Embargo against South Africa	-do-	124-7-13
	G —Bantustans	-do-	Adopted without vote
	H —Political Prisoners in South Africa	-do-	-do-
	I —Assistance to the Oppressed People of South Africa and their National Liberation Movement	-do-	134-3-7
	J —Dissemination of Information on Apartheid	-do-	142-0-3
	K —Women and Children under Apartheid	-do-	Adopted without vote
	L —Role of the Mass Media in International Action against Apartheid	-do-	125-0-19
	M —Role of Non-Governmental Organizations in International Action against Apartheid	-do-	Adopted without vote
	N —Apartheid in Sports	-do-	131-0-14
	O —Declaration on South Africa	-do-	Adopted without vote
	P —Relations between Israel and South Africa	-do-	102-18-22
	Q —Investments in South Africa	-do-	130-0-12
	R —Programme of Work of the Special Committee against Apartheid	17 Dec. 1979	134-0-6

No. of resolution	Title of resolution	Date adopted	Vote
35/206	Policies of apartheid . . .		
	A —Situation in South Africa	16 Dec. 1980	118-10-15
	B —Military and nuclear collaboration with South Africa	-do-	127-4-13
	C —Comprehensive sanctions against South Africa	-do-	115-10-20
	D —Oil embargo against South Africa	-do-	123-7-13
	E —Cultural, academic and other boycotts of South Africa	-do-	123-8-13
	F —Role of transnational corporations in South Africa	-do-	120-7-16
	G —International campaigns against apartheid	-do-	133-0-12
	H —Relations between Israel and South Africa	-do-	103-19-21
	I —International Conference on Sanctions against South Africa	-do-	130-6-8
	J —Assistance to the oppressed people of South Africa and their national liberation movement	-do-	137-3-5
	K —Campaign for the release of political prisoners in South Africa	-do-	Adopted without vote
	L —Dissemination of information on apartheid	-do-	Adopted without vote
	M —Apartheid in sports	-do-	131-0-15
	N —Women and children under apartheid	-do-	132-0-13
	O —Implementation of United Nations resolutions on apartheid by Governments and intergovernmental organizations	-do-	114-10-22
	P —Programme of work of the Special Committee against Apartheid	-do-	141-0-5
	Q —Investments in South Africa	-do-	137-0-9
	R —United Nations Trust Fund for South Africa	-do-	Adopted without vote

*In effect, there seems to be no difference between a resolution adopted without objection and one adopted without vote, because technically both are adopted without vote. However, to accommodate some degree of objection by any Member to some part of the resolution, sometimes the Members concerned may agree to have it adopted without a vote.

Appendix 2

LIST OF SECURITY COUNCIL RESOLUTIONS ON THE RACIAL POLICIES OF THE GOVERNMENT OF SOUTH AFRICA

No. of resolution	Date adopted	Vote
134 (1960)	1 Apr. 1960	9-0-2
181 (1963)	7 Aug. 1963	9-0-2
182 (1963)	4 Dec. 1963	Unanimous
190 (1964)	9 June 1964	7-0-4
191 (1964)	18 June 1964	8-0-3
282 (1970)	23 July 1970	12-0-3*
311 (1972)	4 Feb. 1972	14-0-1
392 (1976)	19 June 1976	By consensus**
417 (1977)	31 Oct. 1977	Unanimous
418 (1977)	4 Nov. 1977	-do-
421 (1977)	9 Dec. 1977	-do-
473 (1980)	13 June 1980	-do-

*As from 31 August 1965 the Security Council was composed of fifteen members instead of eleven which was the case until then.

**Technically, there was no voting or formal objection. A resolution adopted by this manner is, from the legal point of view, weaker than one adopted unanimously where votes are counted. This manner is useful to accommodate a Member who, for some reason, feels unable to vote for the resolution. Indeed, after the adoption of a resolution by consensus, such a Member may well argue that had that resolution been put to vote he would have abstained or expressed reservations on part of it.

NOTES

[1]The term "international community" is here used in its loose sense; it does not indicate the existence of a strict "sense of community" entailing integration and the belief, institutions, and practices strong enough to assure expectations for the peaceful solution of problems. It may be said, however, that the international community is best represented by the UN.

[2]The term "consider" is generally understood within the United Nations context to go beyond mere discussion and to imply the passing of judgment.

[3]For these developments, see UN, Office of Public Information, The *United Nations and Human Rights* (New York, 1973), pp. 40-42.

[4]The Universal Declaration is contained in General Assembly (GA) resolution 217 (III) of 10 December 1948.

[5]The policy of homelands will be explained in chapter 2.

[6]These points will be seen in detail in due course.

[7]UN, General Assembly Official Records (GAOR), Second Session, First Committee, *Summary Record*, 111th Meeting, 17 November 1947, p. 473.

[8]For the strict sense of Council action, see Article 42 of the Charter.

[9]Although mandatory and more comprehensive measures had been adopted against Zimbabwe (Southern Rhodesia), that territory was not a Member State of the UN. It may be noted that sanctions against Zimbabwe were consistently violated by South Africa.

[10]The resolutions adopted by the GA and the Council from 1946 to 1980 on the racial situation in South Africa, with the dates of adoption and the votes cast, are listed in appendices 1 and 2, respectively.

[11]In 1954, in *Brown v. Board of Education of Topeka*, 349 US 294, the U.S. Supreme Court gave up the "separate but equal" doctrine that it had upheld in 1896 in *Plessy v. Ferguson*. It did so on the ground that racial segregation was inherently unequal.

[12]More will be seen in this regard in chapter 6, UN impact on South Africa.

[13]Dora Gaitskell, "Of Human Rights, the UN and Britain," Letter to the Editor, *New York Times*, 23 December 1977, p. A28. Lady Gaitskell, who has long been the United Kingdom delegate to the Third (Social, Humanitarian, and Cultural) Committee of the UN, was replying to a letter to the editor on the subject of selectivity on human rights in the UN.

[14]Stanley Hoffman, "Carter's African Policy," *New York Times*, 13 December 1978, p. A27.

[15]Sidney Hook, "Ideologies of Violence and Social Change" in E. Berkeley Tompkins, ed., with an Introduction, *Peaceful Change in Modern Society* (Stanford, Calif.: The Hoover Institution press, Stanford University, 1971), p. 113.

[16]John Dugard, *Human Rights and the South African Legal Order* (Princeton, N.J.: Princeton University Press, 1978), p. 391.

[17]See, for example, Lincoln P. Bloomfield, *Evolution or Revolution? The United Nations and the Problem of Peaceful Territorial Change* (Cambridge: Harvard University Press, 1957), p. 119; and "The United Nations, the Status Quo, and the Process of Peaceful Change" (Ph.D. dissertation, Harvard University, 1955), p. 3. His book and Ph.D. disser-

tation contain good bibliographies on peaceful change with regard to the League of Nations and the UN.

[18]See Inis L. Claude, Jr., _Swords into Plowshares_, 3d ed., rev. (New York: Random House, 1964), p. 204.

[19]For various definitions of "peaceful change," see Bloomfield, "The United Nations, the Status Quo, and the Process of Peaceful Change," pp. 64-70.

[20]See Hans J. Morgenthau, _Politics among Nations_, 4th ed., rev. (New York: Alfred A. Knopf, 1966), pp. 418-22.

[21]Richard B. Lillich and Frank C. Newman, eds., _International Human Rights: Problems of Law and Policy_ (Boston: Little, Brown and Co., 1979), p. 126.

[22]See Bloomfield, _Evolution or Revolution_, p. 120; also see his "The United Nations, the Status Quo, and the Process of Peaceful Change," p. 256, where he clarified that he included the Spanish case among the issues of peaceful change "only with misgivings," because that case was a matter concerning efforts to alter the form of government in Spain.

[23]Article 107 of the Charter describes an ex-enemy state as one "which during the Second World War has been an enemy of any signatory to the present Charter."

[24]For details, see UN, _Everyman's United Nations_, 8th ed. (New York, 1968), p. 183; also see UN, _Repertoire of the Practice of the Security Council, 1946-51_ (New York, 1954), pp. 306-308.

[25]I. William Zartman, "The African States as a Source of Change," in Richard E. Bissell and Chester A. Crocker, eds., _South Africa into the 1980s_ (Boulder, Colorado: Westview Press, 1979), p. 128.

[26]See Egon Schwelb, _Human Rights and International Community_ (Chicago: Quadraple Books, 1964), pp. 20-21. Articles 22 and 23 of the League Covenant are relevant.

[27]_Documents of United Nations Conference on International Organization_ (Documents of UNCIO), San Francisco, 1945, 21 vols. (United Nations Information Organizations: London and New York, 1945), 3:63.

[28]Ibid., p. 602.

[29]See Louis B. Sohn and Thomas Buergenthal, _International Protection of Human Rights_ (New York: Bobbs-Merrill Co., 1973), p. 511.

[30]Karl Josef Partch, "Les principes de base des droits de l'homme: l'autodétermination, l'égalité et la non-discrimination," in Karel Vasak, gen. ed., _Les Dimensions Internationales des Droits de l'Homme_ (UNESCO, 1978), p. 64.

[31]Leland M. Goodrich, _The United Nations in a Changing World_ (New York: Columbia University Press, 1974), p. 159.

[32]See Theodoor C. Van Boven, "Aperçu du droit international positif des droits de l'homme," in Vasak, _Les Dimensions Internationales_, p. 118.

[33]For the influence of the Universal Declaration, see UN, _United Nations and Human Rights_, pp. 13-15.

[34]UN General Assembly (UNGA), 34th Session, _Provisional Verbatim Record of the Seventeenth Meeting_ (A/34/PV.17), 4 October 1979, pp. 11-15; _New York Times_, 3 October 1979, p. B4.

[35]In resolution 2372 (XXII) of 12 June 1968, the GA proclaimed that South West Africa should thenceforth be known as Namibia.

[36]See, for example, Van Boven, "Aperçu du droit international positif," in Vasak, _Les Dimensions Internationales_, p. 100.

[37]Idem, "Les critères de distinction des droits de l'homme," in Vasak, ibid., pp. 47-48.

[38]M. D. Copithorne, "The Structural Law of the International Human Welfare System," in _The International Law and Policy of Human Welfare_, eds. Ronald St. J. Macdonald, Douglas M. Johnston, and Gerald L. Morris (The Netherlands: Sijthoff and Noordhoff, 1978), p. 156.

[39]The Convention is contained in GA resolution 3068 (XXVIII) of 30 November 1973.

⁴⁰Cited in Nathaniel L. Nathanson and Egon Schwelb, *The United States and the United Nations Treaty on Racial Discrimination* (Washington, D.C.: West Publishing Co., 1975), p. 4.

⁴¹See William W. Bishop, Jr., *International Law: Cases and Materials*, 3d ed. (Boston and Toronto: Little, Brown and Co., 1971), pp. 46-48.

⁴²International Court of Justice, *Legal Consequences for States of the Continued Presence of South Africa in Namibia (South West Africa) notwithstanding Security Council Resolution 276 (1970)*, I.C.J., Advisory Opinion, Reports 1971, p. 76.

⁴³Ibid., p. 123.

⁴⁴Egon Schwelb, "Institutions principales et dérivées sur la Charte," in Vasak, *Les Dimensions Internationales*, p. 315.

⁴⁵Ibid.

⁴⁶UN, GAOR, Thirty-first Session, supp. 10 (A/31/10), *Report of International Law Commission on the Work of its Twenty-eighth Session, 3 May-23 July 1976*, p. 226.

⁴⁷Ibid., pp. 258-59; as recommended by the GA in resolution 34/141 of 17 December 1979, the Commission adopted at its thirty-second session, on first reading, the text of Part I containing article 19 [GAOR, Thirty-fifth Session, supp. 10 (A/35/10), *Report of the International Law Commission on the Work of its Thirty-second Session, 5 May-25 July 1980*].

⁴⁸I.C.J., *Legal Consequences for States*, p. 31.

⁴⁹US, Department of State, *United Nations Conference on International Organization: Selected Documents* [UNCIO: Selected Documents], Pubn. no. 2490 (Washington, D.C.: Government Printing Office, 1946), p. 478.

⁵⁰UNGA, Special Committee against Apartheid, *Verbatim Record of the 416th Meeting* (A/AC.115/PV.416), 21 March 1979, p. 7.

⁵¹UNGA, A/34/PV.17, p. 31.

⁵²Julius K. Nyerere, "America and Southern Africa," *Foreign Affairs* 55 (July 1977): 681.

⁵³*Documents of UNCIO*, vol. 8, pp. 251, 267.

⁵⁴Leland M. Goodrich, Edvard Hambro, and Anne P. Simons, *Charter of the United Nations*, 3d ed., rev. (New York and London: Columbia University Press, 1969), p. 143.

⁵⁵UN, *Report of the United Nations Commission on the Racial Situation in the Union of South Africa* (A/2505), 3 October 1953 [GAOR, Eighth Session, supp. 16], p. 16.

⁵⁶*UNCIO: Selected Documents*, p. 483; also see Sohn and Buergenthal, *International Protection of Human Rights*, p. 511, and Claude, *Swords into Plowshares*, p. 168.

⁵⁷UN, *Yearbook of the United Nations, 1946-47* (New York, 1947), p. 18; also see *UNCIO: Selected Documents*, p. 478.

⁵⁸Hersh Lauterpacht, *International Law and Human Rights* (London: Stevens and Sons, 1950), pp. 213-14.

⁵⁹Ibid., pp. 169, 180.

⁶⁰Joginder Bains Singh, "Domestic Jurisdiction and the Law of the United Nations" (Ph.D. dissertation, University of Michigan, 1953), pp. 169-70.

⁶¹Ibid., pp. 150-51.

⁶²See Minasse Haile, *Domestic Jurisdiction: United Nations Consideration of Domestic Questions and of Their International Effects* (Addis Ababa: Ethiopian Publishing Share Co., 1968), p. 17.

⁶³Ibid., pp. 56-60.

⁶⁴Moses Moskowitz, *International Concern with Human Rights* (New York: Oceana Publications, 1974), p. 54.

⁶⁵Bishop, *International Law*, p. 654.

⁶⁶Dan Ciobanu, *Preliminary Objections Related to the Jurisdiction of the United Nations Political Organs* (The Hague: Martinus Nijhoff, 1975), pp. 38-44.

⁶⁷Ibid., p. 43, fn 44.

[68]Felix Ermacora, "Human Rights and Domestic Jurisdiction," *Recueil Des Cours, 1968-II,* Hague Academy of International Law (Netherlands: Sijthoff, 1969), pp. 405-408, 436, 442-43.

[69]James Leslie Brierly, *The Law of Nations,* 6th ed., ed. by Sir Humphrey Waldock (Oxford: Oxford University Press, 1963), p. 293.

[70]This was shown by the estimates of the 1980 census. Estimates showed that over the past decade South Africa's population had increased by 5 million and that the average annual growth rates for the various ethnic groups were 2.5 percent for Africans, 1.7 percent for whites, 2.2 percent for Coloreds, and 2.4 percent for Asians (Permanent Mission of South Africa to the UN, *South African News Review,* 12 September 1980).

[71]For ease of reference, the term "black" in this study will denote the Africans, the Coloreds, and the Asians in South Africa.

[72]South African Institute of Race Relations (SAIRR), *Laws Affecting Race Relations in South Africa, 1948-1976,* comp. Muriel Horrell (Johannesburg: SAIRR, 1978), p. 10.

[73]M. K. Gandhi, *Satyagraha in South Africa,* trans. Valji Govindji Desai, rev. 2d ed. (Ahmedabad: Navajivan Publishing House, 1950), p. 33.

[74]Ibid., pp. 89-90.

[75]Quoted from President Sir. M. Zafrulla Khan's declaration in I.C.J., *Legal Consequences for States,* p. 62. The white people's objective of domination had been propounded also by Verwoerd's predecessors, J. G. Strydom and D. F. Malan.

[76]See Heribert Adam and Hermann Giliomee, *Ethnic Power Mobilized: Can South Africa Change?* (New Haven: Yale University Press, 1979), p. 17.

[77]Ibid., pp. 61, 116.

[78]See Richard E. Bissell, *Apartheid and International Organizations* (Boulder, Colorado: Westview Press, 1977), pp. 2-3.

[79]For details, see UN, Unit on Apartheid, *Notes and Documents No. 2/71,* "The Dutch Reformed Church in South Africa and the Ideology and Practice of *Apartheid,*" by J. Verkuyl, February 1971; also see *Notes and Documents No. 27/71,* "*Apartheid:* The Laboratory of Racism," by the Right Reverend C. Edward Crowther, June 1971.

[80]UNGA, 34th Session, *Provisional Verbatim Record of the Fifty-ninth Meeting* (A/34/PV.59), 12 November 1979, p. 36.

[81]UNGA, 34th Session, *Provisional Verbatim Record of the Fifty-eighth Meeting* (A/34/PV.58), 9 November 1979, pp. 46-51.

[82]UNESCO Statement on Race (1950) and its Statement on the Nature of Race and Race Differences (1951), dealing mainly with the biological and anthropological aspects of the matter, rejected the theories of race superiority. Its Statement of 1964 attributed differences in achievement to people's cultural history. It also clarified that race mixture has no detrimental biological effects on mankind, but that, to the contrary, it is beneficial by contributing to the preservation of the biological links among human groups. Its Statement of 1967 helped elucidate scientifically the genesis of racialist theories and racial prejudice. These Statements were adopted by experts in their personal capacity, not representing their governments. The Preamble to the Constitution of UNESCO, adopted on 16 November 1945, states that "the great and terrible war which has now ended was a war made possible by the denial of the democratic principles of the dignity, equality and mutual respect of men, and by the propagation, in their place, through ignorance and prejudice, of the doctrine of the inequality of men and races."

[83]See Sohn and Buergenthal, *International Protection of Human Rights,* p. 655; also see the *Report of the Commission on Racial Situation* (A/2505), p. 115.

[84]UNGA, 33rd Session, *Provisional Verbatim Record of the Thirtieth Meeting* (A/33/PV.30), 11 October 1978, p. 16.

[85]Karl W. Deutsch, *Tides Among Nations* (New York: Free Press, 1979), p. 77; for general ideas on economic theories and discrimination, see pp. 71-78.

[86]UNGA, A/34/PV.59, p. 22.

[87]Adam and Giliomee, *Ethnic Power Mobilized*, pp. 133-43.

[88]Marianne Cornevine, *Apartheid—Power and Historical Falsification* (Paris: UNESCO, 1980), p. 34.

[89]Donald G. Baker, "U.S. Perspectives on Change in Southern Africa," in *International Pressures and Political Change in South Africa*, ed. F. McA. Clifford-Vaughan (Cape Town: Oxford University Press, 1978), p. 54.

[90]For the idea and bibliography, see P. L. Moorcraft, "Towards the Garrison State," ibid., pp. 86-105.

[91]R. A. Schrire, "South Africa, the International Community, and the United States," ibid., p. 74.

[92]UN Security Council (UNSC), *Provisional Verbatim Record of the Two Thousand and Forty-fifth Meeting* (S/PV.2045), 1 November 1977, p. 8.

[93]Thomas Karis and Gwendolen M. Carter, *From Protest to Challenge: A Documentary History of African Politics in South Africa, 1882-1964*, 4 vols. (Stanford, California: Hoover Institution Press, 1972-77), vol. 3: *Challenge and Violence, 1953-1964*, by Thomas Karis and Gail M. Gerhart, pp. 712-13. Chief Luthuli was arrested and banned by the South African Government in the 1950s and 1960s.

[94]Ibid., p. 516.

[95]Ibid., p. 796.

[96]UNSC, S/PV.2045, pp. 9-10.

[97]Ibid., p. 8.

[98]For the full text of the Freedom Charter, see Karis and Carter, *From Protest to Challenge*, vol. 3, pp. 205-208.

[99]For a collection of speeches and articles by these leaders and of the documents of many black political, cultural, and educational organizations, see Hendrik W. Van der Merwe et al. eds., *African Perspectives on South Africa: A Collection of Speeches, Articles, and Documents* (Stanford, California: Hoover Institution Press, 1978).

[100]Banning these organizations has not stopped their political activities. As late as June 1979, 18 PAC members were convicted and heavily sentenced on charges of military training to overthrow the state (*Post*, Johannesburg, 28 June 1979, p. 6), and such court cases involving both ANC and PAC have been steadily increasing.

[101]Dugard, *Human Rights and the South African Legal Order*, p. 6. He compares the legal position of human rights in South Africa to the American Bill of Rights and modern human rights conventions and explains that parliamentary sovereignty (supremacy) and a primitive legal positivism have combined to produce a legal system with no constitutional safeguards for individual liberty in South Africa.

[102]More will be seen on this subject in part 3 under "Constitutional Proposals".

[103]Section 46 (c) of the Constitution (1961) provides that no person is qualified to be a member of the House of Assembly unless that person is white.

[104]Constitution, Section 108 (1).

[105]See the *Rand Daily Mail* (Johannesburg), 3 May 1980.

[106]Republic of South Africa, *House of Assembly Debates* (Hansard), Pretoria, Third Session-Sixth Parliament, 14 June 1979, no. 18, col. 8786.

[107]Dugard, *Human Rights and the South African Legal Order*, p. 4.

[108]With regard to equality, the apartheid laws are inconsistent with many of the conventions or constitutions of the UN specialized agencies. The Declaration of Philadelphia of ILO contains the fundamental principle that "all human beings irrespective of race, creed or sex have the right to pursue both their material well-being and their spiritual development in conditions of freedom and dignity, of economic security and equal opportunity." In 1961, the International Labour Conference adopted a resolution calling on South Africa to withdraw from membership until such time as it had abandoned apartheid. In June 1963, the Governing Body of ILO decided to exclude South Africa from ILO meetings. On 11 March 1966, South Africa withdrew from ILO. South Africa had similarly withdrawn from UNESCO in 1955.

In 1964, its voting privileges were suspended by the World Health Organization (WHO). The Conference of Food and Agriculture Organization (FAO) decided in 1963 to exclude South Africa from its work. The same year, South Africa gave notice of withdrawal from membership, which became effective on 18 December 1968. On 30 April 1975, the World Meteorological Congress suspended South Africa from the membership of the World Meteorological Organization until it renounced its policy of racial discrimination. In June 1977, the Board of Governors of the International Atomic Energy Agency decided not to redesignate South Africa as a member (for details of South Africa's withdrawal and expulsion from international organizations, see Bissell, *Apartheid and International Organizations*).

[109]Republic of South Africa, *House of Assembly Debates* (Hansard), Third Session-Sixth Parliament, 2 to 9 February 1979, no. 1, Questions and Replies, col. 12.

[110]Ibid., 26 February to 2 March 1979, no. 4, Questions and Replies, col. 283.

[111]Ibid., First Session-Sixth Parliament, 17 to 21 April 1978, no. 11, Questions and Replies, col. 644.

[112]Republic of South Africa, *Senate Debates* (Hansard), Fourth Session-Sixth Parliament, no. 3, 17 to 20 March 1980, Questions and Replies, col. 6.

[113]Recent changes in the labor legislation in South Africa will be seen in part 3.

[114]Patrick Laurence, "Politics is a Business of Who Gets What," *Rand Daily Mail* (Johannesburg), 20 November 1979, p. 12.

[115]SAIRR, *Race Relations in South Africa*, p. 298.

[116]*Economist* (London), 14 January 1978, p. 50.

[117]As witnessed by large-scale school boycotts by Colored students from April to July 1980.

[118]Republic of South Africa, *House of Assembly Debates* (Hansard), Third Session-Sixth Parliament, 2 to 9 February 1979, no. 1, Questions and Replies, cols. 27-28.

[119]Ibid., col. 22.

[120]See Johan Adler, Deputy Consul General of South Africa in New York, "Letter to the Editor," *New York Times*, 14 November 1977, p. 32.

[121]The author of this book participated in a meeting of the Ad Hoc Working Group of Experts on Southern Africa, Commission on Human Rights, held in London, United Kingdom, from 30 July to 3 August 1979, where victims of torture gave evidence.

[122]U.S. Congress, *Country Reports on Human Rights Practices for 1979*, Report submitted to the Committee on Foreign Affairs, U.S. House of Representatives, and Committee on Foreign Relations, U.S. Senate, by the Department of State, 4 February 1980, p. 184.

[123]See Amnesty International, *Report 1979* (London: Amnesty International Publications, 1979), pp. 32-34.

[124]"Human Rights in the World," *International Commission of Jurists Review* (Geneva), no. 20 (June 1978), p. 15.

[125]For details on this point, see Dugard, *Human Rights and the South African Legal Order*, pp. 37-49.

[126]Eugene Victor Walter, *Terror and Resistance: A Study of Political Violence* (New York: Oxford University press, 1969), p. 25.

[127]T. A. Critchley, *The Conquest of Violence: Order and Liberty in Britain* (London: Constable and Co. Ltd., 1970), p. 26.

[128]See Elizabeth S. Landis, "Denial of Human Rights in Namibia," *Objective Justice*, 8 (Spring 1976): 32-46. She examines the articles of the Universal Declaration versus law and practice in Namibia and concludes that almost all articles of the Universal Declaration have been violated by the South African Government. As the apartheid laws of Namibia are the extension of those in South Africa, the same conclusions are, a priori, applicable to South Africa itself.

[129]For details about legislative and other measures of racial discrimination in South Africa, see UN, Commission on Human Rights, *Violations of Human Rights in South Africa* (E/CN.4/1270), 31 January 1978, chap. 1; also see SAIRR, *Race Relations in South Africa*.

For a general view of South Africa's racial discrimination, see Bissell, *Apartheid and International Organizations*, pp. 1-13.

[130]The item was inscribed in the agenda in 1946 as Treatment of Indians in the Union of South Africa, in 1949 as Treatment of People of Indian Origin in the Union of South Africa, and in 1961 as Treatment of People of Indian and Indo-Pakistan Origin in the Union of South Africa.

[131]GA resolution 44 (I) of 1946.

[132]GA resolution 265 (III) of 1949. The reference to Pakistan was made to cover the people of Pakistani origin, as Pakistan was admitted to the UN membership in 1947 and participated in India's complaint.

[133]GA resolution 395 (V) of 1950.

[134]GA resolution 615 (VII) of 1952. As announced by the President of the GA on 21 December 1952, the Member States appointed to serve on the Good Offices Commission were Cuba, Syria, and Yugoslavia.

[135]UNGA, *Report of the United Nations Good Offices Commission* (A/2473), 14 September 1953, p. 3.

[136]Ibid., *A/2723*, 15 September 1954, p. 3.

[137]GA resolution 616 (VII) of 1952.

[138]The Commission would be composed of Mr. Ralph J. Bunche, Mr. Hernan Santa Cruz, and Mr. Jaime Torres Bodet. As Mr. Bunche and Mr. Bodet were unable to accept the appointment, on 30 March 1953 Mr. Dantès Bellegarde and Mr. Henri Laugier were appointed instead.

[139]M. Moskowitz has noted in *International Concern with Human Rights* (p. 52) that this declaration was nothing less than a demand for "one-man-one-vote."

[140]See Singh, "Domestic Jurisdiction and the Law of the United Nations," p. 192.

[141]See Sohn and Buergenthal, *International Protection of Human Rights*, p. 658; also see *Report of the Commission on Racial Situation*, pp. 116-17.

[142]*Report of the Commission on Racial Situation*, p. 118.

[143]UN, *Second Report of the United Nations Commission on the Racial Situation in the Union of South Africa* (A/2719), 26 August 1954 (GAOR, Ninth Session, 1954, supp. 16), pp. 87-90.

[144]UN, *Repertory of Practice of United Nations Organs*, vol. 1, supp. 1 (New York, 1958), p. 39.

[145]UN, *Third Report of the United Nations Commission on the Racial Situation in the Union of South Africa* (A/2953), 26 August 1955 (GAOR, Tenth Session, 1955, supp. 14), p. 99.

[146]See GA resolution 719 (VIII) of 1953.

[147]GA resolution 721 (VIII) of 1953. As has been seen, under Article 14 the Assembly may, subject to the provisions of Article 12, recommend measures for the "peaceful adjustment" of any situation which is likely to impair friendly relations.

[148]See GA resolutions 816 (IX) of 1954, 919 (X) of 1955, and 1015 (XI) of 1957.

[149]UN, *Repertory of Practice of United Nations Organs*, vol. 1, supp. 1, p. 31.

[150]See GA resolution 820 (IX) of 1954.

[151]UN, *Everyman's United Nations*, p. 157; for the statement made by the South African representative in September 1958, see GAOR, Thirteenth Session, *Verbatim Record*, Seven Hundred and Fifty-seventh Plenary Meeting, 24 September 1958, pp. 134-36.

[152]GA resolution 917 (X) of 1955.

[153]GA resolution 1016 (XI) of 1957.

[154]UN, *Annual Report of the Secretary-General on the Work of the Organization, 16 June 1956-15 June 1957* (A/3594), 1957 (GAOR, Twelfth Session, supp. 1), p. 57.

[155]GA resolution 1178 (XII) of 1957.

[156]GA resolutions 1179 (XII) of 1957 and 1302 (XIII) of 1958.

[157]GA resolution 1248 (XIII) of 1958.

[158]GA resolution 1375 (XIV) of 1959. According to the established practice of the UN, the term "all States" refers to States Members of the UN, members of a specialized agency and of the International Atomic Energy Agency, and parties to the Statute of the International Court of Justice.

[159]GA resolution 1460 (XIV) of 1959.

[160]GA resolutions 1597 (XV) and 1662 (XVI) of 1961.

[161]GA resolution 1598 (XV) of 13 April 1961.

[162]GA resolution 1663 (XVI) of 28 November 1961.

[163]UN, *Yearbook 1959* (New York, 1960), p. 57; for details of the statement, see GAOR, Fourteenth Session, *Verbatim Record*, Eight Hundred and Eleventh Meeting, 28 September 1959, pp. 227-33.

[164]"Negotiation" is the first means contained in Art. 33 of the Charter regarding the peaceful settlement of disputes.

[165]GA resolutions on the budget, for example, are legally binding on Member States (Art. 17 of the Charter). For the nature, scope, and legal effects of Assembly resolutions, as well as for a good bibliography on the subject, see Stephen G. Xydis, "The General Assembly," in *The United Nations: Past, Present, and Future*, ed. James Barros (New York: Free Press, 1972), pp. 89-93.

[166]The change of the name of the Union of South Africa to that of the Republic of South Africa occurred because in 1961 South Africa withdrew from the British Commonwealth and became a Republic. Because of its racial policies, South Africa had been under strong pressures from other Commonwealth members either to revise its policies or to withdraw from the Commonwealth.

[167]GA resolution 1761 (XVII) of 1962. By GA resolutions 2054 (XX) of 1965 and 2671 (XXV) of 1970, the Special Committee was enlarged. On 8 December 1970, its name was changed from the Special Committee on the Policies of Apartheid of the Government of the Republic of South Africa to that of Special Committee on Apartheid. By resolution 3324D (XXIX) of 1974, it was changed to Special Committee Against Apartheid. In resolution 34/93R of 1979, the Assembly requested its President to expand the membership of the Special Committee, in consultation with the regional groups and bearing in mind the principle of equitable geographical distribution.

[168]GA resolution 2202A (XXI) of 1966.

[169]Resolutions 1978 (XVIII) of 1963, 2054 (XX) of 1965, 2202 (XXI) of 1966, 2506 (XXIV) of 1969, and 2624 (XXV) of 1970. As will be seen, the Council had adopted sanctions (voluntary, not under Chapter VII of the Charter) against South Africa in 1963.

[170]Resolutions 2054A (XX) of 1965, 2202A (XXI) of 1966, 2307 (XXII) of 1967, 2396 (XXIII) of 1968, 2506B (XXIV) of 1969, 2671F (XXV) of 1970, 2775F (XXVI) of 1971, 2923E (XXVII) of 1972, 3151G (XXVIII) of 1973, 3324B (XXIX) of 1974, 3411G (XXX) of 1975, and 31/6D of 1976.

[171]Resolutions 1978B (XVIII) of 1963, 2506A (XXIV) of 1969, 2764 (XXVI) of 1971, 2923A (XXVII) of 1972, 3055 (XXVIII) of 1973, 3324C (XXIX) of 1974, 3411B (XXX) of 1975, 31/6C of 1976, 32/105E of 1977, 33/183F of 1979, 34/93H of 1979, and 35/206K of 1980.

[172]UNSC, *Report of the Secretary-General* (S/5457), 19 November 1963.

[173]Resolutions 1978B (XVIII) of 1963, 2054B (XX) of 1965, 2202B (XXI) of 1966, 2671E (XXV) of 1970, 2774 (XXVI) of 1971, 2923A (XXVII) of 1972, 3055 (XXVIII) of 1973, 3324C (XXIX) of 1974, 3411 (XXX) of 1975, 31/6B of 1976, 32/105A of 1977, 33/183A of 1979, 34/93B of 1979, and 35/206R of 1980. By the end of 1980, the Fund had received $11,467,202 from 86 Member States and other donors including organizations and individuals.

[174]Resolutions 2396 (XXIII) of 1968, 2506B (XXIV) of 1969, 2671F (XXV) of 1970, 2775F (XXVI) of 1971, 2923E (XXVII) of 1972, 3055 (XXVIII) of 1973, 3151G (XXVIII) of 1973, 3324C (XXIX) of 1974, 3411 (XXX) of 1975, 31/6 I of 1976, 32/105E, J and

K of 1977, 33/183K of 1979, 34/93 I of 1979, and 35/206A of 1980.

[175]UN, *Yearbook 1970*, p. 132.

[176]Ibid., p. 139.

[177]GA resolution 32/105J; in fact, there are two liberation movements in South Africa, namely, ANC and PAC. Both of them are recognized by the Organization of African Unity and the UN. In the UN terminology, especially after 1976, when the whole movement in the abstract is meant it is referred to as the national liberation movement; otherwise, they are referred to as liberation movements.

[178]UNGA, 32nd Session, *Provisional Verbatim Record of the One Hundred and Second Meeting* (A/32/Pv.102), 14 December 1977, p. 47.

[179]Ibid., p. 32.

[180]Ibid., pp. 103-105.

[181]The Declaration on South Africa is contained in GA resolution 34/93 O of 1979.

[182]GA resolution 35/206A of 1980.

[183]See, for example, GA resolutions 2775F (XXVI) of 1971 and 2923E (XXVII) of 1972.

[184]For example, GA resolutions 3151G (XXVIII) of 1973 and 31/6 I of 1976.

[185]GA resolution 33/183K of 1979.

[186]GA resolution 2054A (XX) of 1965.

[187]GA resolution 2307 (XXII) of 1967.

[188]GA resolution 2923E (XXVII) of 1972.

[189]GA resolution 3055 (XXVIII) of 1973.

[190]GA resolution 3324C (XXIX) of 1974.

[191]GA resolutions 31/6 I of 1976, 32/105K of 1977, 33/183L of 1979, 34/93A of 1979, and 35/206J of 1980.

[192]For example, GA resolutions 2054B of 1965, 2775G (XXVI) of 1971, and 2923D (XXVII) of 1972.

[193]For example, GA resolutions 2396 (XXIII) of 1968, 2775G (XXVI) of 1971, and 2923D (XXVII) of 1972.

[194]GA resolution 2775B (XXVI) of 1971.

[195]GA resolution 2671C (XXV) of 1970.

[196]GA resolution 3151E (XXVIII) of 1973.

[197]GA resolution 3151D (XXVIII) of 1973.

[198]GA resolution 3324D (XXIX) of 1974.

[199]GA resolution 3411B (XXX) of 1975.

[200]GA resolution 3411F (XXX) of 1975.

[201]GA resolution 3151C (XXVII) of 1973. The Fund became operational in January 1975. By the end of 1980, it had received $619,226 from forty-one Member States.

[202]GA resolutions 32/105H of 1977, 33/183 I of 1979 and 35/206L of 1980; for a comprehensive report on UN information activity against apartheid until 1976, see GA, *Report of the Special Committee against Apartheid* (A/31/22/Add.3; S/12150/Add.3), 26 October 1976.

[203]GA resolution 2202 (XXI) of 1966.

[204]GA resolution 2671F (XXV) of 1970.

[205]GA resolution 2923E (XXVII) of 1972.

[206]GA resolution 3151G (XXVIII) of 1973.

[207]The Convention is contained in GA resolution 3068 (XXVIII) of 1973.

[208]GA resolution 2202 (XXI) of 1966.

[209]GA resolution 2307 (XXII) of 1967.

[210]See, for example, GA resolution 31/6J of 1976.

[211]GA resolution 32/105B of 1977.

[212]GA resolutions 31/6G of 1976 and 32/105L of 1977.

[213]GA resolution 33/183B of 1979.

[214]GA resolutions 2396 (XXII) of 1968 and 2671 (XXV) of 1970.

[215]GA resolution 2775D (XXVI) of 1971.

[216]More will be seen on this issue in the chapter on the UN impact on South Africa.

[217]GA resolution 31/6F of 1976.

[218]The Declaration is contained in GA resolution 32/105M of 1977.

[219]For the draft convention and the controversial article 10, see UN, Department of Public Information, *Press Release*, GA/AP/1138, 10 September 1980; also see UN, *Report of the Ad Hoc Committee on the Drafting of an International Convention against Apartheid in Sports* [GAOR, Thirty-fifth Session, supp. 36 (A/35/36], 1980.

[220]GA resolution 2396 (XXIII) of 1968.

[221]GA resolution 2506 (XXIV) of 1969.

[222]GA resolutions 2671F (XXV) of 1970, 2775F (XXVI) of 1971, 2923E (XXVII) of 1972, 3324C (XXIX) of 1974, 3411B (XXX) of 1975, 3411G (XXX) of 1975, 31/6C of 1976, 31/6 I of 1976, 32/105J of 1977, 33/183K of 1979, 34/93A of 1979, 34/93 O of 1979, and 35/206A and G of 1980.

[223]See Partch, "Les principes de base des droits de l'homme," p. 72.

[224]A. H. Robertson, *Human Rights in the World* (Manchester: Manchester University Press, 1972), p. 33.

[225]See Moskowitz, *International Concern with Human Rights*, pp. 42-53.

[226]GA resolution 2671F (XXV) of 1970.

[227]GA resolution 2775E (XXVI) of 1971.

[228]GA resolution 3411D (XXX) of 1975.

[229]GA resolution 31/6A of 1976.

[230]GA resolutions 32/105N of 1977, 34/93G of 1979, and 35/206A of 1980.

[231]GA resolution 2775F (XXVI) of 1971.

[232]See, for example, GA resolution 2636A (XXV) of 1970.

[233]The vote on the draft resolution was 96 in favor, 16 against, and 9 abstentions.

[234]GA resolution 3411G (XXX) of 1975.

[235]GA resolution 3324E (XXIX) of 1974.

[236]GA resolution 31/6 I of 1976.

[237]For military and nuclear collaboration, see GA resolutions 32/105F of 1977, 33/183G and M of 1979, 34/93D and E of 1979 and 35/206B and H of 1980; for economic collaboration, see resolutions 31/6H of 1976, 32/105G of 1977 and 33/183H and 34/93C of 1979; for investments in South Africa, see resolutions 31/6K of 1976, 32/105 O of 1977, 33/183 O and 34/93Q of 1979 and 35/206Q of 1980; for trade union action, see resolutions 2575H (XXVI) of 1971 and 32/105C of 1977.

[238]GA resolution 33/183B of 1979.

[239]GA resolution 34/93C of 1979.

[240]GA resolutions 34/93A, D, E, F, and Q of 1979.

[241]GA resolution 35/206G of 1980.

[242]From 1962 to 1979, inclusive, UN membership increased by 48 to 152, most of them Afro-Asian countries. Even earlier, by the end of 1961, when the UN had 104 members, the original fifty-one members of the Organization were already in the minority (For UN membership, see Department of Public Information, *Press Release*, M/2257, 25 August 1980). As of 25 September 1981, the UN membership stood at 156.

[243]See Brian Crozier, *A Theory of Conflict* (London: Hamish Hamilton, 1974), pp. 10-11.

[244]GA resolution 2625 (XXV) of 1970 on the Declaration on Principles of International Law concerning Friendly Relations provides that "every State has the duty to refrain from any forcible action which deprives peoples . . . of their right to self-determination. In their actions against, and resistance to, such forcible action in pursuit of the exercise of their right to self-determination, such peoples are entitled to seek and to receive support in accordance with the purposes and principles of the Charter." GA resolution 3070 (XXVIII) of 1973

reaffirmed "the legitimacy of the peoples' struggle for liberation from colonial and foreign domination and alien subjugation by all available means including armed struggle." GA resolution 3103 (XXVIII) of 1973, adopted before the Diplomatic Conference on the Reaffirmation and Development of International Humanitarian Law Applicable in Armed Conflicts (1974), laid down "basic principles of the legal status of the combatants struggling against colonial and alien domination and racist regimes." These principles are now covered by the additional protocols to the 1949 Geneva Conventions and the Additional Protocol of 1977.

[245]In the resolution which it adopted on 14 September 1981 at its eighth emergency special session, on the question of Namibia, the GA called upon Member States, specialized agencies and international organizations to render increased and sustained support and material, financial, military and other assistance to the South West Africa People's Organization to enable it to intensify its struggle for the liberation of Namibia. It also called upon the international community to extend, as a matter of urgency, all support and assistance, including military assistance, to the front-line States in order to enable them to defend their sovereignty and territorial integrity against the renewed acts of aggression by South Africa. But, the question of Namibia is one of decolonization.

[246]For example, GA resolutions 3055 (XXVIII) of 1973 and 3324C (XXIX) of 1974.

[247]These changes will be seen in the chapter on UN impact on South Africa.

[248]SC resolution 134 (1960) of 1 April 1960, adopted with the abstentions of France and the United Kingdom.

[249]UN, *Report of the Secretary-General on certain steps taken in regard to the implementation of Security Council resolution S/4300 of 1 April 1960 concerning the situation in the Union of South Africa* (S/4635), 23 January 1961; also interim reports S/4305 of 19 April 1960 and S/4551 of 11 October 1960.

[250]SC resolution 181 (1963) of 7 August 1963, on which again France and the United Kingdom abstained.

[251]UN, *Report by the Secretary-General in pursuance of the resolution adopted by the Security Council on 7 August 1963* (S/5438), 11 October 1963.

[252]SC resolution 182 (1963) of 4 December 1963, adopted unanimously.

[253]The Group of Experts was composed of Mrs. Alva Myrdal of Sweden, Sir Edward Asafu-Adjaye of Ghana, Sir Hugh Foot of the United Kingdom, and Mr. Josip Djerdja of Yugoslavia. However, Mr. Djerdja resigned in March 1964 and was replaced by Mr. Dey Ould Sidi Baba of Morocco.

[254]UN, *Report of the Group of Experts established in pursuance of the Security Council resolution of 4 December 1963* (S/5658), 20 April 1964, pp. 19-35 passim.

[255]Ibid., p. 7.

[256]SC resolution 190 (1964) of 9 June 1964, adopted with the abstentions of Brazil, France, the United Kingdom, and the United States.

[257]SC resolution 191 (1964) of 18 June 1964, adopted with the abstentions of Czechoslovakia, France, and the Soviet Union.

[258]UN, *Letter dated 13 July 1964 from the representative of South Africa to the Secretary-General* (S/5817), 14 July 1964 [Security Council Official Records (SCOR), Nineteenth Year, 1964, special supp. 1].

[259]UN, *Letter dated 16 November 1964 from the representative of South Africa to the Secretary-General* (S/6053), 19 November 1964 (SCOR, Nineteenth Year, 1964, special supp. 1).

[260]UN, *Report of the Expert Committee established in pursuance of Security Council resolution 191 (1964)* (S/6210), 2 March 1965 (SCOR, Twentieth Year, 1965, special supp. 2).

[261]See GA resolution 2307 (XXII) of 1967.

[262]See GA resolution 2396 (XXIII) of 1968.

[263]See UN, *Report of the Security Council, 16 July 1967-15 July 1968* [GAOR, Twenty-third Session, supp. 2 (A/7202)], pp. 118-19.

[264]See UN, *Report of the Security Council, 16 July 1968-15 July 1969* [GAOR, Twenty-fourth Session, supp. 2 (A/7602)], p. 95.

[265]SC resolution 282 (1970) of 23 July 1970, adopted with the abstentions of France, the United Kingdom, and the United States.

[266]The reference to political rights in this and other resolutions of the Council and the GA is superflous because political rights are already contained in the Universal Declaration and the two Covenants on human rights and are covered by the term "human rights and fundamental freedoms." It does, however, serve to emphasize the importance of political rights.

[267]See SC resolutions 311 (1972), 392 (1976), 417 (1977), and 473 (1980).

[268]SC resolution 311 (1972) of 4 February 1972, adopted with the abstention of France alone.

[269]GA resolutions 2923E (XXVII) of 1972, 3151A to G (XXVIII) of 1973, 3324 (XXIX) of 1974, and 3411G (XXX) of 1975. As already seen, in October 1974 the Council considered the specific request for the expulsion of South Africa from UN membership.

[270]SC resolution 417 (1977) of 31 October 1977, adopted unanimously.

[271]UN, *Report of the Secretary-General on the Implementation of Resolution 418 (1977) on the Question of South Africa Adopted by the Security Council* (S/12673), 28 April 1978, p. 3.

[272]SC resolution 418 (1977) of 4 November 1977, adopted unanimously; the Council's action under this resolution was a decision, not a recommendation.

[273]UNSC, *Provisional Verbatim Record of the Two Thousand and Forty-sixth Meeting* (S/PV.2046), 4 November 1977, pp. 18-19.

[274]Ibid., p. 11.

[275]Ibid., pp. 16-17.

[276]Ibid., p. 23.

[277]SC resolution 421 (1977) of 9 December 1977, adopted unanimously.

[278]SC resolution 473 (1980) of 13 June 1980, adopted unanimously.

[279]GA resolutions 265 (III) of 1949, 395 (V) of 1950, 511 (VI) of 1952, 615 (VII) of 1952, 816 (IX) of 1954, 919 (X) of 1955 and 1015 (XI) of 1957.

[280]GA resolutions 719 (VIII) of 1953, 1015 (XI) of 1957, 1179 (XII) of 1957, 1302 (XIII) of 1958, 1460 (XIV) of 1959, 1597 (XV) of 1961, and 1662 (XVI) of 1961.

[281]GA resolutions 395 (V) of 1950, 511 (VI) of 1952, 615 (VII) of 1952, and 719 (VIII) of 1953.

[282]GA resolutions 44 (I) of 1946 and 719 (VIII) of 1953.

[283]GA resolutions 1179 (XII) of 1957, 1302 (XIII) of 1958, 1460 (XIV) of 1959, 1597 (XV) of 1961, and 1662 (XVI) of 1961.

[284]GA resolutions 1302 (XIII) of 1958, 1460 (XIV) of 1959, 1597 (XV) of 1961, and 1662 (XVI) of 1961.

[285]Ibid.

[286]GA resolution 616A (VII) of 1952.

[287]GA resolution 616B (VII) of 1952.

[288]GA resolution 721 (VIII) of 1953.

[289]GA resolution 820 (IX) of 1954.

[290]GA resolution 917 (X) of 1955.

[291]GA resolutions 1016 (XI) of 1957 and 1178 (XII) of 1957.

[292]GA resolutions 1248 (XIII) of 1958 and 1375 (XIV) of 1959.

[293]GA resolutions 1598 (XV) and 1663 (XVI) of 1961.

[294]GA resolution 1761 (XVII) of 1962.

[295]GA resolutions 1881 (XVIII) and 1978V (XVIII) of 1963.

[296]Those resolutions were listed in the preceding chapter.

[297]See GA resolution 2054A (XX) of 1965.

[298]Those resolutions were listed in the preceding chapter.

[299]Resolutions 1978 (XVIII) of 1963, 2054 (XX) of 1965, 2202 (XXI) of 1966, 2506 (XXIV) of 1969, 2624 (XXV) of 1970, and 2775 (XXVI) of 1971.

[300]GA resolution 2396 (XXIII) of 1968.

[301]GA resolutions 2671F (XXV) of 1970, 3151G (XXVIII) of 1973.

[302]GA resolutions 2202A (XXI) of 1966, 2307 (XXII) of 1967, 2396 (XXIII) of 1968, 2506B (XXIV) of 1969, 2671F (XXV) of 1970, 2923E (XXVII) of 1972, 3068 (XXVIII) of 1973, 3151G (XXVIII) of 1973, 3324E (XXIX) of 1974, 3411G (XXX) of 1975, 31/6 I of 1976, 33/193L of 1979 and 35/206A of 1980.

[303]GA resolution 2307 (XXII) of 1967.

[304]GA resolutions 2396 (XXIII) of 1968, 2506 (XXIV) of 1969, 33/183F of 1979, 34/93H of 1979 and 35/206K of 1980.

[305]GA resolution 2506A (XXIV) of 1969.

[306]GA resolution 2506B (XXIV) of 1969.

[307]GA resolution 2671F (XXV) of 1970.

[308]GA resolution 2764 (XXVI) of 1971.

[309]GA resolution 2775F (XXVI) of 1971.

[310]GA resolution 2923A (XXVII) of 1972.

[311]GA resolution 2923E (XXVII) of 1972.

[312]GA resolution 3068 (XXVIII) of 1973.

[313]GA resolution 3151G (XXVIII) of 1973.

[314]GA resolution 3324C (XXIX) of 1974.

[315]GA resolution 3324E (XXIX) of 1974.

[316]GA resolution 3411G (XXX) of 1975.

[317]GA resolution 31/6A of 1976.

[318]GA resolution 31/6C of 1976.

[319]GA resolution 31/6D of 1976.

[320]GA resolution 31/6H of 1976.

[321]GA resolution 31/6 I of 1976.

[322]GA resolution 32/105F of 1977.

[323]GA resolution 32/105J of 1977.

[324]GA resolution 32/105K of 1977.

[325]GA resolution 33/183A of 1979.

[326]GA resolution 33/183B of 1979.

[327]GA resolution 34/93A of 1979.

[328]GA resolution 35/206A of 1980.

[329]GA resolution 35/206 J of 1980.

[330]GA resolution 35/206 K of 1980.

[331]GA resolution 35/206 N of 1980.

[332]GA resolution 35/206 I of 1980.

[333]See GA resolutions 3324B (XXIX) of 1974 and 31/6D of 1976.

[334]SC resolution 134 (1960) of 1 April 1960.

[335]SC resolution 181 (1963) of 7 August 1963.

[336]SC resolution 182 (1963) of 4 December 1963.

[337]SC resolution 190 (1964) of 9 June 1964.

[338]SC resolution 191 (1964) of 18 June 1964.

[339]SC resolution 282 (1970) of 23 July 1970.

[340]SC resolution 311 (1972) of 4 February 1972.

[341]SC resolution 392 (1976) of 19 June 1976.

[342]SC resolution 417 (1977) of 31 October 1977.

[343]SC resolution 418 (1977) of 4 November 1977.

[344]SC resolution 421 (1977) of 9 December 1977.

[345]UNSC, S/PV.2046, pp. 9-11.

[346]Ibid., pp. 16-17.

[347]Ibid., p. 8; also see UNSC, *Provisional Verbatim Record of the Two Thousand and Forty-fourth Meeting* (S/PV.2044), 31 October 1977, pp. 21-22.

[348]UNSC, S/PV. 2046, p. 23.

[349]Ibid., p. 4.

[350]He glossed over the fact that no such means exist for blacks in South Africa and that opponents of apartheid have been ruthlessly repressed.

[351]UNSC, *Letter dated 4 November 1977 from the Chargé d'Affaires of the Permanent Mission of South Africa to the United Nations addressed to the Secretary-General* (S/12439), 4 November 1977.

[352]UNSC, *Note by the President of the Security Council* (S/13549), 21 September 1979.

[353]UNSC, *Letter dated 24 September 1979 from the Permanent Representative of South Africa to the United Nations addressed to the President of the Security Council* (S/13552), 24 September 1979.

[354]SC resolution 473 (1980) of 13 June 1980.

[355]UN, *Repertory of Practice of United Nations Organs*, vol. 1 (New York, 1955), p. 67.

[356]UN, GAOR, 1st Session, 2nd Part, General Committee, *Summary Record*, 19th Meeting, 24 October 1946, pp. 69-70.

[357]UN, GAOR, 1st Session, 2nd Part, *Verbatim Record*, Fiftieth Plenary Meeting, 7 December 1946, p. 1006.

[358]UN, GAOR, 1st Session, 2nd Part, Joint Committee of the First and Sixth Committees, *Summary Record*, 1st Meeting, 21 November 1946, pp. 1-2.

[359]Ibid., pp. 3, 18.

[360]UN, GAOR, 2nd Session, First Committee, *Summary Record*, 110th Meeting, 15 November 1947, p. 460.

[361]UN, GAOR, 2nd Session, *Verbatim Record*, One Hundred and Nineteenth Plenary Meeting, 20 November 1947, pp. 1114-15.

[362]UN, *Repertory of Practice of United Nations Organs*, vol. 1, p. 67.

[363]GA resolution 44 (I) of 1946.

[364]UN, GAOR, 7th Session, Ad Hoc Political Committee, *Summary Record*, 13th Meeting, 12 November 1952, pp. 65-67.

[365]UN, *Repertory of Practice of United Nations Organs*, vol. 1, p. 96.

[366]Ibid., supp. 1, vol. 1, p. 39.

[367]Ibid. (1972), supp. 3, vol. 1, pp. 73, 111, 115, 122, 127.

[368]UN, GAOR, 1st Session, 2nd Part, Joint Committee of the First and Sixth Committees, *Summary Record*, 1st Meeting, 21 November 1946, p. 7. It should be noted that the representatives of China were those of Chiang Kai-Shek until 25 October 1971 when the Assembly adopted a resolution recognizing instead the representatives of the People's Republic of China.

[369]UN, GAOR, 1st Session, 2nd Part, *Verbatim Record*, Fiftieth Plenary Meeting, 7 December 1946, p. 1020.

[370]UN, GAOR, 1st Session, 2nd Part, Joint Committee of the First and Sixth Committees, *Summary Record*, 3rd Meeting, 26 November 1946, pp. 28-29.

[371]Ibid., 2nd Meeting, 25 November 1946, p. 16.

[372]Ibid., pp. 14-16.

[373]UN, GAOR, 1st Session, 2nd Part, General Committee, *Summary Record*, 19th Meeting, 24 October 1946, p. 71.

[374]UN, GAOR, 2nd Session, First Committee, *Summary Record*, 110th Meeting, 15 November 1947, p. 463.

[375]Ibid., 111th Meeting, 17 November 1947, p. 467.

[376]Ibid., 110th Meeting, 15 November 1947, p. 460.

[377]Ibid., 109th Meeting, 15 November 1947, p. 448.

[378]UN, GAOR, 2nd Session, *Verbatim Record*, One Hundred and Nineteenth Plenary Meeting, 20 November 1947, p. 1114.

[379]UN, GAOR, 7th Session, Ad Hoc Political Committee, *Summary Record*, 18 Meeting, 17 November 1952, p. 98.

[380]Ibid., 15th Meeting, 13 November 1952, p. 76.

[381]Ibid., 14th Meeting, 12 November 1952, p. 72. [It is ironic that some of the Western Powers which had initiated or supported the historic Uniting for Peace Resolution of 1950, on the ground that under Articles 10 and 11 of the Charter the Assembly had extensive powers to discuss and recommend anything within the purview of the Charter, would argue that the Assembly was not competent to consider South Africa's racial situation.]

[382]Ibid., 17th Meeting, 15 November 1952, p. 90.

[383]Ibid., 20th Meeting, 20 November 1952, p. 117.

[384]See Bissell, *Apartheid and International Organizations*, p. 17.

[385]See UN, *Repertoire of the Practice of the Security Council, supp. 1959-63* (New York, 1965), p. 301; also see GAOR, 15th Session, Special Political Committee, *Summary Record*, 242nd Meeting, 5 April 1961, p. 77.

[386]UN, GAOR, 16th Session, Special Political Committee, *Summary Record*, 274th Meeting, 31 October 1961, pp. 69-70.

[387]UN, GAOR, 13th Session, Special Political Committee, *Summary Record*, 94th Meeting, 21 October 1958, p. 41.

[388]UN, GAOR, 17th Session, Special Political Committee, *Summary Record*, 327th Meeting, 8 October 1962, pp. 7-8.

[389]Ibid., 329th Meeting, 11 October 1962, pp. 13-14.

[390]Ibid., 334th Meeting, 19 October 1962, pp. 37-38.

[391]Ibid., 337th Meeting, 26 October 1962, pp. 55-56, and 339th Meeting, 30 October 1962, pp. 66-67.

[392]UN, GAOR, 27th Session, Special Political Committee, *Summary Record*, 819th Meeting, 20 October 1972, p. 81.

[393]As already seen, it took fifteen years for the United Kingdom Government to say that the Assembly was competent to deal with the matter because of the *sui generis* nature of the issue.

[394]See, for example, Lauterpacht, *International Law and Human Rights*, pp. 169, 180, 213-14; Singh, "Domestic Jurisdiction and the Law of the United Nations," pp. 96, 216-17.

[395]UN, GAOR, 1st Session, 2nd Part, Joint Committee of the First and Sixth Committees, *Summary Record*, 1st Meeting, 21 November 1946, pp. 3-4.

[396]UN, GAOR, 2nd Session, First Committee, *Summary Record*, 106th Meeting, 12 November 1947, p. 421.

[397]For the categorization of the rights and freedoms of the Universal Declaration, see Nehemiah Robinson, *The Universal Declaration of Human Rights* (New York: Institute of Jewish Affairs, 1958); René Cassin, *La Declaration Universelle des Droits de l'Homme de 1948* (Paris: Institut de France, 1958); Maurice Cranston, *What are Human Rights?* (New York: Basic Books, Inc., 1962); H. Lauterpacht, *International Law and Human Rights* (London: Stevens and Sons, 1950); and D. D. Raphael (ed.), *Political Theory and the Rights of Man* (Bloomington: Indiana University Press, 1967).

[398]See Charter Articles 1 (3), 13 (1), 55, and 76 (c).

[399]See Sohn and Buergenthal, *International Protection of Human Rights*, p. 652.

[400]Lauterpacht, *International Law and Human Rights*, pp. 148-49.

[401]In a speech that he made on 3 September 1963, Dr. H. F. Verwoerd said that "South Africa is unequivocally the symbol of anti-communism in Africa" and "also still a bastion in Africa for Christianity and the Western world" [Cited in W. A. Landman, *A Plea for Understanding: A Reply to the Reformed Church in America* (Cape Town, South Africa:

Dutch Reformed Church, 1968), p. 111]. Also, immediately after Ronald Reagan's election victory for the presidency of the U.S., and jubilant at the defeat of President Carter who might have ultimately supported economic sanctions against South Africa over the dispute on Namibia, the South African Broadcasting Corporation announced that the election results marked the defeat of pseudo-liberalism, permissiveness, state intervention, appeasement and anti-patriotism and meant that "Western Christian culture' still had a chance to triumph over communism" ["South Africa Seems Gratified," *New York Times*, 6 November 1980, p. A10].

[402]*South African Digest* (Pretoria), 13 April 1979, p. 20.

[403]For details, see Joseph Lelyveld, "Despite Plenty, Hunger is Rife in South Africa," *New York Times*, 23 November 1980, pp. 1, 22.

[404]See Permanent South African Mission to the United Nations, *South African News Review*, 14 October 1980. The Prime Minister was reported telling a public meeting in Pretoria that "the political rights of the Coloreds had produced problems and that ways had to be found to bring them into public affairs."

[405]*Documents of UNCIO*, vol. 3, p. 425.

[406]Lauterpacht, *International Law and Human Rights*, p. 94.

[407]Ibid., pp. 427-28.

[408]The South African majority does not enjoy the equality of the Stoics, nor the equality of the Greek *polis* (although it was equality by citizenship, not by birth, and excluded such people as the slaves), nor the equality of the Roman Law as *Persona*.

[409]"The People's Programme," *Sechaba*, September 1980, p. 5.

[410]See, for example, ECOSOC resolutions 1330 (XLIV) and 1331 (XLIV) of 31 May 1968 and 1419 (XLVI) of 6 June 1969; also see ECOSOC, Commission on Human Rights, Sub-Commission on Prevention of Discrimination and Protection of Minorities, Question of Slavery and the Slave Trade in All Their Practices and Manifestations, Including the Slavery-like Practices of Apartheid and Colonialism, *Report of the Working Group on Slavery* (E/CN.4/Sub.2/447), 20 August 1980; for the historical development of apartheid as a collective form of slavery, see ECOSOC, Commission on Human Rights, Sub-Commission on Prevention of Discrimination and Protection of Minorities, Apartheid as a Collective Form of Slavery, *Report of the Secretary-General* (E/CN.4/Sub.2/449), 18 July 1980.

[411]UN, GAOR, 1st Session, 2nd Part, Joint Committee of the First and Sixth Committees, *Summary Record*, 4th Meeting, 27 November 1946, pp. 33-34.

[412]UN, GAOR, 1st Session, 2nd Part, *Verbatim Record*, Fifty-second Plenary Meeting, 8 December 1946, p. 1061.

[413]Lauterpacht, *International Law and Human Rights*, pp. 192-99.

[414]UN, *Repertoire of the Practice of the Security Council, 1946-51*, p. 453.

[415]See UN, *Repertory of Practice of United Nations Organs*, supp. 3, vol. 1, p. 100.

[416]See Sohn and Buergenthal, *International Protection of Human Rights*, pp. 672-83.

[417]UN, *Repertoire of the Practice of the Security Council, supp. 1959-63*, p. 300.

[418]Ibid.

[419]Ibid., p. 301.

[420]Ibid.

[421]Ibid.

[422]Ibid., p. 302.

[423]See Sohn and Buergenthal, *International Protection of Human Rights*, pp. 691-98.

[424]UN, *Repertoire of the Practice of the Security Council, supp. 1964-65* (New York, 1968), p. 204.

[425]Ibid., p. 205.

[426]Claude, *Swords into Plowshares*, pp. 166-67.

[427]UN, *Repertory of Practice of United Nations Organs*, supp. 3, vol. 1, p. 104.

[428]See Sohn and Buergenthal, *International Protection of Human Rights*, p. 725.

[429]According to rule 39, the Council "may invite members of the Secretariat or other

persons, whom it considers competent for the purpose, to supply it with information or to give other assistance in examining matters within its competence." It is interesting to note that the Council's rules of procedure are still provisional.

[430]UN, SCOR, Thirty-second Year, *Verbatim Record*, Two Thousand and Forty-third Meeting, 28 October 1977, pp. 5-7.

[431]UNSC, S/PV.2044, pp. 21-22.

[432]UNSC, S/PV.2045, p. 31.

[433]UNSC, S/PV.2046, p. 37.

[434]Ibid., pp. 43-47.

[435]It must be clarified that it was the General Assembly that had agreed that apartheid itself was a threat to world peace, not the Security Council.

[436]UNSC, *Provisional Verbatim Record of the Two Thousand and Fifty-sixth Meeting* (S/PV.2056), 26 January 1978, p. 38.

[437]Clyde Ferguson and William R. Cotter, "South Africa—What is to be Done?" *Foreign Affairs* 56 (January 1978): 259.

[438]With regard to African countries' demands that the UN impose comprehensive and mandatory sanctions on South Africa, they are sometimes blamed for hypocritically demanding sanctions while many of them have trade relations with South Africa. True, many African countries have been historically involved in trade with South Africa and have even become economically dependent on it by geographical or other circumstances. Such dependence, however, does not necessarily mean that they should acquiesce in apartheid that is humiliating not only to South African blacks but also to blacks everywhere. In fact, recently some African states have attempted to free themselves from economic dependence on South Africa. Nine African states, namely, Angola, Botswana, Lesotho, Malawi, Mozambique, Swaziland, Tanzania, Zambia, and Zimbabwe, which are all dependent on South Africa for food supplies or for its harbors and railways, have held conferences to seek ways and means to eliminate or reduce their dependence on South Africa and, on 27 November 1980, received a pledge of $650 million for that purpose from international organizations and developed nations (see "Groups Pledge $650 Million for 9 Black African Nations," *New York Times*, 28 November 1980, p. A7).

[439]Specialized agencies are affiliated with the UN, through agreements with ECOSOC, under Article 63 of the Charter. They are intergovernmental organizations as described under Article 57. With regard to assistance by specialized agencies to blacks in South Africa, see UN, ECOSOC, *Assistance to the Oppressed People of South Africa and their National Liberation Movement by Agencies and Institutions within the United Nations System* (E/1980/78), 23 June 1980.

[440]Many NGOs are affiliated with the UN, in consultative status with ECOSOC, under Article 71 of the Charter. In August 1978, for example, NGOs held an International Conference for Action Against Apartheid in Geneva, Switzerland. Also, an International Non-Governmental Organization Action Conference on Sanctions against South Africa was held in Geneva from 30 June to 3 July 1980.

[441]United States, Department of State, "Human Rights in South Africa," *Current Policy*, no. 181, 13 May 1980. The statement was made on 13 May 1980 before the subcommittees on Africa and on International Organizations of the House Committee on Foreign Affairs.

[442]Richard E. Bissell, "How Strategic is South Africa?" in Bissell and Crocker, *South Africa into the 1980s*, p. 222.

[443]For details of the EEC Code of Conduct, see Lillich and Newman, *International Human Rights*, pp. 465-68; for details on the Sullivan Principles, see UN, Centre against Apartheid, *Notes and Documents No. 4/80*, "The Sullivan Principles: Decoding Corporate Camouflage," by Elizabeth Schmidt, March 1980.

[444]See UN, Department of Public Information, *Press Release*, GA/AP/1087, 24 March 1980 (hearing on labor and trade union aspects of apartheid at the 451st Meeting of the Special Committee against Apartheid), pp. 2-6.

[445]See Anthony Lewis, "State of Violence: II," *New York Times*, 8 December 1977, p. A23.

[446]*Rand Daily Mail* (Johannesburg), "South Africa is Drifting into Lasting Unrest," 19 June 1980, p. 3.

[447]Adam and Giliomee, *Ethnic Power Mobilized*, p. 300.

[448]The question under consideration then was South Africa's attempt to enter into a "dialogue" with its neighbouring states.

[449]The Council was then considering the item "Relationship between the United Nations and South Africa," referred to it by the Assembly.

[450]See UNSC, *Provisional Verbatim Records of the One Thousand and Eight Hundreth Meeting* (S/PV/1800), 24 October 1974, pp. 28-53 passim.

[451]*African Research Bulletin* (Exeter, England), vol. 11, 15 November 1974.

[452]Republic of South Africa, *House of Assembly Debates* (Hansard), Pretoria, First Session-Sixth Parliament, 6-10 March 1978, no. 6, col. 2823.

[453]*The Economist* (London), 31 December 1977, p. 65.

[454]*Rand Daily Mail* (Johannesburg), 2 May 1979, p. 13.

[455]Republic of South Africa, *House of Assembly Debates* (Hansard), Pretoria, First Session-Sixth Parliament, 6-10 February 1978, no. 2, cols. 821-84.

[456]Ibid., 17-21 April 1978, no. 11, cols. 5227-30. For the Gleneagles Agreement, see Sports Policies under Internal Changes below.

[457]See Republic of South Africa, *House of Assembly Debates* (Hansard), Pretoria, Third-Session-Sixth Parliament, 23 May 1979, no. 15, cols. 7123-24.

[458]For details, see the *Economist* (London), 26 November 1977, pp. 47-48.

[459]See "Mr. Vorster's Mandate," Editorial, *New York Times*, 2 December 1977, p. A26.

[460]See the *New York Times*, 16 December 1977, p. A7.

[461]Ibid., 12 January 1978, p. 18; also see "Increasing the Pressure on Pretoria," Editorial, *New York Times*, 23 December 1977, p. A28.

[462]*New York Times*, 15 February 1978, p. A5.

[463]See, for example, the *New York Times*, 11 March 1978, p. 1; 15 March 1978, p. A.22; 19 March 1978, sec. 3, p. 1; and 22 April 1978, p. L25.

[464]Dick Clark, "U.S. Corporate Interests in South Africa," *Report to the Committee on Foreign Relations*, U.S. Senate, January 1978, p. 13.

[465]Quoted by the *South African Digest* (Pretoria), 22 February 1980, p. 26.

[466]Anthony Lewis, "With All Deliberate Speed," *New York Times*, 15 December 1977, p. A31.

[467]John F. Burns, "Sanctions and South Africa," *New York Times*, 29 October 1977, p. 3.

[468]Chester A. Crocker, "The United States and Africa," *Africa Report* 26 (September-October 1981), pp. 6-8.

[469]Foreign Policy Study Foundation, *South Africa: Time Running Out*, Report of the Study Commission on U.S. Policy Toward Southern Africa, Berkeley: University of California Press, 1981.

[470]See UN, Centre against Apartheid, *Notes and Documents no. 4/77*, "Sports Boycott in the International Campaign against *Apartheid*," by Richard E. Lapchick, February 1977.

[471]For text of Gleneagles Agreement, see Dennis Brutus and Robert Baker, eds., "Papers from the Conference on International Sport, Politics, Racism and Apartheid," *Journal of Sport and Social Issues* 2 (Fall/Winter, 1978): 55-56.

[472]See UN, Centre against Apartheid, *Notes and Documents no 25/77*, "Apartheid in Sports: Business as usual," by Trevor Richards, August 1977.

[473]Caryle Murphy, "New South African Policy on Sports Causes Collision of Principle, Practice," *Washington Post*, 25 February 1978, p. A13.

[474]*New York Times*, 13 February 1978, p. 1.

[475]*South African Digest* (Pretoria), 20 April 1979, pp. 25-26.

[476]*Financial Mail* (Johannesburg), 21 December 1979, p. 1247.

[477]*Rand Daily Mail* (Johannesburg), Editorial, "Our Standpoint on the Sports Issue," 17 January 1980, p. 8.

[478]Ibid., 31 March 1981, p. 12.

[479]Republic of South Africa, *House of Assembly Debates* (Hansard), Pretoria, First Session-Sixth Parliament, 24-28 April 1978, no. 12, cols. 5558-60.

[480]*Rand Daily Mail* (Johannesburg), 9 January 1980.

[481]Simon Jenkins, "The Tribal Glue," *Economist* (London), South Africa Survey, 21 June 1980, p. 21.

[482]Ibid., p. 19.

[483]*Post* (Johannesburg), 15 November 1979.

[484]Simon Jenkins, "The Tribal Glue."

[485]*Sunday Post* (Johannesburg), 28 October 1979.

[486]*Economist* (London), 10 May 1980, p. 35.

[487]John Darnton, "Apartheid, as Real and Painful as Ever," *New York Times*, 30 October 1977, sec. 4, p. 1.

[488]See John F. Burns, "South Africa Modifying Apartheid Without Weakening White Power," *New York Times*, 6 April 1978, p. 1.

[489]John de St. Jorre, "South Africa: Is Change Coming?" *Foreign Affairs* 60 (Fall 1981): 108.

[490]*South African Digest* (Pretoria), Information Newsletter, 13 June 1980.

[491]*New York Times*, Editorial, "Speak Forcefully to South Africa," 20 June 1980, p. A30.

[492]Republic of South Africa, *Government Gazette*, vol. 182, no. 7152, 1 August 1980.

[493]Helen Zille, "Academics Criticize Schlebusch Plans," *Rand Daily Mail* (Johannesburg), 4 October 1979, p. 3.

[494]See *South African Digest* (Pretoria), Information Newsletter, 20 June 1980.

[495]Ibid.

[496]Adam and Giliomee, *Ethnic Power Mobilized*, p. 296.

[497]See Martin Schneider, "The Citizen Connection," *Rand Daily Mail* (Johannesburg), 10 May 1978, p. 9.

[498]See Fleur de Villiers, "South Africa Facing Its Worst Political Upheaval," *Sunday Times* (Johannesburg), 7 May 1978, p. 1.

[499]Amnesty International, *Report 1979*, p. 32.

[500]Adam and Giliomee, *Ethnic Power Mobilized*, p. 3.

[501]African National Congress of South Africa, Observer Mission to the U.N. and Representation to the U.S.A. (New York), *Press Release* [June 1980].

[502]*Rand Daily Mail* (Johannesburg), 5 October 1979, p. 5.

[503]John F. Burns, "South Africa Says Blast May Signal Guerrilla War," *New York Times*, 9 December 1976, p. 3.

[504]*South African Digest* (Pretoria), "Pattern of Violence," 2 February 1979, p. 18.

[505]Ibid., 16 November 1979, p. 4.

[506]Simon Jenkins, "The Tribal Glue."

[507]For attacks on police stations in Orlando and Ermelo in November 1979, see *Rand Daily Mail* (Johannesburg), 5 November 1979 and *Post* (Johannesburg), 6 November 1979.

[508]*Rand Daily Mail* (Johannesburg), 2 June 1980.

[509]Ibid.

[510]*Newsweek*, 30 June 1980.

[511]*Rand Daily Mail* (Johannesburg), 7 June 1980.

[512]Patrick Lawrence, "Collaboration: Where is the Point of No Return," *Rand Daily Mail* (Johannesburg), 31 October 1979.

[513]*South African Digest* (Pretoria), 16 November 1979, p. 25.

[514]"Attack on the Coloureds," *Sechaba* (London), Official Organ of the ANC, May 1980, p. 11.

[515]Ameen Akhalvaya, "A Three-way Power Tug-o'war," *Rand Daily Mail* (Johannesburg), 31 October 1979, pp. 10-11.

[516]Ibid.

[517]Simon Jenkins, "The Tribal Glue."

[518]*New York Times*, Editorial, "Speak Forcefully to South Africa;" also see *Rand Daily Mail* (Johannesburg), 5 November 1979, p. 10.

[519]*The Economist* (London), "South Africa: Backwards, Fast," 10 May 1980, p. 35.

[520]David Ottaway, "Africa: U.S. Policy Eclipse," *Foreign Affairs* 58 (America and the World 1979): 646.

[521]Allister Sparks, Commentary, *Rand Daily Mail* (Johannesburg), 3 November 1977, p. 4.

[522]Tom Wicker, "The Nightmare Ahead," *New York Times*, 29 December 1978, p. A23.

[523]Helen Zille, "Editor Airs Nat Race Law Debate," *Rand Daily Mail* (Johannesburg), 14 January 1980, p. 3.

[524]Idem, "Apartheid Must Go Says Top Academic," ibid., 12 November 1979, p. 5.

[525]Benjamin Progrund, "Waiting for Nat Change," *Rand Daily Mail* (Johannesburg), 21 March 1980.

[526]Quoted from *Evening Post* in *South African Digest* (Pretoria), 27 April 1979, p. 21.

[527]*Post* (Johannesburg), 30 January 1980, p. 9.

[528]*Star* (Johannesburg), 22 December 1979, p. 9.

[529]*Rand Daily Mail* (Johannesburg), commentary, "A Unique Voice," 9 July 1980.

[530]On this point see Colin Legum, "The African Crisis," *Foreign Affairs* 57 (America and the World 1978): 642; also see Henry Bienen, "U.S. Foreign Policy in a Changing Africa," *Political Science Quarterly* 93 (Fall 1978): 452, 461.

[531]Burns, "Sanctions and South Africa."

[532]Pogrund, "Waiting for Nat Change."

[533]Helen Zille, "The New Verligte Nat Vision," *Rand Daily Mail* (Johannesburg), 17 October 1979.

[534]*New York Times*, 1 December 1977.

[535]Stanley Uys, "A Closer Look at Afrikanerdom," *Rand Daily Mail* (Johannesburg), 19 October 1979.

[536]Adam and Giliomee, *Ethnic Power Mobilized*, pp. 8-10.

[537]Benjamin Pogrund, "PW and BJ—the Same Bars," *Rand Daily Mail* (Johannesburg), 20 March 1980.

[538]See UN, Department of Public Information, *Press Release ILO/2066*, 19 June 1980.

[539]John F. Burns, "A Peaceful Shift is Seen by Blacks in South Africa," *New York Times*, 4 April 1978, p. 5.

[540]*New York Times*, 14 November 1977, p. L5.

[541]*Star* (Johannesburg), 15 December 1979.

[542]*New York Times*, 9 June 1978, p. A3.

[543]Zartman, "The African States as a Source of Change," pp. 107, 129.

BIBLIOGRAPHY

A. *United Nations Documents and Publications*
(Chronological)

United Nations. *Documents of United Nations Conference on International Organization, San Francisco, 1945.* 21 vols. United Nations Information Organizations: London and New York, 1945.

United Nations. General Assembly Official Records (GAOR). 1st Session, 2nd Part. General Committee. *Summary Record.* 19th Meeting, 24 October 1946.

————. ————. 1st Session, 2nd Part. Joint Committee of the First and Sixth Committees. *Summary Record.* 1st Meeting, 21 November 1946; 2nd Meeting, 25 November 1946; 3rd Meeting, 26 November 1946; 4th Meeting, 27th November 1946.

————. ————. 1st Session, 2nd Part. *Verbatim Record.* Fiftieth Plenary Meeting, 7 December 1946; Fifty-second Plenary Meeting, 8 December 1946.

————. *Yearbook of the United Nations, 1946-47.* New York: 1947.

————. ————. 2nd Session. First Committee. *Summary Record.* 106th Meeting, 12 November 1947; 110th Meeting, 15 November 1947; 111th Meeting, 17 November 1947.

————. ————. 2nd Session. *Verbatim Record.* One Hundred and Nineteenth Plenary Meeting, 20 November 1947.

————. ————. 7th Session. Ad Hoc Political Committee. *Summary Record.* 13th to 20th Meetings, 11 to 20 November 1952.

————. *Report of the United Nations Commission on the Racial Situation in the Union of South Africa* (A/2505), 3 October 1953. GAOR. Eighth Session, 1953, supp. 16.

————. *Second Report of the United Nations Commission on the Racial Situation in the Union of South Africa* (A/2719), 26 August 1954. GAOR. Ninth Session, 1954, supp. 16.

————. *Repertoire of the Practice of the Security Council, 1946-51.* New York: 1954.

————. *Repertory of Practice of United Nations Organs.* vol. 1. New York: 1955.

————. *Third Report of the United Nations Commission on the Racial Situation in the Union of South Africa* (A/2953), 26 August 1955. GAOR. Tenth Session, 1955, supp. 14.

————. *Annual Report of the Secretary-General on the Work of the Organization, 16 June 1956-15 June 1957* (A/3594), 1957. GAOR, Twelfth Session, supp. 1.

————. GAOR. 13th Session. Special Political Committee. *Summary Record.* 94th Meeting, 21 October 1958.

————. *Repertory of Practice of United Nations Organs.* vol. 1, supp. 1. New York: 1958.

————. GAOR. 14th Session. *Verbatim Record.* Eight Hundred and Eleventh Plenary Meeting, 28 September 1959.

————. *Yearbook of the United Nations,* 1959. New York: 1960.

————. *Report of the Secretary-General on Certain Steps Taken in Regard to the Implementation of Security Council Resolution S/4300 of 1 April 1960 Concerning the Situation in the Union of South Africa* (S/4635), 23 January 1961.

————. GAOR. 15th Session. Special Political Committee. *Summary Record.* 242nd Meeting, 5 April 1961.

————. ————. 16th Session. Special Political Committee. *Summary Record.* 274th Meeting, 31 October 1961.

————. ————. 17th Session. Special Political Committee. *Summary Record.* 327th Meeting, 8 October 1962; 329th Meeting, 11 October 1962; 334th Meeting, 19 October 1962; 337th Meeting, 26 October 1962; 339th Meeting, 30 October 1962.

————. *Report by the Secretary-General in Pursuance of the Resolution Adopted by the Security Council on 7 August 1963* (S/5438), 11 October 1963.

————. *Report of the Secretary-General* (S/5457), 19 November 1963.

————. *Report of the Group of Experts Established in Pursuance of the Security Council Resolution of 4 December 1963* (S/5658), 20 April 1964.

————. *Letter Dated 13 July 1964 from the Representative of South Africa to the Secretary-General* (S/5817), 14 July 1964. Security Council Official Records (SCOR). Nineteenth Year, 1964, special supp. 1.

————. *Letter dated 16 November 1964 from the Representative of South Africa to the Secretary-General* (S/6053), 19 November 1964. SCOR. Nineteenth Year, 1964, special supp. 1.

————. *Repertoire of Practice of the Security Council, supp. 1959-63.* New York: 1965.

————. *Report of Expert Committee Established in Pursuance of Security Council Resolution 191 (1964)* (S/6210), 2 March 1965. SCOR. Twentieth Year, 1965, special supp. 2.

————. *Everyman's United Nations.* 8th ed. New York: 1968.

————. *Repertoire of the Practice of the Security Council, supp. 1964-65.* New York: 1968.

————. *Report of the Security Council, 16 July 1967-15 July 1968* [GAOR, Twenty-Third Session, supp. 2 (A/7202)].

————. *Report of the Security Council, 16 July 1968-15 July 1969* [GAOR, Twenty-Fourth Session, supp. 2 (A/7602)].

————. *Yearbook of the United Nations,* 1970. New York: 1972.

————. International Court of Justice. *Legal Consequences for States of the Continued Presence of South Africa in Namibia (South West Africa) notwithstanding Security Council Resolution 276 (1970).* Advisory Opinion, I.C.J. Reports 1971.

————. Unit on Apartheid. *Notes and Documents no. 2/71.* "The Dutch Reformed Church in South Africa and the Ideology and Practice of *Apartheid.*" By Dr. J. Verkuyl, February 1971.

————. ————. *Notes and Documents no. 27/71.* "*Apartheid*: The Laboratory of Racism." By the Right Reverend C. Edward Crowther, June 1971.

————. GAOR. 27th Session. Special Political Committee. *Summary Record.* 819th Meeting, 20 October 1972.

————. Office of Public Information. *The United Nations and Human Rights.* New York: 1973.

————. Security Council. *Provisional Verbatim Record of the One Thousand and Eighth Hundreth Meeting* (S/PV. 1800), 24 October 1974.

————. Office of Public Information. "Denial of Human Rights in Namibia." *Objective Justice* 8 (Spring 1976). By Elizabeth S. Landis.

————. GAOR. 31st Session, supp. 10 (A/31/10). *Report of the International Law Commission on the Work of its Twenty-eighth Session,* 3 May-23 July 1976.

————. General Assembly. *Report of the Special Committee against Apartheid* (A/31/22/Add. 3, S/12150/Add. 3), 26 October 1976.

————. Centre against Apartheid. *Notes and Documents no. 4/77.* "Sports Boycott in the International Campaign against *Apartheid.*" By Richard E. Lapchick, February 1977.

————. ————. *Notes and Documents no. 25/77.* "Apartheid in Sports: Business as Usual." By Trevor Richards, August 1977.

————. SCOR. Thirty-Second Year. *Verbatim Record.* Two Thousand and Forty-third Meeting, 28 October 1977.

————. Security Council. *Provisional Verbatim Record of the Two Thousand and Forty-fourth Meeting* (S/PV. 2044), 31 October 1977.

————. ————. *Provisional Verbatim Record of the Two Thousand and Forty-fifth Meeting* (S/PV. 2045), 1 November 1977.

————. ————. *Provisional Verbatim Record of the Two Thousand and Forty-sixth Meeting* (S/PV. 2046), 4 November 1977.

————. ————. *Letter dated 4 November 1977 from the Chargé d'Affaires of the Permanent Mission of South Africa to the United Nations Addressed to the Secretary-General* (S/12439), 4 November 1977.

————. General Assembly. 32nd Session. *Provisional Verbatim Record of the One Hundred and Second Meeting* (A/32/PV.102), 14 December 1977.

————. Security Council. *Provisional Verbatim Record of the Two Thousand and Fifty-sixth Meeting* (S/PV. 2056), 26 January 1978.

————. Commission on Human Rights. *Violations of Human Rights in Southern Africa* (E/CN. 4/1270), 31 January 1978, chap. 1.

————. Report of the Secretary-General on the Implementation of Resolution 418 (1977) on the Question of South Africa Adopted by the Security Council (S/12673), 28 April 1978.

————. General Assembly. 33rd Session. *Provisional Verbatim Record of the Thirtieth Meeting* (A/33/PV. 30), 11 October 1978.

————. ————. Special Committee against Apartheid. *Verbatim Records of the 416th Meeting* (A/AC. 115/PV. 416), 21 March 1979.

————. Security Council. *Note by the President of the Security Council* (S/13549), 21 September 1979.

————. ————. *Letter dated 24 September 1979 from the Permanent Representative of South Africa to the United Nations Addressed to the President of the Security Council* (S/13552), 24 September 1979.

————. General Assembly. 34th Session. *Provisional Verbatim Record of the Seventeenth Meeting* (A/34/PV. 17), 4 October 1979.

————. ————. 34th Session. *Provisional Verbatim Record of the Fifty-eighth Meeting* (A/34/PV. 58), 9 November 1979.

————. ————. 34th Session. *Provisional Verbatim Record of the Fifty-ninth Meeting* (A/34/PV. 59), 12 November 1979.

————. Department of Public Information. *Press Release GA/AP/1087*, 24 March 1980.

————. Centre against Apartheid. *Notes and Documents no. 4/86.* "The Sullivan Principles: Decoding Corporate Camouflage." By Elizabeth Schmidt, March 1980.

————. Department of Public Information. *Press Release ILO/2066*, 19 June 1980.

————. Economic and Social Council. *Assistance to the Oppressed People of South Africa and Their National Liberation Movement by Agencies and Institutions within the United Nations System* (E/1980/78), 23 June 1980.

————. ————. Commission on Human Rights. Sub-Commission on Prevention of Discrimination and Protection of Minorities. Apartheid as a Collective Form of Slavery. *Report of the Secretary-General* (E/CN. 4/Sub. 2/449), 18 July 1980.

————. GAOR. 35th Session, supp. 10 (A/35/10). *Report of the Interna-*

tional Law Commission on the Work of its Thirty-Second Session, 5 May-25 July 1980.

————. Economic and Social Council. Commission on Human Rights. Sub-Commission on Prevention of Discrimination and Protection of Minorities, Question of Slavery and the Slave Trade in All Their Practices and Manifestations, Including the Slavery-like Practices of Apartheid and Colonialism. *Report of the Working Group on Slavery* (E/CN. 4/Sub. 2/447), 20 August 1980.

————. Department of Public Information. *Press Release M/2257,* 25 August 1980.

————. ————. *Press Release GA/AP/1138,* 10 September 1980.

————. *Report of the Ad Hoc Committee on the Drafting of an International Convention against Apartheid in Sports* [GAOR, Thirty-fifth Session, supp. 36 (A/35/36)], 1980.

B. *Books*

Adam, Heribert, and Giliomee, Hermann. *Ethnic Power Mobilized: Can South Africa Change?* New Haven: Yale University Press, 1979.

Amnesty International. *Report 1979.* London: Amnesty International Publications, 1979.

Bishop Jr., William W. *International Law: Cases and Materials.* 3d ed. Boston and Toronto: Little, Brown and Co., 1971.

Bissell, Richard E. *Apartheid and International Organizations.* Boulder, Colorado: Westview Press, 1977.

Bissell, Richard E., and Crocker, Chester A. eds. *South Africa into the 1980s.* Colorado: Westview Press, 1979.

Bloomfield, Lincoln P. *Evolution or Revolution? The United Nations and the Problem of Peaceful Territorial Change.* Cambridge: Harvard University Press, 1957.

Brierly, James Leslie. *The Law of Nations.* 6th ed., edited by Sir Humphrey Waldock. Oxford: Oxford University Press, 1963.

Cassin, René. *La Declaration Universelle des Droits de L'homme de 1948.* Paris: Institut De France, 1958.

Ciobanu, Dan. *Preliminary Objections Related to the Jurisdiction of the United Nations Political Organs.* The Hague: Martinus Nijhoff, 1975.

Claude, Jr., Inis L. *Swords into Plowshares.* 3d ed. rev. New York: Random House, 1964.

Clifford-Vaughan, F. McA., ed. *International Pressures and Politcal Change in South Africa.* Cape Town: Oxford University Press, 1978.

Copithorne, M. D. "The Structural Law of the International Human Welfare System." In *The International Law and Policy of Human Welfare.*

Edited by Ronald St. J. Macdonald, Douglas M. Johnston, and Gerald L. Morris. The Netherlands: Sijthoff and Noordhoff, 1978.

Cornevine, Marianne. *Apartheid—Power and Historical Falsification*. Paris: UNESCO, 1980.

Cranston, Maurice. *What are Human Rights?* New York: Basic Books, Inc., 1962.

Critchley, T. A. *The Conquest of Violence: Order and Liberty in Britain*. London: Constable and Co. Ltd., 1970.

Crozier, Brian. *A Theory of Conflict*. London: Hamish Hamilton, 1974.

Deutsch, Karl W. *Tides among Nations*. New York: Free Press, 1979.

Dugard, John. *Human Rights and the South African Legal Order*. Princeton, New Jersey: Princeton University Press, 1978.

Gandhi, M. K. *Satyagraha in South Africa*. Translated by Valji Govindji Desai. rev. 2nd ed. Ahmedabad: Navajivan Publishing House, 1950.

Goodrich, Leland M. *The United Nations in a Changing World*. New York: Columbia University Press, 1974.

Goodrich, Leland M.; Hambro, Edvard; and Simons, Anne P. Charter of the United Nations, 3d ed. rev. New York and London: Columbia University Press, 1969.

Haile, Minasse. *Domestic Jurisdiction: United Nations Consideration of Domestic Questions and of Their International Effects*. Addis Ababa: The Ethiopian Publishing Co., 1968.

Hook, Sidney. "Ideologies of Violence and Social Change." In *Peaceful Change in Modern Society*. Edited, with an introduction, by E. Berkeley Tompkins. Stanford, Calif.: The Hoover Institution press, 1971.

Karis, Thomas, and Carter, Gwendolen M. *From Protest to Challenge: A Documentary History of African Politics in South Africa*, 1882-1964. 4 vols. Stanford, California: Hoover Institution Press, 1972-77.

Landman, W. A. *A Plea for Understanding: A Reply to the Reformed Church in America*. Cape Town, South Africa: Dutch Reformed Church, 1968.

Lauterpacht, H. *International Law and Human Rights*. London: Stevens and Sons, 1950.

Lillich, Richard B., and Newman, Frank C. eds. *International Human Rights: Problems of Law and Policy*. Boston: Little, Brown and Co., 1979.

Morgenthau, Hans J. *Politics among Nations*. 4th ed. rev. New York: Alfred A. Knopf, 1966.

Moskowitz, Moses. *International Concern with Human Rights*. New York: Oceana Publications, 1974.

Nathanson, Nathaniel L., and Schwelb, Egon. *The United States and the United Nations Treaty on Racial Discrimination*. Washington, D.C.: West Publishing Co., 1975.

Raphael, D. D. ed. *Political Theory and the Rights of Man*. Bloomington: Indiana University Press, 1967.

Robertson, A. H. *Human Rights in the World*. Manchester: Manchester University Press, 1972.

Robinson, Nehemiah. *The Universal Declaration of Human Rights*. New York: Institute of Jewish Affairs, 1958.

South African Institute of Race Relations. *Laws Affecting Race Relations in South Africa, 1948-1976*. comp. Muriel Horrell. Johannesburg: South African Institute of Race Relations, 1978.

Schwelb, Egon. *Human Rights and International Community*. Chicago: Quadraple Books, 1964.

Sohn, Louis B., and Buergenthal, Thomas. *International Protection of Human Rights*. New York: Bobbs-Merrill Co., 1973.

U.S. Department of State. *United Nations Conference on International Organization: Selected Documents*. Pubn. 2490. Washington, D.C.: Government Printing Office, 1946.

Van der Merwe, Hendrik W.; Charton, Nancy C. J.; Kotzé, D. A.; and Magnusson, Ake. eds. *African Perspectives on South Africa: a Collection of Speeches, Articles, and Documents* (Stanford, California: Hoover Institution Press, 1978).

Vasak, Karel. gen. ed. *Les Dimensions Internationales des Droits ae L'homme* [The International Dimensions of Human Rights]. Paris: UNESCO. 1978.

Walter, Eugene Victor. Terror and Resistance: A Study of Political Violence. New York: Oxford University Press, 1969.

Xydis, Stephen G. "The General Assembly." In *The United Nations: Past, Present, and Future*, pp. 89-93. Edited by James Barros. New York: Free Press, 1972.

C. Periodicals and Newspapers

"A Unique Voice." Commentary. *Rand Daily Mail* (Johannesburg), 9 July 1980.

Adler, Johan. Deputy Consul-General of South Africa to New York. Letter to the Editor. *New York Times*, 14 November 1977.

Africa Research Bulletin (Exeter, England), vol. 11, 15 November 1974.

Akhalyava, Ameen. "A Three-way Power Tug-o'-War." *Rand Daily Mail* (Johannesburg), 31 October 1979.

"Attack on the Coloureds." *Sechaba* (London), Official Organ of the African National Congress of South Africa, May 1980, pp. 11-12.

Bienen, Henry. "U.S. Foreign Policy in a Changing World." *Political Science Quarterly* 93 (Fall 1978): 443-64.

Brutus, Dennis, and Baker, Robert. eds. "Papers from the Conference on International Sport, Politics, Racism and Apartheid." *Journal of Sport and Social Issues* 2 (Fall/Winter, 1978): 55-56.

Burns, John F. "South Africa Says Blast May Signal Guerrilla War." *New York Times*, 9 December 1976.

————. "Sanctions and South Africa." *New York Times*, 29 October 1977.

————. "A Peaceful Shift is Seen by Blacks in South Africa." *New York Times*, 4 April 1978.

————. "South Africa Modifying Apartheid Without Weakening White Power." *New York Times*, 6 April 1978.

Crocker, Chester A. "The United States and Africa." *Africa Report* 26 (September-October 1981): 6-8.

Darnton, John. "Apartheid as Real and Painful as Ever." *New York Times*, 30 October 1977, sec. 4, p. 1.

De St. Jorre, John. "South Africa: Is Change Coming?" *Foreign Affairs* 60 (Fall 1981): 106-22.

De Villiers, Fleur. "South Africa Facing Its Worst Political Upheaval." *Sunday Times* (Johannesburg), 7 May 1978.

Economist (London), 26 November, 31 December 1977; 14 January 1978.

Ferguson, Clyde, and Cotter, William R. "South Africa: What is to be Done?" *Foreign Affairs* 56 (January 1978): 253-74.

Financial Mail (Johannesburg), 21 December 1979.

Gaitskell, Dora. "Of Human Rights, the UN and Britain." Letter to the Editor. *New York Times*, 23 December 1977.

"Groups Pledge $650 Million for 9 Black African Nations." *New York Times*, 28 November 1980.

Hoffman, Stanley. "Carter's African Policy." *New York Times*, 13 December 1978.

"Increasing the Pressure on Pretoria." Editorial. *New York Times*, 23 December 1977.

International Commission of Jurists. "Human Rights in the World." *International Commission of Jurists Review* (Geneva), no. 20 (June 1978): 15-18.

Jenkins, Simons. "The Tribal Glue." *Economist* (London), South Africa Survey, 21 June 1980.

Laurence, Patrick. "Collaboration: Where is the Point of No Return." *Rand Daily Mail* (Johannesburg), 31 October 1979.

————. "Politics is a Business of Who Gets What." *Rand Daily Mail* (Johannesburg), 20 November 1979.

Legum, Colin. "The African Crisis." *Foreign Affairs* 57 (America and the World 1978): 633-51.

Lelyveld, Joseph. "Despite Plenty, Hunger is Rife in South Africa." *New York Times*, 23 November 1980.

Lewis, Anthony. "State of Violence: II." *New York Times*, 8 December 1977.

————. "With All Deliberate Speed." *New York Times*, 15 December 1977.

"Mr. Vorster's Mandate." Editorial. *New York Times*, 2 December 1977.

Murphy, Caryle. "New South African Policy on Sports Causes Collision of Principle, Practice." *Washington Post*, 25 February 1978.

New York Times, 14 November, 1, 16 December 1977; 12 January, 13, 15 February, 11, 15, 19 March, 22 April, 9 June 1978; 3 October 1979.

Nyerere, Julius K. "America and Southern Africa." *Foreign Affairs* 55 (July 1977): 671-84.

Ottoway, David. "Africa: U.S. Policy Eclipse." *Foreign Affairs* 58 (America and the World 1979): 637-58.

"Our Standpoint on the Sports Issue." *Editorial. Rand Daily Mail* (Johannesburg), 17 January 1980.

"Pattern of Violence." *South African Digest* (Pretoria), 2 February 1979.

Pogrund, Benjamin. "P W and B J—the Same Bars." *Rand Daily Mail* (Johannesburg), 20 March 1980.

―――. "Waiting for Nat Change." *Rand Daily Mail* (Johannesburg), 21 March 1980.

Post (Johannesburg), 28 June, 15 November 1979; 30 January 1980.

Rand Daily Mail (Johannesburg), 2 May, 5 October, 5 November 1979 9 January, 2, 7 June 1980; 31 March 1981.

Schneider, Martin. "The Citizen Connection." *Rand Daily Mail* (Johannesburg), 10 May 1978.

"South Africa is Drifting into Lasting Unrest." *Rand Daily Mail* (Johannesburg), 19 June 1980.

"South Africa: Backwards, Fast." *Economist* (London), 10 May 1980.

"South Africa Seems Gratified." *New York Times*, 6 November 1980, p. A10.

South African Digest (Pretoria), 13 20, 27 April, 16 November 1979; 22 February 1980.

―――. "Information Newsletter," 13, 20 June 1980.

Sparks, Alister. Commentary. *Rand Daily Mail* (Johannesburg), 3 November 1977.

"Speak Forcefully to South Africa." Editorial. *New York Times*, 20 June 1980.

Star (Johannesburg), 15, 22 December 1979.

Sunday Post (Johannesburg), 28 October 1979.

"The People's Programme," *Sechaba*, September 1980.

Uys, Stanley. "A Close Look at Afrikanerdom." *Rand Daily Mail* (Johannesburg), 19 October 1979.

Wiecker, Tom. "The Nightmare Ahead." *New York Times*, 29 December 1978.

Zille, Helen. "Academics Criticize Schlebusch Plans." *Rand Daily Mail* (Johannesburg), 4 October 1979.

―――. "The New Verligte Nat Vision." *Rand Daily Mail* (Johannesburg), 17 October 1979.

————. "Apartheid Must Go Says Top Academic." *Rand Daily Mail* (Johannesburg), 12 November 1979.

————. "Editor Airs Nat Race Law Debate." *Rand Daily Mail* (Johannesburg), 14 January 1980.

D. *Parliamentary Debates of South Africa*
(Chronological)

Republic of South Africa. *House of Assembly Debates* (Hansard). First Session-Sixth Parliament, 6-10 February 1978, no. 2, cols. 821-84.

————. ————. First Session-Sixth Parliament, 6-10 March 1978, no. 6, col. 2823.

————. ————. First Session-Sixth Parliament, 17-21 April 1978, no. 11, cols. 5227-30; Questions and Replies, col. 644.

————. ————. First Session-Sixth Parliament, 24-28 April 1978, no. 12, cols. 5558-60.

————. ————. Third Session-Sixth Parliament, 2-9 February 1979, no. 1, Questions and Replies, cols. 12, 27-28.

————. ————. Third Session-Sixth Parliament, 26 February-2 March 1979, no. 4, Questions and Replies, col. 283.

————. ————. Third Session-Sixth Parliament, 23 May 1979, no. 15, cols. 7123-24.

————. ————. Third Session-Sixth Parliament, no. 18, 14 June 1979, col. 8786.

————. ————. Fourth Session-Sixth Parliament, 17-20 March 1980, no. 3, Questions and Replies, col. 6.

E. *Theses and Other Publications*

African National Congress of South Africa. Observer Mission to the UN and Representation to the U.S.A. (New York). *Press Release* [June 1980].

Bloomfield, Lincoln P. "The United Nations, The Status Quo, and the Process of Peaceful Change." Ph.D. dissertation, Harvard University, 1955.

Clark, Dick. "U.S. Corporate Interests in South Africa." Report to the Committee on Foreign Relations. U.S. Senate, January 1978.

Ermacora, Felix. "Human Rights and Domestic Jurisdiction." *Recueil Des Cours, 1968-II*. Hague Academy of International Law. Netherlands: Sijthoff, 1969.

Foreign Policy Study Foundation. *South Africa: Time Running out*. Report of the Study Commission on U.S. Policy Toward Southern Africa. Berkeley: University of California Press, 1981.

Permanent Mission of South Africa to the UN, *South African News Review*, 12 September, 14 October 1980.

Republic of South Africa. *Government Gazette*, vol. 182, no. 7148, 1 August 1980.

Singh, Joginder Bains. "Domestic Jurisdiction and the Law of the United Nations." Ph.D. dissertation, University of Michigan, 1953.

U.S. Congress. *Country Reports on Human Rights Practices for 1979*. Report submitted to the Committee on Foreign Affairs, U.S. House of Representatives, and Committee of Foreign Relations, U.S. Senate, by the Department of State, 4 February 1980.

U.S. Department of State. "Human Rights in South Africa." *Current Policy*, no. 181, 13 May 1980.

INDEX